BETWEEN HERMENEUTICS AND SCIENCE

AN ESSAY ON THE EPISTEMOLOGY OF PSYCHOANALYSIS

PSYCHOLOGICAL ISSUES

HERBERT J. SCHLESINGER, *Editor*

BETWEEN HERMENEUTICS AND SCIENCE

AN ESSAY ON THE EPISTEMOLOGY OF PSYCHOANALYSIS

CARLO STRENGER, Ph.D.

Psychological Issues
Monograph 59

INTERNATIONAL UNIVERSITIES PRESS, INC.
Madison, Connecticut

Library of Congress Cataloging-in-Publication Data

Strenger, Carlo.
  Between hermeneutics and science : an essay on the epistemology of psychoanalysis / Carlo Strenger.
    p. cm. — (Psychological issues ; monograph 59)
  Includes bibliographical references and index.
  ISBN 0-8236-0497-7
  1. Psychoanalysis. 2. Epistemology. I. Title. II. Series.
  [DNLM: 1. Psychoanalytic Theory. W1 PS572 v. 59 / WM 460 S915b]
RC506.S77 1991
616.89'17—dc20
DNLM/DLC
for Library of Congress   91-7025
                                                                   CIP

Manufactured in the United States of America

CONTENTS

PREFACE AND ACKNOWLEDGMENTS

When I set out to write and think about the issues addressed here, I believed that I had clear-cut answers to the criticisms voiced against psychoanalysis. I thought it was possible to give a model which would show in detail why psychoanalytic reasoning is sound and why the clinical method can ascertain the truth of psychoanalytic propositions.

One of the great advantages of writing is that it gives ideas a certain objectivity, a certain detachment from one's own mind. Ideas which seem persuasive when they are entertained, arguments which seemed tight when only thought of vaguely, must stand on their own once they are on paper. My experience was that many things which had seemed clear to me before became problematic once I had written them.

The question that this essay is concerned with is: how much of what psychoanalysis claims to know on the basis of clinical work can indeed be known on this evidence? What type of knowledge is psychoanalytic knowledge? The answers I have arrived at are not simple. I found myself unable to accept either of the two currently popular positions: I do not think that psychoanalysis is akin to natural science and that it has no relation whatsoever to the humanities, nor do I believe that it is a purely hermeneutic discipline which need not bother with controlled research, since it deals with meanings and not with causes. I have tried to find my way in between these two extremes, and I offer my own views for consideration—even though they are far from constituting a tightly woven systematic whole.

During the years in which I thought and wrote about these questions I gave courses on related matters at the graduate program for history and philosophy of science at Hebrew

University, I saw patients in psychoanalytic therapy, and I went through my own analysis. The movement between daily clinical work and my own experience as an analysand on the one hand and theoretical reflection about what I was doing and experiencing on the other hand were both fruitful and at times difficult. If one writes purely about theoretical issues, one is less bothered by reality, so to speak. The sheer inner coherence of one's ideas is what counts. It is more difficult to come to grips with and make sense of one's own experience as it is lived and yet maintain a sense of direction about the theoretical view one wants to propound.

I wanted to make sense of the analytic experience on a relatively high level of abstraction and avoid two shortcomings: one is to develop a model of what psychoanalysis is supposed to be on the basis of some preconceived model derived from the philosophy of science. None of the philosophical models of what scientific knowledge is has turned out to be very useful in understanding what we actually do. Scientists often felt that the models had very little in common with what they were doing in their daily practice. Similarly psychoanalysts have often felt that the criticisms leveled against their discipline were based on a complete misconception of what they were actually doing.

The second shortcoming is intrinsic to descriptions in terms close to clinical practice: what we do in our daily clinical work, without relating to criticisms of psychoanalytic claims to knowledge. Such accounts can be very useful in sharpening our understanding of what psychoanalytic thinking is all about. The recent paradigm of such work is Schafer's profound *The Analytic Attitude* (1983) to which I am in many ways indebted. The problem is that such work does not really appease epistemological doubts about the modes of thinking involved in psychoanalysis. By integrating my clinical experience with a more philosophical level of abstraction, I have tried to give an account of psychoanalytic clinical thought which is neither disjoined from experience nor insensitive to recent critiques of psychoanalysis.

I point time and time again to the need for controlled research on psychoanalysis and to a rethinking of its foundations. It might have been desirable to summarize existing research and thought on these issues, but this would have required an additional book. I feel quite comfortable with this omission as there are three recent books which can be consulted in these matters.

The first is Wallerstein's *Forty-Two Lives in Treatment* (1986a) which summarizes the largest single piece of research ever done on clinical psychoanalysis, the Menninger study. It covers an enormous amount of clinical material and shows many of the complexities involved in such research.

The second is Morris Eagle's *Recent Developments in Psychoanalysis* (1984a) which deals with a question I deem to be of foremost importance: to what extent does actual theoretical and clinical thought diverge from the classic paradigm of Freud's structural model? Eagle's work succeeds admirably in identifying an underlying convergence in strands of psychoanalytic thinking as different as the works of G. S. Klein and W. R. D. Fairbairn.

The third is Daniel Stern's fascinating *The Internal World of the Infant* (1985) which is a paradigm of the integration of infant research and psychoanalytic thought. It shows how direct observation of infants paired with a keen psychoanalytic imagination can correct misconceptions about actual child development arising from the reconstructive method. In addition, it shows how such research can generate fruitful hypotheses concerning processes and content in clinical work.

I would like to express my gratitude to the people who have contributed in one way or another to this work. First and foremost I would like to thank Joseph Sandler. He has in many ways contributed to my grasp of psychoanalytic theory and practice during the years I studied and worked with him. His advice and encouragement have been very important to me.

Meir Winokur read the first version of this essay from the beginning to the end, chapter by chapter as I wrote them. His sensitive and constructive comments helped me at moments at which I was not sure that I was still on the right track. I would also like to thank Albert Solnit who read the whole first version and gave valuable advice.

Herbert Schlesinger, the editor of *Psychological Issues*, and the two anonymus readers of the manuscript were helpful as well.

Their comments encouraged me to rework the manuscript, clarify and strengthen my argument. I have incorporated most of their advice in this final version.

Shelley Ostroff, a dear friend, edited the whole manuscript for me. She put up with my obstinate reluctance to give up earlier formulations, improved the style of this essay, and taught me a lot about writing in general and in English, which is not my native language. The remaining stylistic deficiencies are of course my sole responsibility.

I have discussed many problems with Ruth Stein over the last years. She has endured my mood swings ranging from exaggerated optimism to total pessimism concerning the defensibility of psychoanalytic clinical wisdom. By sharing her own experience and thinking about these matters with me, she has sharpened my understanding of what psychoanalysis is about. She was also part of a study group in psychoanalysis which included Meir Perlow, Itamar Levi, and Dafna Gorkin-Ladin; this group provided interesting food for thought on theoretical and clinical issues.

Much of the process of writing this essay consisted of my gradually acknowledging that things were more complex, less reassuring and conclusive than I would have liked them to be. Much of the flexibility I needed to come to terms with this I gained in my analysis with Rena Hrushovski Moses which occurred while I was working on this book. This experience provided one of the most important touchstones of my ideas as they developed. Throughout many hundreds of hours I have come to appreciate her rich, sensitive, and humane conception of psychoanalysis and I had firsthand experience of what non-dogmatic analysis can be like. The ideas expressed here in many ways reflect what I have received from working with her.

This essay is dedicated to my parents who have given me strength, support, and love on my meandering way, even though it did not always correspond to their values and hopes.

FOREWORD

Psychoanalysis has undergone significant developments during the last five decades. The number of schools of thought, the variety of styles of work and types of patients we work with have increased significantly. Our understanding of clinical and developmental processes is greater than ever. Despite—perhaps because—of this, psychoanalysis is in certain respects in a crisis. The multiplicity of approaches within psychoanalysis and the increasing complexity of our understanding of the factors involved in clinical work have called several of the central tenets of psychoanalysis into question. The proliferation of theories and the existence of many alternative forms of psychotherapy which are no less successful in ameliorating illness than psychoanalysis raise issues of great importance.

We have too often reacted to criticisms coming from outside psychoanalysis as sheer inconveniences. Psychoanalysts have thought that they really knew that their theories were true, and that it was only the lack of acquaintance with the analytic process that led nonanalysts to be critical of psychoanalytic theories and practice. The time has come to reflect on the nature of our knowledge more profoundly. Too many conflicting theories are believed to be "true" to accept the "truth" of any one of them at face value. Yet, in spite of this, it must be said that the psychoanalyst's unease with critiques leveled from outside has some validity, even though more often than not the portrait of psychoanalytic practice which underlies those critiques is a caricature of what we actually do. In fact, our thinking is less erratic, less remote from commonsense reasoning than philosophers and academic psychologists have assumed.

Carlo Strenger's *Between Hermeneutics and Science* is a welcome response to the unsettled and unsettling condition of psycho-

analysis. Strenger is in many ways singularly qualified for the
task of reflecting on the nature of psychoanalytic knowledge.
On the one hand, he is a clinical psychologist who knows psychoanalysis not only in theory but also from firsthand practice;
on the other, he has been trained as a philosopher and has been
teaching in that field. This allows him to use recent developments in philosophy to elucidate many crucial issues around
psychoanalysis; and he does so with great skill. His present essay
is an attempt to formulate the nature of psychoanalytic clinical
knowledge in a way which can satisfy both the psychoanalytic
clinician and the critic unacquainted with analytic practice.
Strenger draws on the clinical experience of others as well as
on his own in his description of psychoanalytic reasoning. His
presentation eschews the shortcomings of critiques reflecting
misunderstandings of psychoanalysis, which are almost inevitable when external critics deal with what we do. Strenger also
manages to avoid the pitfall of assuming that the critics of psychoanalysis must be wrong just because they have no clinical
experience. His philosophical background makes him acutely
aware of the epistemological problems with which thinking and
practice are faced. His account is in many ways a defense of
psychoanalytic clinical thinking. His vivid descriptions and analyses show how the psychoanalytic clinician is using modes of
thought which are much closer to common sense than many
critics believe. He shows clearly how we can reasonably claim
to know about unconscious processes and contents of our patient's minds, and he gives a convincing account of how we can
reconstruct our patient's past from the material emerging
within the analytic process.

Strenger does not shy away from pointing out the weaknesses
and limitations of psychoanalytic knowledge. He shows relentlessly that many psychoanalytic authors have been overly optimistic about the extent to which we can know how human
beings develop and the degree to which the curative factors in
psychoanalysis and in psychotherapy can be specified. His defense of psychoanalysis against the more extreme critics does
not invite us to rest quietly on our achievements. He points out
the junctures and issues at which we need more systematic empirical evidence and at which we must rethink those very basic

assumptions which often remain unquestioned.

Between Hermeneutics and Science is likely to be read profitably by psychoanalysts, academic psychologists, philosophers, and anyone else interested in psychoanalysis. Psychoanalysts will find many of their intuitions about how we think and work spelled out with a clarity rarely to be found in the literature. Reading Strenger will also lead many of us to reflect more profoundly on how much (or how little) we really know. He presents the criticisms leveled against psychoanalysis in a way which makes them more palatable to those of us who feel that a straw man rather than actual psychoanalytic theory and practice has been the target of many of the attacks we have had to endure. The clinician reading this book will have a stimulus to be less dogmatic and more sensitive to the presuppositions of his clinical work.

Academic psychologists and philosophers may gain from this work a deeper understanding of what psychoanalysis is about. They will find a lucid account of psychoanalytic thinking and a vivid description of psychoanalytic clinical practice. This may alleviate some of their prejudices against psychoanalysis without their having to accept the truth of psychoanalysis *ex cathedra*. It is therefore to be hoped that this monograph will contribute both to the current self-reflection of psychoanalysis and to a dialogue with other disciplines.

Joseph Sandler
Freud Memorial Professor of Psychoanalysis
in the University of London

INTRODUCTION

This essay is an attempt to come to terms with an intellectual tension, which I think many people in the field of psychoanalysis experience. On the one hand, there is clinical work—be it in the classical analytic setting or in analytically oriented psychotherapy: we work with patients, sometimes for long periods, and we see a process of change occur. This process does not seem to be only the result of the therapeutic relationship, crucial as it is. Throughout a therapy, especially a successful one, a distinct sense of gradually finding and formulating a truth about the patient occurs.

The patient's progress is felt to be linked to an increasing understanding of his mental life and biography (by both the therapist and the patient himself). The sense of conviction that we are not just involved in creating a useful myth about the patient rests partially on two factors: the patient's experience of insight is not one of intellectually seeing that a certain interpretation explains the material well. It is rather a combination of strong emotional experiences induced by the interpretive work and the narrative fit, which enhance the plausibility of the interpretation. Often a sense of relief occurs, when lifelong fears, anxieties, and pains are placed in a context, which gives them more meaning and makes them less threatening.

Similarly there is the personal analysis which induces a change in our experience of self and others, the weakening of neurotic patterns, problems and anxieties. The process of going through transferences, resisting and resolving them, and the interweaving of this process with a gradually emerging sense of growing coherence in our biographies, both past and present, is experienced from within. The combination of the personal analysis and the work with patients creates an especially powerful amal-

1

gam: therapeutic processes are simultaneously experienced from two points of view. There is the experience of growing empathy with our patients, because we have had analogous experiences ourselves, and also because of a growing capacity to acknowledge and to use constructively our own countertransference.

All of this creates the tendency to assume that the conceptual framework which organizes the totality of these experiences is a true theory of human nature. Psychoanalytic theory has an additional property which is conducive to accepting it as a true, general, theory. Freud himself quite early regarded psychoanalysis as more than just a theory of the etiology of neurotic symptoms. Throughout his work he unfolded a picture of psychoanalysis as a general view of the *condition humaine* and of many manifestations of culture, from myth through art to the dynamics of mass psychology. And it is indeed a powerful explanatory framework: there are probably few, if any, other theories in the twentieth century which have so strongly influenced the self-understanding of Western culture. The combination of personal experience, both as therapist and analysand, and the general capacity of psychoanalytic theory to elucidate manifestations of human nature is difficult to resist in the conviction it engenders.

On the other hand, there are the criticisms which have been voiced against psychoanalysis from the very beginning of its history. Psychoanalysis has grounded most of its claims on clinical data, which by their very nature violate one of the central requirements of scientific research: evidence in favor of theories should be public and replicable. The necessity of protecting patients' anonymity, as well as the very nature of the analytic process, makes the analytic situation a very private one. In addition, until the age of the tape recorder, there was no technical possibility of coming close to recording even the verbal data. Now that the technical possibility exists, it turns out that every transcript, precise as it may be, still fails to capture the richness of the actual analytic experience.

Furthermore, there is the notorious incapacity of psychoanalytic theory to provide predictions sufficiently precise to yield uncontroversial and clear-cut evidence measuring up to the standards of the natural sciences. Even the great explanatory power of psychoanalytic theory poses methodological problems. Karl Raimund Popper (1963) gave the classic formulation of the complaint that psychoanalysis, by its very tendency to explain *every* kind of data, is not falsifiable, since it seems to be consistent with every conceivable state of affairs. This seemed especially true with respect to the way analysts tended to dismiss criticisms of psychoanalysis as manifestations of resistance, thus immunizing the theory by using it to explain away any attempt to criticize it.

The situation of psychoanalysis has become more precarious since, in the last few decades, numerous alternative forms of psychotherapy have emerged. Some of those—in particular behavior therapy—proved to be far more efficient than psychoanalysis in eliminating symptoms such as compulsions and phobias which were once the exclusive domain of psychoanalysis. In addition, even among the approaches represented by psychoanalysis, there are a number of competing theoretical approaches. American ego psychology, Kleinian analysis, object relation theory, and Kohutian self psychology are just overarching categorizations of the much vaster multitude of theoretical and therapeutic nuances to be found under the general label of psychoanalysis today.

The plethora of coexisting theoretical and practical approaches to the field of clinical psychology and psychotherapy may make us skeptical about all of them. Such skepticism may be strongest about a theory like psychoanalysis which, while being a framework with an enormous scope, has failed to come up with methodologically unproblematic and clear-cut confirming evidence.

The practicing clinician of psychoanalytic persuasion therefore faces the following dilemma: on the one hand, the experiences as a person and as a therapist lead him to take psychoanalysis as a powerful and presumably true theory of human nature; on the other hand, there is the methodological self-consciousness which he should have acquired by his academic training. This part of the clinician's intellectual identity makes it difficult not to be suspicious of the claims of a theory which in many respects fails to stand up to the requirements of the scientific community.

I would like to add a personal remark here: my personal intellectual predicament is characterized by the tensions just sketched, but it is also somewhat more complicated. Through my professional involvement in philosophy and a collateral interest in intellectual history, I am well acquainted with the problems around the seductive quality of systems of thought, which are sufficiently powerful to provide explanations for all the phenomena to be encountered, and which have yet been rejected in the course of history. This implies that I cannot help harboring some suspicion directed toward the overall psychoanalytic conviction engendered in me by my own personal biography and clinical activities. My inclinations push me to attempt to do justice both to the experiential conviction as well as to the intellectual demand for clarity and justification for theoretical convictions and also practical decisions (like that concerning the form of psychotherapy one wants to specialize in).

In this essay I am not trying to approach the problem outlined within a conceptual vacuum. I have found it both natural and productive to use two theoretical frameworks involved in lively discussions to represent the two sides of my own self fighting the struggle between clinician and methodologist.

The side representing the experientially convinced human being and clinician is a metatheoretical position, which has emerged throughout roughly the last 15 years in the psychoanalytic literature. I will call this the *hermeneuticist conception of psychoanalysis,* which I will present in chapter 2. This view has defended the idea that psychoanalysis is not part of the natural sciences, and should thus not be measured by their standards. It gives clinical experience a unique place in the confirmation of psychoanalytic theory and is thus well suited to provide the conceptual framework for the defense of the experiential truth constituting one side of the dilemma I want to deal with.

The side of philosophically oriented, methodological critique of psychoanalysis has in recent years been taken up by the respected philosopher of science, Adolf Grünbaum. In a series of publications culminating in his book *The Foundations of Psy-*

choanalysis (1984), he has presented a critique of the evidential foundations of psychoanalysis, unprecedented in its clarity and incisiveness. His arguments and claims will be the topic of chapter 1.

The bulk of this essay (chapters 3 to 6) is an attempt to present versions of claims of the hermeneuticist conception of psychoanalysis, which stand up to the sharp critique it has been subjected to by Grünbaum. I try to give a model of psychoanalytic interpretive activity, which makes it plausible that analytic interpretations can to some extent be "tested on the couch," to use Grünbaum's own phrase. Furthermore, I try to come to grips with the multitude of coexisting approaches in psychotherapy by presenting a pluralist perspective to explain why such approaches need not be inconsistent with each other (chapter 6). Much of what follows is therefore an attempt to give a conceptual foundation to the intuition that the experiential truth attained in the clinical setting can be justified.

In the final chapter I will turn to the limitations of the hermeneuticist defense of psychoanalysis. In particular, I want to argue that the hermeneuticists have disregarded the crucial role of background knowledge in the epistemic assessment of psychoanalysis. This has been pernicious and has made the hermeneuticist conception of psychoanalysis vulnerable to more criticism than necessary. I will conclude by sketching a perspective on psychoanalysis as a general research program and as a *Weltanschauung*.

PART I

RECENT CONTRIBUTIONS IN THE EPISTEMOLOGY OF PSYCHOANALYSIS

1

ADOLF GRÜNBAUM'S CRITIQUE OF PSYCHOANALYSIS

The philosophical literature on psychoanalysis has often been vitiated by a central defect. Authors like Popper condemned psychoanalysis as unscientific in order to illustrate the strength of their theories. Others endorsed it as a paradigm for some general thesis, e.g., the existence of a schism between the natural sciences and the humanities. There hardly had been a philosopher who bothered to examined psychoanalytic theory in detail, without too many preconceptions, to find out to what extent it has a sound epistemic foundation.

In his *The Foundations of Psychoanalysis* Adolf Grünbaum, a well-known philosopher of science, has taken up this task in an impressive way. He displays a remarkable knowledge of the psychoanalytic literature and his arguments are lucid and well-documented, allowing for fruitful discussion and critique. He has a clear question and pursues it relentlessly through almost 300 pages: psychoanalysts generally claim that the best—if not the only—way to investigate the truth of psychoanalytic theory is within the setting of analytic treatment. Grünbaum wants to find out whether this method is capable of providing valid confirmation for the theory.

After detailed analysis he arrives at a negative answer. He claims to have shown that it is impossible to make sure that the data obtained in the analytic situation are uncontaminated, i.e., not the result of suggestion. Furthermore, he contends that there is no way to prove within the setting of analytic therapy

9

that its therapeutic results are not due to a placebo effect. Therefore clinical work cannot by itself provide the foundation for accepting psychoanalytic theory.

It is important not to misread Grünbaum as stating that psychoanalysis is wrong. The question regarding its truth, he believes, is an empirical one that cannot be settled by philosophical analysis. All he claims is that the truth value of the theory cannot be ascertained simply by practicing psychoanalysis. Instead, it is necessary to conduct controlled longitudinal and experimental studies if we want to know whether the theory guiding clinical practice is true, and whether therapeutic results are indeed due to the guidance of our theories.

Any such thesis must be backed by a view of the structure of psychoanalytic theory, i.e., a reconstruction of the logical nature of psychoanalytic propositions. Grünbaum views psychoanalytic theory of neurosis as a set of propositions stating causal connections between types of childhood events (e.g., repression of sexual wishes) and resulting psychopathological symptoms. Psychoanalytic theory of dreams and slips of tongue states causal relationships between repressed mental contents and the phenomena to be explained.

There is a strong current in both psychoanalytic and philosophical writings (Habermas, 1968, G. S. Klein, 1976; Ricoeur, 1970; Schafer, 1976; see also chap. 2) which attacks this kind of interpretation of psychoanalytic theory. These theorists claim that psychoanalysis is not concerned with causal relations but deals with meanings and motives, and they believe to have thus rebutted the methodological charges often raised against psychoanalysis. These writers have also claimed that the epistemic weaknesses apply only to metapsychology and not to what has been labeled the clinical theory of psychoanalysis.

It is therefore a further advantage of Grünbaum's book that it is concerned exclusively with the clinical theory, thus precluding the defense that he is attacking a straw man, an anachronistic view of psychoanalysis. Grünbaum devotes his introduction, a third of the book, to attacking the hermeneuticist interpretation of psychoanalysis which to his mind is based mainly on conceptual muddles. He thus tries to clear the ground for his claim that psychoanalysis is essentially concerned with causal connections, which provides the background for his arguments in the main part of the book.

Clearly, not all aspects of *The Foundations of Psychoanalysis* can be taken up within this chapter. In the first section I will present Grünbaum's views on the epistemic foundations of the psychoanalytic theory of neurosis, which is the structural paradigm for his critique of other parts of psychoanalysis; and in the second section I will summarize his most important arguments against the hermeneuticist interpretation of psychoanalysis. Although I believe all of Grünbaum's arguments to be worthy of serious consideration, I disagree with many of his conclusions. In the final section I will indicate the line of thought I believe to be most fruitful in answering his charges.

a)   GRÜNBAUM'S CRITIQUE OF THE CLINICAL METHOD

Anyone who claims that analytic therapy is the setting in which psychoanalytic theory can and should be tested must be able to specify how the data obtained in this setting can be validated. Grünbaum's thesis in a nutshell is that clinical work alone cannot yield such validation. His main assumption (which I shall question later on) is that the psychoanalytic theory of neurosis is a conjunction of hypotheses about causal connections between types of events in childhood and forms of psychopathology in adult life. Grünbaum is aware that the theory of the nature of these events has changed considerably in the course of the historical development of psychoanalysis.

There are several ways in which processes in analytic treatments are supposed to confirm the clinical theory. First, there is the fact that therapies guided by the theory can cure neuroses, which is taken as a proof for the truth of the interpretations given by the analyst. Second, while patients do not accept all interpretations, acceptance can under certain circumstances confirm these interpretations. Third, some interpretations cause the patient to produce further material like childhood memories, dreams, etc., which correspond to the content of the analyst's intervention. Such processes are believed to confirm psychoanalytic etiological hypotheses, since interpretations are intended to uncover the pathogens of the patient's neurosis by undoing repressions.

Grünbaum claims that none of these phenomena can be taken as confirmations of the truth of interpretations and *a fortiori* not as confirmations of psychoanalytic theory. Acceptance of an interpretation by a patient can be due to suggestion, and the same holds true for the production of other confirming material. Psychoanalysis itself has been aware of this danger for a long time, and especially of the patient's need to please the analyst by being a "good analysand." As for the therapeutic results of psychoanalysis, Grünbaum argues that even if they were very impressive, one would have to make sure that they are not due to a placebo effect, i.e., completely independent of the truth of the interpretations given to patients. If this is not ensured, clinical work cannot provide a rational foundation for accepting psychoanalytic theory.

Grünbaum enthusiastically praises Freud for having recognized these problems and for having formulated the only good epistemological defense of psychoanalysis he could detect in the literature to date. On pages 139–140 Grünbaum summaries Freud's "daring hypothesis," as he calls it, as follows:

(1) Only the psychoanalytic method of interpretation and treatment can yield or mediate to the patient correct insight into the unconscious pathogens of his psychoneurosis, and

(2) the analysand's correct insight into the etiology of his application is, in turn, *causally necessary* for the therapeutic conquest of his neurosis.

Grünbaum calls this conjunction, which provides the gist of an argument given by Freud in his *Introductory Lectures on Psychoanalysis* (1916–17), the necessary condition thesis. What this thesis ensures, if it is true, is that only true insight has therapeutic effect, and therefore it provides a validation of data gained in the analytic setting. Grünbaum emphasizes Freud's epistemological and methodological sophistication and repeatedly criticizes later analytic authors for not having recognized the crucial importance of the necessary condition thesis, which he takes to be the only valid defense of the idea that psychoanalysis can be tested "on the couch."

One of the empirical implications of the necessary condition thesis is that only psychoanalysis or analytically oriented therapy should have curative effects on neuroses. The fact that these therapies do not always cure does not in itself falsify the necessary condition thesis, but the existence of any nonanalytic, successful form of psychotherapy does. The most clear-cut example of such a falsifying instance is, of course, behavior therapy, which for certain monosymptomatic neuroses is even clearly superior to psychoanalysis in therapeutic efficiency. The necessary condition thesis has turned out to be empirically wrong.

Therefore, Grünbaum argues, the one and only reason that has ever been given to believe that psychoanalysis can be tested exclusively or mainly by clinical methods is invalid. This does not entail the falsity of psychoanalysis as a whole, but it does show (or so Grünbaum thinks) that "Without this vindication or some other as yet unknown epistemic underpinning, not even the tortures of the thumbscrew or of the rack should persuade a rational being that free association can *certify* pathogens or other causes!" (p. 186). A dramatic statement, whatever one may think of its truth value.

Grünbaum's main contention is thus that the method of clinical investigation is essentially vitiated, and that it cannot by itself ensure the validation of its data. Grünbaum, however, does not remain content with this. He continues in several chapters in which he tries to show that even if clinical data were not problematic in the way described, they would still not constitute acceptable evidence for some of the cornerstones of psychoanalytic theory.

I want to summarize one important point. Grünbaum argues that therapeutic success cannot be taken to confirm the hypothesis of the repression etiology of neurosis. Let us assume that by lifting some repression, we cure a patient's symptom. This would still not mean that the original repression of this specific content was causally responsible for the onset of the neurosis. All we could claim on the given data is that the maintenance of the repression was causally responsible for the *maintenance* of the symptom. We cannot infer from processes during therapy to any causal connection between childhood events and the present neurosis.

In a later chapter, Grünbaum formulates his point in general terms, showing that such inductive inference violates the basic canons of inductive logic. His argument is that, even if we were to find that an overwhelming proportion of people suffering from neurosis N went through childhood event P, this would not yet show that P is causally relevant to N. It could still turn out that the same proportion of people *not* suffering from N have gone through P, in which case P would not at all be causally linked to N. This possibility could only be ruled out through the study of control groups. Grünbaum thus provides additional support for his conclusion that extraclinical research must be undertaken if the psychoanalytic theory of neurosis is to be confirmed.

b)   GRÜNBAUM ON THE HERMENEUTICIST CONCEPTION OF PSYCHOANALYSIS

One could respond to Grünbaum's critique with the contention that he is fighting a straw man. There is a vast literature, headed by Roy Schafer, G. S. Klein, and Merton Gill, who have argued for years that psychoanalysis should not be misunderstood as a natural science. Instead, they claim, one must see it as a hermeneutic enterprise which by its nature has different criteria of validation than the natural sciences. Psychoanalysis does not (or, at any rate, should not) talk about causal connections between events; it talks about meaning structures and narrative coherence. If we follow these authors, Grünbaum's interpretation of psychoanalysis may be viewed as anachronistic, and *eo ipso* his criticisms may be seen as misguided.

The hermeneuticist alternative is the topic of a quite polemical attack, which Grünbaum mounts in the 90-page introduction to his book. His main targets are what he considers to be logical blunders in the writings of Habermas, Ricoeur, G. S. Klein, and Roy Schafer. Many of Grünbaum's contentions *are* justified and I defer their discussion to chapter 3. This section concentrates on two of Grünbaum's central arguments of a more general nature.

The first argument (pp. 50–56) concerns claims made by hermeneuticist authors that the confirmation of analytic interpretations hinges on the narrative coherence they bring into the patient's associations and his patterns of behavior. They make them meaningful, intelligible, and this is the mark of their rightness.

Against this Grünbaum puts forth an interesting contention. Imagine exorcists who interpret schizophrenic symptoms in women by saying that they are satanically possessed. It may very well be possible that the narratives they construct around the schizophrenic behavior make it meaningful. Furthermore, it could be that their exorcist procedures have a temporary therapeutic effect. Yet "even if these therapeutic effects were impressive, we would hardly credit the shamans or exorcists with having unraveled the otherwise 'meaning' of the witchcraft or possession symptoms. For we reject their underlying causal ontology, which determines what kind of 'meaning' their quest will uncover" (p. 54). Therefore the fact that psychoanalysts succeed in making sense of their patients' associations and symptoms can confirm neither their interpretations nor the theory underlying them. This is a powerful argument indeed, and I shall return to it in the next section.

The second point Grünbaum raises against the hermeneuticists concerns their tendency to think that an explanation in terms of reasons is logically incompatible with explanations in terms of causes (pp. 69–83). Their arguments take two essential forms: (a) The method of psychoanalysis is suitable for uncovering reasons *qua* motives but not for ascertaining causes, since clinical investigation cannot confirm causal laws of the form "always when A then B." Psychoanalytic propositions must therefore be formulated in terms of reasons and not of causes. (b) Motives of reasons cannot be causes, since the logic of reason-explanations is intrinsically different from the logic of causal explanations.

Grünbaum shows in some detail (pp. 73–76) that the first argument is based on a simplistic notion of cause. There are many fields, like general medicine, in which causal relations are stated and investigated, although the antecedents of these relations are neither causally necessary nor sufficient for the concurrence of the consequences, like in the nexus between smoking and lung cancer. We then speak of causal relevance without postulating exceptionless causal laws. As for point b), we must mention—thus strengthening Grünbaum's point—that the thesis of the incompatibility of explanations by reasons and by causes is a doctrine which was held by neo-Wittgensteinian philosophers in the '50s and '60s. This position has been shown to be wrong mainly by the seminal work of Donald Davidson (1980), and to my mind conclusively so (see chap. 3). To the extent that hermeneuticist theses are based on this view, their conceptual foundations are weak. Whether it is doomed to failure, as Grünbaum thinks, is one of the questions to which I shall turn now.

c)   A Preliminary Assessment of Grünbaum's Critique

Grünbaum's epistemological verdict concerning the possibility of testing psychoanalysis on the couch is clear-cut. In his view analytic theory is replete with causal hypotheses which are epistemically inaccessible to the clinical method. I want to stress that his argument is internally cogent. *If* the structure of psychoanalysis corresponds to Grünbaum's reconstruction, it would indeed be unclear how the analytic setting could contribute to the confirmation of the theory.

I think that Grünbaum's reconstruction is inadequate. It is certainly right to attempt to make the logical structure of a theory as clear as possible if its epistemic credentials are to be examined. But this need not entail oversimplification—and of this Grünbaum is guilty. I am not charging him on this point because he exemplifies his contentions by hypotheses which have long been discarded, like the early form of the repression etiology of hysteria. Grünbaum is aware of the fact that psychoanalysis has changed since the 1890s, and he correctly thinks that, for his purposes, it is the structure of the hypotheses which matters and not their changing content.

My contention, however, is that the *structure* of psychoanalytic theory has changed since its beginnings, and not only the content of this or that etiological hypothesis. This is true even in Freud's time, and not only for developments after his death. These changes have affected the epistemic properties of the theory and are therefore relevant to Grünbaum's subject.

The historical development of psychoanalysis was driven, among other things, by the discovery that etiological hypotheses of the form (and not only the content) of the early etiology of hysteria always proved mistaken. The same childhood events could lead to neuroses in some cases and not in others. It is the way they were experienced, and the person's adaptational resources during the process of development, which determine the pathogenicity of these events.

The complexities uncovered by clinical experience gradually led to a widening of psychoanalytic perspective. Phenomena such as the negative therapeutic reaction were responsible for the emergence of the structure model in the 1920s. The idea of feeling states as motives for defense and the later introduction of the adaptational point of view came to be the groundwork of ego psychology. Psychoanalysis thus changed from a set of etiological hypotheses into a theory of human nature in general. Its core is a theory of development and of mental functioning under conditions of conflict, which forms the frame for the understanding of psychopathological phenomena (for more details, see chapter 4). Psychoanalysis has become the most complex theory of twentieth-century psychology, covering an enormous scope. At present it is impossible to isolate simple etiological hypotheses from this body of thought without distorting its nature.

There is no doubt that the theory has become progressively less transparent from an epistemological point of view, and Grünbaum seems to have trouble accepting this. In his effort to show—against Popper—that psychoanalysis is falsifiable, he repeatedly compliments Freud with phrases like "the epoch-making repression etiology" (p. 179) and "the daring Necessary Condition Thesis" (p. 140). Grünbaum likes such hypotheses because they can be examined in isolation and have an easily statable empirical content—properties which as such are certainly laudable. In contrast, he calls Freud's *Inhibitions, Symptoms and Anxiety* the "disapprovingly fuzzy 1926 essay on anxiety" (p. 165). In view of the fact that this work constitutes one of the milestones of the development of psychoanalytic theory, such a label is surprising, to say the least. I believe that only excessive concern for epistemic simplicity can be responsible for such failure of judgment in an incisive mind like Grünbaum's.

We must concede that it is extremely difficult to provide an adequate reconstruction of the logical and epistemic structure of psychoanalysis. The hermeneuticist alternative as it presents itself in the literature today is not satisfying. In part it rests on a weak conceptual foundation (see section b), and it is vulnerable to the very strong argument, already made. Grünbaum's most impressive contention against the hermeneuticist defense of psychoanalysis is that narrative coherence cannot function as the criterion of the truth of an interpretation, since there is always a multitude of interpretations that make narrative sense. Yet some of these would be rejected right away because of their underlying causal ontology. This claim could be justified on purely logical grounds, but for the present it may suffice to make it intuitively plausible by mentioning two examples. Both Greek mythology and monotheistic interpretation of human experience are narratively highly coherent. But the first would be rejected by all, the second by most Western intellectuals. It is therefore not sufficient to cite narrative coherence of analytic interpretations as the only support for the theory which guides them.

The following lines of thought will be elaborated in later chapters, and they should serve to weaken the force of some of Grünbaum's claims. To begin with, we must differentiate between two levels of coherence. First, there is what could be called *internal* narrative coherence. By this term I refer to the intelligibility that an interpretation confers to some material, e.g., patients' associations. Such interpretations are guided by what I call a hermeneutic frame, which provides criteria for the selection of the material to be interpreted and for the *a priori* plausibility of interpretations. Such frames can include wandering souls, punishing Gods, archetypes, unconscious fantasies and drives, etc., depending on the cultural context. Hermeneutic frames—psychoanalysis is one of them—are judged by the extent to which they cohere with the causal ontology implicit in the generally accepted theories of the relevant culture. This *external coherence* constitutes a measure for the *a priori* plausibility of hermeneutic frames and scientific theories in general. The inner coherence of the specific interpretations generated by hermeneutic frames corresponds to the accuracy of predictions in the confirmation of scientific theories (this is taken up in more detail in chapter 7).

The factor of external coherence has been neglected by the hermeneuticist literature in general and by psychoanalysis in particular. Within the latter context it can easily be shown that arguments concerning external coherence play an important role in discussions between psychoanalytic schools. Many of the criticisms adduced against Kleinian theory by authors influenced by ego psychology are good examples of this. They reject Kleinian hypotheses because they are inconsistent with many of the facts about early child development often known from nonpsychoanalytic psychology (Kernberg, 1980).

The structure of the confirmation of hermeneutic frames is a complex affair, and I shall say more about it later on. It is clear, however, that without considerations regarding external coherence, psychoanalysis has sufficient support. None of this denies that psychoanalysis definitely needs to be investigated experimentally, for example, the question of therapeutic efficiency. In general this need is less desperate than Grünbaum believes because the clinical method has more means for the validation of its data than he assumes. The reason he underestimates this capacity is probably due to a misinterpretation of the nature of insight provided by analysands. Grünbaum seems to take insight for knowledge about causal relations, while in reality it is rather a restructuring of experience. What the patient has perceived as alien to himself and unintelligible is now experienced as meaningful and part of himself.

Analysts spend a great deal of their training on sharpening their sensorium for feeling states, moods, and forms of interaction. As they become better, they are able to differentiate between genuine insight and defensive intellectualization. It is true that such nuances are not easily perceptible to an untrained observer, but this is no argument for their inexistence. Otherwise, the same would apply to the musical structure of a Bach fugue or very small differences in pitch between tones, which can generally only be identified by experienced musicians. The analyst's sensorium is an important tool in the validation of his data, and analytic work would be impossible without it.

There is a genuine problem here: having recourse to the analyst's abilities of the sort just mentioned in defense of psychoanalysis is often perceived as intellectually dishonest by non-analysts. They can easily come to think that this is just a way to immunize analytic theory from criticism, and fairness demands that we admit that such suspicion is not always misplaced. A good analysis of the structure of psychoanalysis would have to indicate the exact points at which the analyst's abilities play a rationally defensible role in the confirmation of the theory (see chap. 4).

Finally, the need to clear up the muddles around the questions whether psychoanalysis is concerned with reasons or with causes must be mentioned. Grünbaum is absolutely right in forcefully rejecting the idea that reasons cannot be causes (pp. 69–83; see also section b of this chapter). But he is no less wrong in believing that reason-explanations must therefore have the same logic as explanations in the natural sciences.

The work of the philosopher Donald Davidson (1980) contains several of the conceptual tools needed for an elucidation of crucial problems in the philosophy of psychoanalysis. In particular, Davidson has shown that reasons *are* causes; nevertheless there *cannot* be strict causal laws in terms of reasons. If exploited correctly, this insight can be used to do justice both to Grünbaum's insistence that psychoanalytic explanations have a strong causal element and to the hermeneuticist intuition that the logic of psychoanalytic explanation differs in important ways from explanation in the natural sciences (see chap. 3).

d)   IMPLICATIONS OF THE CURRENT STATE OF
PSYCHOTHERAPY RESEARCH

Recently Grünbaum has been challenged by Paul Kline on the grounds that Grünbaum has not taken into account the rather remarkable amount of empirical research supporting many of the concepts of psychoanalytic theory. There are two volumes summarizing this research (Fisher and Greenberg, 1977; Kline, 1981). Both volumes conclude that there are several theoretical constructs in the Freudian corpus which are supported reasonably well by the evidence. Examples are: the anal personality type, the Oedipus complex, several defense mechanisms such as repression and projection, and some more.

Grünbaum's main answer (1986, p. 269) is: he does not think that any of the studies mentioned by either Kline or Fisher and Greenberg demonstrate anything with respect to the cornerstone of Freudian theory: the repression etiology of neuroses. At best these studies provide some support for several theoretical constructs. Hence, Grünbaum believes, there is no reason to reassess the conclusions he arrived at in *The Foundations of Psychoanalysis,* namely, that the tenets of Freudian theory remain empirically unsupported.

One question Grünbaum's reply raises is whether psychoanalytic theory should be regarded as resting on a central pillar which supports the whole rest of the theory. This is certainly implied by Grünbaum's metaphor of the cornerstone of psychoanalysis, which he applies to the repression etiology. If we assume that Grünbaum is right in this respect, the next question is whether the only way to test Freudian theory is to tackle the repression etiology hypothesis directly. This is an important point since the difficulty in tackling such complex developmental hypotheses by controlled research methods is enormous. I raise these questions here only in order to defer discussion to the last chapter of this essay.

At present I want to focus on another aspect highlighted by the present state of research on psychoanalysis. The first strong impression generated by the work of Kline (1981) and Fisher and Greenberg (1977) is the extent to which central concepts of Freudian theory have *not* been confirmed. This holds true even for concepts for which some favorable evidence is quoted, such as the Oedipus complex. Kline's conclusion of his review on the topic is that there is some evidence for the existence of the phenomenon (p. 435). He emphasizes that the evidence does not at all pertain to Freud's far-reaching claim that the

Oedipus complex is central to personality development in general and the genesis of neuroses in particular.

It is a valuable experience for anyone working in psychoanalysis to go through the two review volumes by Fisher and Greenberg, and Kline. The result can easily shake profound convictions to a considerable extent. None of the authors concludes that the hypotheses have not been substantiated. But it is extremely difficult to get positive evidence for very central ideas in psychoanalytic theory. This includes the importance of the Oedipus complex, the pathogenicity of repression, oral character traits, and the like.

A further strong impression generated by these volumes is the extent to which it is unclear what exactly the contents of psychoanalytic theory are. To give just one example: Fisher and Greenberg devote two chapters to Freud's theory of the genesis of paranoia as a defense against homosexual impulses. This theory of the genesis of paranoia has already been questioned many years ago by such authors as Sullivan (1956, pp. 156–158) and Arieti (1955, p. 141). The tendency of present-day psychoanalysis is to seek the developmental origins of severe pathologies in very early stages. Homosexual themes in paranoia tend to be considered as epiphenomenal rather than causative.

Similar points apply to developments in the conception of the anal period of development. The work of Margaret Mahler and her associates (1975) has put the issue of separation-individuation into the focus of the developmental period coinciding with the anal phase of the classical theory. It is worth noting that the processes hypothesized by Mahler et al. were derived from direct observation of toddlers rather than from reconstructive reasoning. They have found application in psychoanalytic theory of psychopathology (Kernberg, 1980).

This does not imply that the classical conception of the anal phase and Mahler's conception of separation-individuation are necessarily inconsistent with each other. It is very difficult to say clearly what *the* psychoanalytic conception of X (oral, anal, phallic phases, paranoia, schizophrenia, etc.) is, where X can be almost anything. There are at this point several competing hypotheses on about every topic dealt with in psychoanalysis.

Fisher and Greenberg and Kline have solved this problem by

sticking exclusively to research on the hypotheses in Freud's works. This is in many ways certainly a wise strategy. The price paid is that quite often the scrutinized concepts and hypotheses may strike the contemporary analytic practitioner and theorist as outdated.

The multitude of competing approaches to be found today is not to be deplored. I tend to see it as an indication that psychoanalysis is intellectually alive and not frozen. The problem generated by the present situation lies elsewhere. As long as there was only one major theory to be found in psychoanalysis, the clinician could easily comfort himself in the following manner: "Maybe it is true that the theory I work with is not sufficiently substantiated empirically. But it is the only one to be had anyway. Since I must do something, I might as well use the theory which seems most likely to be approximately true on *a priori* grounds as well as on the basis of clinical experience, unsystematic and biased as that may be."

This attitude is no longer viable today. The domain of psychotherapy is not exclusively dominated by psychoanalysis, and even within psychoanalysis there are many approaches which in several respects diverge significantly. A brief glance at the issue of *Contemporary Psychoanalysis* (1987) devoted to the variety of approaches easily convinces us that psychoanalysis has ceased to be homogeneous. It is not at all easy to pinpoint what the common core of the approaches labeled psychoanalytic is (a question I will return to in the final chapter).

If the perspective is widened and nonpsychoanalytic approaches are considered as well, the predicament of the psychoanalytic therapist becomes even more precarious. The classic review of the existing studies comparing outcome of different psychotherapeutic approaches comes to an unsettling conclusion: the evidence suggests that not one of the better established forms of psychotherapy (psychodynamic, experiential, behavioral, and cognitive) can claim superiority over the others. The notable exception is a clear advantage of behavioral approaches to monosymptomatic, clearly delineated disturbances like phobias, compulsions, and sexual dysfunctions (Bergin and Lambert, 1978, p. 170).

Research on the factors operative in psychotherapy has remained quite inconclusive to date. Yet some hypotheses seem slightly supported by the present state of the evidence (Parloff et al., 1978): one is that Roger's triad of genuinenes, empathy, and nonpossessive warmth as personality characteristics of the therapist seems to have some correlation with positive outcome of therapy. The next is that a warm and supportive attitude of the therapist seems to influence outcome positively. There are some more specific findings which I will not mention, since I want to turn to two surprising negative findings: one is that the effectiveness of the therapist's personal therapy remains undemonstrated. The other is that the evidence for the therapist's experience as a determinant of outcome is surprisingly weak (p. 273).

The last two findings are especially surprising from the point of view of psychoanalysis, since its whole training system is based on the two assumptions yet lacking support. Again the authors of this review do not infer that the hypotheses that the therapist's experience is important in determining success and that personal therapy enhances outcome of therapies conducted must be dropped. The point is that there is as yet no evidence that these factors are operative. A further negative finding must be mentioned: it is not at all clear that insight is of special importance in determining success of therapy.

These results carry some obvious consequences for psychoanalysis. One is that what Grünbaum calls the necessary condition thesis cannot be maintained in the face of the evidence. Insight into the infantile roots of neurosis is not a necessary condition for the cure of neurosis. Another is that the emphasis of psychoanalysis on insight as the major factor operative in psychoanalytic therapy is quite problematic given that it has not been substantiated in psychotherapy research.

The general problem emerging for psychoanalysis from current research seems to me to be the following: there are many forms of psychotherapy which seem to be equal to psychoanalysis in therapeutic effect. Hence the most parsimonious hypothesis about the factors operative in psychotherapy is that there must be some factors common to all or most forms of psychotherapy which ought to account for most of the observed effect. This hypothesis runs counter to a profound conviction which has been central to psychoanalysis since Freud, namely, that there is an essential difference between psychoanalytic therapy and all other forms of psychotherapy: only psychoanalysis cures by exposing the roots of neurosis, whereas other therapies (if at all successful) are superficial, as they only treat symptoms by some suggestive mechanism. (This idea went along with the long ago falsified predictions that such therapies would turn out to be useless because of symptom substitution.)

The spectrum of attitudes toward this problem ranges across the following options. The most negative is Eysenck's (1985): psychoanalysis should be rejected as a whole; it is a superseded theory and research program. The intermediary is Grünbaum's: psychoanalysis has no reasonable empirical foundation, and such foundation will never come from clinical data. It must be sought in extraclinical research. The most positive is that taken by Brenner (1982, p. 4): the clinical method is sound scientific practice and psychoanalysis is a well-founded theory.

Along this spectrum there are many more intermediary positions. Grünbaum's work has focused on the question of whether the data gathered in the clinical setting have any validity. Two levels of this question can be distinguished. One is whether clinical data as they have been presented traditionally by psychoanalysts can be used as evidence. The other is whether *any* data ever to be gained from the clinical setting, however controlled, will confirm psychoanalytic theory.

As we have seen, Grünbaum thinks that clinical data will never suffice to confirm crucial aspects of psychoanalytic theory. His view is grounded on the idea that the repression etiology of the neuroses is the cornerstone of psychoanalytic theory and that this hypothesis can only be substantiated through extraclinical research. In a later publication (1986) he acknowledges that some not yet known method of clinical investigation may be able to shed some more light on the processes of analytic therapy, but he remains quite skeptical in this respect (p. 279).

Edelson (1984) has proposed several research designs based on clinical material. Edelson thus basically concurs with those who say that clinical evidence as it has been presented by psychoanalysts until now is methodologically problematic. His point is that there are ways to use clinical material which could provide probative evidence for at least some hypotheses of clinical psychoanalysis. Hence Edelson, unlike Grünbaum, is not skeptical with respect to future clinical data.

Edelson's proposals are interesting in themselves, but they do not address a problem preoccupying many practitioners and theorists in psychoanalysis. Grünbaum's indictment is that clinical data do not warrant any conclusion about the truth or falsity of psychoanalytic theories. Yet the practicing clinician generally has acquired a profound conviction about the truth of the particular version of psychoanalysis he works with. Thousands of hours of therapeutic sessions have made sense to him because he organized them along the lines proposed by his theoretical framework. Developments and processes took place along the lines predicted by his theory. In the best cases a deep conviction emerged both in him and in his patients that truths about their mental lives, past and present, were emerging. Is all this experiential conviction to be discarded *qua* evidence for the theory he works with?

I think that it is this experiential conviction which makes it so difficult for many clinicians in psychoanalysis to be seriously interested in controlled research. They feel that at best such research confirms clinical wisdom they have learned about long ago, and at worst it does not succeed in proving what they know to be true on the basis of their clinical experience. If we want to be careful, we must of course say: what they *think* they know on the basis of their clinical experience.

What then are we to make of this experiential conviction? One option has already been mentioned: it is simply to reject it as a source of evidence which can be taken seriously. This is a rather unpalatable option for the clinician. If he cannot trust the sensorium he has built up throughout his career as a viable source for the understanding of human beings, his skills as a clinician do not do anything they are supposed to do.

Another option is that taken implicitly or explicitly by many psychoanalytic clinicians. They do not bother about controlled research, and they are simply sure that they know the truth about their domain. This option is unpalatable for intellectual reasons: first, experiential conviction has served as a foundation for too many systems of thought in intellectual history which have turned out to be false. Examples range from animism through the geocentric world view and Aristotelian physics to a variety of religions. Second, psychoanalysis makes it very difficult to take experiential conviction as a sole basis for knowledge claims. There are today quite a variety of schools within psychoanalysis, each claiming to have the best understanding of analytic phenomena. Not all of them can be exclusively right, and yet all of them say that their view is strictly based on clinical experience.

This essay is in many ways an attempt to find a way between two extremes: total rejection of ordinary clinical experience as evidence and overestimation of its powers. My aim is to present a model which shows to what extent clinical reasoning can be reasonably assessed. One of the emphases throughout this book will be that rationality is wider than the scientific method. Psychoanalytic reasoning is shown to be similar in many respects to ways of reasoning in other intellectual disciplines such as history and law. If one accepts that these disciplines are accessible to rational argumentation, psychoanalysis is a rationally acceptable discipline as well. A second, no less important, line of thought emphasizes time and again where the limits of clinical wisdom are, and where psychoanalysis is in desperate need of thorough, controlled research in order to find out the truth about its own subject domain.

2

THE HERMENEUTICIST CONCEPTION
OF PSYCHOANALYSIS

In the course of the last 15 years it has become quite fashionable to talk about psychoanalysis as a hermeneutic discipline. A quick glance through any recent issue of *Psychoanalysis and Contemporary Thought* (which is the journal containing most metatheoretical material in psychoanalysis today) makes this quite obvious. The aim of this chapter is to introduce this conception in the following way: in section a I present the main aspects of philosophical hermeneutics as it has emerged in the present century; section b is devoted to the philosophers who have dealt with psychoanalysis, and who have influenced the Hermeneuticist Conception of Psychoanalysis. I will then state what I consider to be its five major theses which have not been consistently differentiated in the literature. This conflation has been harmful.

Before embarking onto the presentation of hermeneutics I should add a terminological remark. It is preferable to speak of the hermeneutic*ist* rather than hermeneut*ic* conception of psychoanalysis for a simple reason: the term "hermeneutic" is used to characterize intellectual disciplines (generally in the humanities). The conception of psychoanalysis discussed here is a certain viewpoint, or a school of thought, claiming that psychoanalysis is a hermeneut*ic* discipline. In analogy to other schools of thought (positiv*ist*, real*ist*, relativ*ist*) I prefer to add the same suffix to the term "hermeneutic."

29

a) THE DEVELOPMENT OF HERMENEUTICS

The history of hermeneutics as a discipline can be roughly divided into three major periods. The first ranges from the sixteenth to the end of the eighteenth century. It was initiated by the disputes about the correct exegesis of the Holy Scriptures, which arose with the Reformation. Luther stressed that the Bible could and should be read without the guidance and constraints imposed by the Catholic church. This led a number of authors to write treatises attempting to formulate rules for the understanding of the Scriptures, and soon these questions were applied to legal texts as well. In this first period hermeneutics was mainly a practically oriented discipline aimed at the construction of a *canon of rules* for interpretation (for this and what follows I rely on Gadamer and Boehm, 1976).

The second period is associated with the rise of Romanticism and the preoccupation with how earlier historical periods could be understood. The context of the discussion was an attempt to differentiate between the natural sciences concerned with general laws and the humanities concerned with individual events, periods, and persons. The main exponent of this dichotomy at the time was Herder (Berlin, 1976) who was to become an important influence on Goethe. Romantic hermeneutics received its final form in the work of Friedrich Schleiermacher (Gadamer and Boehm, 1976). His central concern was to show that the exegesis of the Holy Scriptures was founded on the same principles as textual understanding in every other context. The ensuing discussion concerning the methodology of textual exegesis and historical research culminated in the edifice of German philology of the nineteenth century. This second period can thus be put under the heading of the search for a methodology for the humanities (the *Geisteswissenschaften*).

The onset of the third period, that of modern hermeneutics, is mainly associated with the name of Wilhelm Dilthey, who wrote important historical works during the last three decades of the nineteenth century. In addition, he was interested in the conditions of the possibility of objective knowledge in the humanities. As opposed to the writers of the previous two periods of hermeneutics, he did not believe that a canon of rules for interpretation could be found. He asked a more fundamental question: what is the nature of historical understanding, and what is the essence of the meanings to be sought for? This led him to the thesis that the process of interpretation consists in a reenactment of the experience of the author by his interpreter—a doctrine which came to be associated with Collingwood (1946) in England later on.

The third phase of hermeneutics is characterized by a more strictly theoretical approach. The idea of a practically applicable canon of rules for interpretation was seen to be unrealizable. Dilthey's view of interpretation as reenactment was unrealistic as well: it was not at all clear what exactly had to be reenacted, and how the interpreter could know that his reenactment was right. The question which became urgent was therefore: if there is no set of rules which defines the criteria for the correctness of textual understanding, what does guarantee the objectivity of some given interpretation?

It was Martin Heidegger (1899–1976) who provided the conceptual framework within which the discipline of philosophical hermeneutics was to evolve in the twentieth century. Heidegger is one of the major figures of continental philosophy of this period, but his philosophy is too complex to be expounded here. Instead, I want to summarize briefly three major theses of philosophical hermeneutics as they found expression in the major text of the contemporary hermeneutic movement, *Truth and Method*, written by Hans-Georg Gadamer, one of Heidegger's most important students.

The first is that understanding is not an activity human beings engage in primarily or only when they approach linguistic phenomena. It is rather the basic mode of human existence in all its manifestations. To be a human being is to be constantly structuring his or her world in terms of meaning. Our capacity to understand texts is therefore not restricted to texts, but is derived from our more basic activity of interpreting the world.

The second major thesis has become quite famous under the name "hermeneutic circle." A reader setting out to interpret a text must assume that there is something to be understood there, that he is not faced with a meaningless jumble of sounds or of ink stains. Furthermore, the interpreter must have many preconceptions about what it is to communicate something through a text, what type of texts there are, and the like. The idea of the hermeneutic circle is intimately linked to the thesis that understanding is a basic modality of human existence. Understanding a text is to integrate it into the horizons of intelligibility by which we structure our world.

The result is in a sense circular: the interpreter sets out to understand by presuming, to begin with, what kind of meanings there are to be found. If he does not succeed in fitting the text into his frame of intelligibility, he has failed to understand the text; the text remains literally meaningless to him. The process of interpretation seems to be caught up in itself: if the interpreter can only find meanings of the type he reads into the text, he cannot correct his own understanding. Gadamer's view on this is that the process of correcting one's presuppositions must always be partial. Only if we succeed in partially integrating the text into our preexisting frames of meaning can we notice that we fail to understand it in part. This failure will manifest itself by the text's recalcitrance to bend completely to our previous frame, which we can then try to enlarge in a way allowing us to accommodate the unintelligible parts.

An example will make this point intuitively clearer. The most basic thesis of Freud's *Interpretation of Dreams* is that dreams are meaningful. Dream reports are classical examples of texts (in the widest sense of the word), which on the face of it resist integration into any of our preexisting notions of meaningfulness. Freud's basic thesis that dreams are wish fulfillments is hermeneutically speaking an assimilation of dreams to an activity known and intelligible to us: the fantasizing of a wished-for state of affairs, i.e., imagining it with a partial pretension that it is actual. But dreams do not fit easily into this frame. Freud therefore widens our context of intelligibility by adding the idea of motivated censure of dreams, and the hypothesis that some of the wishes expressed by dreams are not rooted in the present. The introduction of the idea of infantile, repressed wishes and of censorship places seemingly nonsensical aspects of dreams a context in which they can be understood.

The third thesis of philosophical hermeneutics gave Gadamer's *magnum opus* its somewhat misleading name *Truth and*

Method. The title is misleading since the thesis is precisely that there is *no* such thing as a method for arriving at and validating an interpretation of texts. This idea can again be seen to follow from the two previous ones. Understanding is the activity of placing texts (spoken, written, dreamed, etc.) into the structure of what we previously take to be meaningful. The interpreter's task cannot be to objectify the text completely. One of the metaphors Gadamer uses to characterize the process of interpretation is that the interpreter enters into a dialogue with the text. Being in a dialogue is not to be completely detached, but rather to be interacting with one's partner. Gadamer carries his idea quite far. At first sight it seems that the metaphor is not quite accurate. In a dialogue both partners interact with and influence each other, which seems simply not to hold for the relation between text and interpreter. The interpreter, one might think, may be changed by the text, but not vice versa. Gadamer radicalizes his view by arguing that texts do not have eternally fixed meanings independent of the reader. If the interpreter must assimilate the text to his own framework of meaning, he enriches the text and enlarges the significance to be found.

Actually this is not quite precise: the interpreter cannot really put himself in the author's place. Gadamer thinks that Dilthey's idea of reenactment is misleading. The interpreter cannot step out of his own horizon of intelligibility and adopt the author's. He can only try to assimilate the author's text into his own horizon, by widening his own conceptions of meaningfulness. Gadamer does not take this to mean, though, that every act of interpretation distorts the text; the opposite is true. Since the interpreter can see more than the author, he can often understand the author better than the author himself does or did. The interaction between text and reader can therefore be one of mutual enrichment.

But this also means that there cannot be a hermeneutic method. The criterion of successful interpretation must ultimately remain the interpreter's experience of truly having appropriated the text. The interpretation cannot be measured relative to some external, absolute standard. Only the fact that the text has become transparent within the horizon of intelligibility of the interpreter (or interpretive community) can serve as the hallmark of appropriation.

The question then arises of how interpretive practice can be salvaged from falling into subjectivity. If the criterion for successful understanding is the experience of having understood the text, every interpreter can only rely on his own intuitions, which would make objectivity and rational discussion of interpretations impossible.

The answer proposed by philosophical hermeneutics is as follows: interpreters of texts and spoken utterances are not individuals detached from socially constituted forms of life. I mentioned Gadamer's first thesis, which was that understanding is an activity essential to human existence in general and not restricted to the decoding of linguistic phenomena. Every individual grows into a world structured by the meanings embodied in the form of life of his society. His horizons of intelligibility are thus not private to him but shared by the members of his culture.

The result is that every individual interpreter must be seen as part of an *interpretive community*. His criteria for successful understanding of texts are grounded in the meaning-structures underlying the culture, which has formed him as a human being. This growing into an interpretive community can attain more specific manifestations if he goes through training in some hermeneutic discipline in the humanities or some of the social sciences (psychoanalysis would be a good example here). His initiation into the discipline occurs less by the learning of explicit rules than by participation in the interpretive *practice* of the respective community.

Correspondingly interpretive practice allows for objectivity despite the impossibility of providing algorithmlike rules for the correctness of interpretations. The intersubjectivity is guaranteed by the fact that individual interpreters are part of the same tradition or form of life. Their criteria for judging interpretations are embodied in their skills, enabling them to participate in their common practice (see also Fish, 1980, part 2; Taylor, 1985, part 3). This idea of the possibility that objectivity of interpretation is constituted by the common practice of interpreters, rather than by a methodology which can be formalized, has become extremely influential in modern philosophy (e.g., Taylor, 1985; Wittgenstein, 1953; Kripke, 1984) far beyond the school of philosophical hermeneutics, and it will play an important role in this essay (chaps. 3 and 4). The crucial step taken in this approach is to drop the picture of objectivity as the mirroring of an unconceptualized reality. Instead objectivity is understood, in a Kantian way, as intersubjectivity.

b)   THE PHILOSOPHICAL ROOTS OF THE HERMENEUTICIST
INTERPRETATION OF PSYCHOANALYSIS

Philosophical interest in psychoanalysis took two basic forms. One was the examination of psychoanalysis from the point of view of the philosophy of science which tended to be critical of the epistemic credentials of psychoanalysis. A major exponent of this approach was presented in chapter 1. The second type of philosophical writings on psychoanalysis, which is the topic of this section, approached psychoanalysis as a (or even *the*) major psychological theory of the twentieth century. They were interested in the basic structure of psychological explanation —sometimes more generally in the structure of the social sciences and/or humanities—and analyzed psychoanalysis as a paradigm for their field of interest.

I will start with the English philosophers (primarily located in Oxford and Cambridge), who showed interest in psychoanalysis mainly in the 1950s and 1960s. Most of these writers belonged to the school of the philosophy of ordinary language, whose major figures were Ludwig Wittgenstein, Gilbert Ryle, and John L. Austin. The general thrust of the work inspired by these men was the careful analysis of the logical structure of segments of ordinary language. The idea was such that activity could help both to dissolve certain philosophical puzzles by clarifying linguistic confusions and to make explicit the pictures of segments of reality embodied in ordinary language. In this tradition there were several philosophers who took psychoanalysis to be an extremely valuable psychological theory but who thought that Freud had had a wrong conception of the nature of his own work (e.g., Flew, 1949; McIntyre, 1958; Peters, 1949; Toulmin, 1949). He thought that he was formulating a theory about previously unknown causes of human behavior. But, they claimed, in giving psychological explanations of human behavior, he was not dealing with the *causes* at all. In reality, such explanations were really descriptions of behavior as motivated action. An action and the reason motivating it were not two distinct events; rather they were logically connected descriptions of one event as intentional and directed. What Freud had therefore really been doing was to extend the range of behaviors to be described as intentional action by including events like slips of tongue, neurotic symptoms, and dreams.

The philosophical theses of the English authors about psychoanalysis were therefore (a) that reason-explanations were not causal; (b) that psychoanalysis gave reason-explanations for action; and (c) that psychoanalytic explanations could therefore not be assimilated to natural science models of causal explanations.

As we turn to the European continent, it is apparent that the whole framework of the philosophical interest in psychoanalysis changed quite drastically. The two major figures here are Paul Ricoeur of France and Jürgen Habermas of Germany.

Ricoeur is a prolific writer who has engaged in several large-scale projects since the late 1940s, only one of which is of interest here. The major task of hermeneutics is to provide of a theory of the interpretation of symbols, where a symbol is defined as "any structure of signification in which a direct, primary, literal meaning designates, in addition, another meaning which is indirect, secondary and figurative, and which can be apprehended only through the first" (Ricoeur, 1974, p. 148). By this he means the approach which considers the text as *hiding* its meaning. The interpreter's task is to be suspicious of the underlying motives and currents in the text and thus to unmask its hidden meaning. Ricoeur's main work on psychoanalysis is a 500-page book which contains, among other things, a very careful analysis of the interrelation of natural science thinking and hermeneutics in Freud's work. Ricoeur was the first author who provided a systematic interpretation of psychoanalysis as a hermeneutic discipline.

Habermas, like Ricoeur, is a very prolific writer who, for

more than two decades, has been pursuing a major project which is an attempt to formulate the foundations for a critical theory of society, which seeks to provide the normative basis for a critique of existing institutions and practices in Western society. Habermas dealt with psychoanalysis in his book, *Knowledge and Human Interest* (1968, Engl. tr., 1971). His major concern was to show that there was a special kind of knowledge, for which psychoanalysis was his main paradigm. This is the self-knowledge which, by its every existence, frees man from underlying causal laws which coerce man only so long as he does not understand them.

Habermas interprets the psychoanalytic concept of repression hermeneutically as the excommunication of certain mental contents from the person's language. The person's incapacity verbally to formulate his own wishes and fears forces him to follow them blindly. The analytic process is one of self-reflection, through which the person can reintegrate the excommunicated parts into his language. In Habermas's view of psychoanalysis it is this very attainment of self-knowledge which emancipates the person from the rule of the unknown.

A corollary of this understanding of psychoanalysis is that Habermas (quite similarly to the English philosophers) thinks that Freud misconceived the nature of his own enterprise. He speaks of the "scientific self-misunderstanding" of metapsychology (1968, chap. 11) which led Freud to cast his contribution to mankind's self-reflection into the language of nineteenth-century mechanistic science.

c)   THE FIVE THESES OF THE HERMENEUTICIST CONCEPTION
OF PSYCHOANALYSIS

The different strands of philosophical thought about psychoanalysis have had a strong influence on the current self-reflection of psychoanalysis. The problem is that this influence was of a somewhat diffuse nature and that issues were obscured by the conflation of five distinct and logically independent theses.

At first glance, these philosophical views have some traits in common. All of them put special emphasis on some close connection between psychoanalysis and language. All of them claim that psychoanalysis should not be considered as belonging to the natural sciences and that Freud's metatheoretical understanding of his own theory was misleading. Certainly a somewhat vague antiscientistic current underlies all positions mentioned. All of these philosophers oppose the positivistic view that there is only one model of rational theory construction and testing which corresponds to the structure of modern physics.

A number of authors have been involved in the formulation of the hermeneuticist conception of psychoanalysis (e.g., Gill, 1983; Klein, 1976; Goldberg, 1984; Schafer, 1976, 1983; Spence, 1982a). The most sustained attempt to reinterpret psychoanalysis as a hermeneutic discipline has been Roy Schafer's. His writings on the topic started to appear in 1970 and his output during the years afterward was quite remarkable (1976, 1978, 1980, 1983). Since his writings add up to something like a theory, which includes both a clinical and metatheoretical perspective, I will mostly focus on his writings in the chapters to come to exemplify certain points in the hermeneuticist conception of psychoanalysis. This will not bias the discussion; although others have differed from him in some details, none has delineated the hermeneuticist point of view with the same stamina.

The essence of the hermeneuticist conception of psychoanalysis can be organized into five theses. These are briefly presented here and discussed in the following section.

Thesis 1: Metapsychology should be discarded. Freudian metapsychology is seen to derive from Freud's nineteenth-century mechanistic conceptions of science. It should be discarded (a) because it cannot be tested by clinical work, and (b) because it embodies a misleading, mechanistic picture of man. Instead, psychoanalysis should focus on the clinical theory Freud created (Klein, 1976, chaps. 1 and 2; Schafer, 1976, chaps. 1, 4, and 5; Gill, 1983). The philosophical roots of this thesis are to be found in all the authors mentioned in section b.

Thesis 2: Psychoanalysis should avoid subpersonal terminology and use only personal terms. G. S. Klein (1976), Schafer (1976), and

Gill (1983) have forcefully advocated this thesis. The same formulation has been advocated for all of psychology by several authors (Gauld and Shotter, 1977; Dreyfus, 1979; Harre, 1983). The psychoanalytic authors have—I believe wrongly—identified this thesis with the one that metapsychology should be abandoned. Additionally, Schafer (1976) has taken this thesis to imply that psychoanalysis should adopt his action language. The thesis in its general version is that the subject of psychoanalytic theory and interpretation should not be drives, forces, and mechanisms but persons who perceive, desire, defend, etc.

Thesis 3: Psychoanalysis does not explain behavior in terms of causes. This thesis has been defended most vigorously by Schafer (1976, esp. chap. 10). In his version it has two aspects. One is that psychoanalysis is not concerned with causal links between childhood events and neurotic symptoms to be found in adults. The other is that even when the patient's behavior is explained in terms of his present mental states, these are not causal explanations. Both of these aspects are closely linked to the English neo-Wittgensteinians mentioned in section b above.

Thesis 4: Psychoanalysis is concerned with meanings. In this general form, this thesis will probably be acceptable to most analysts. In its stronger, more typically hermeneuticist version it states that psychoanalytic theory is a systematic elaboration of *story lines* arranged along the lines of an account of psychosexual development. These story lines are then used to organize the patient's experience in an enlightening manner (G. S. Klein, 1976, chapter 1; Spence, 1982a; Schafer, 1983). Here a central tenet of both Ricoeur's and Habermas's views can be encountered.

Thesis 5: There are always many possible interpretations of human behavior and psychoanalysis is one of them. Schafer (1983) strongly emphasizes what he calls "a relativist position" (p. 277) and makes it an integral of his general perspective on psychoanalysis. Others with a similar outlook are Goldberg (1984) and Gill (1983). These authors do not think that such interpretive pluralism (they call it relativism) constitutes a problem, whereas Spence (1982a) and Eagle (1980, 1984) do. The philosophical roots of this pluralism can be found in hermeneutics (Gadamer,

Ricoeur), poststructuralist philosophy, and literary theory (for an excellent presentation, see Culler, 1981).

d) THE HERMENEUTICIST CONCEPTION AS AN EPISTEMIC DEFENSE OF PSYCHOANALYSIS

It would have been possible to add a sixth thesis to the list of the previous section. I have preferred not to do so since the point to be made is of a more general nature, overarching the more specific theses presented. The hermeneuticist conception of psychoanalysis is to a large extent a radical attempt to invalidate methodological criticisms made against psychoanalysis. Instead of trying to answer charges about the unverifiability of psychoanalytic propositions one by one, they want to discard them as irrelevant.

The line of defense could be summarized as follows: philosophers of science and other critics have measured psychoanalysis by the standards of natural science, but psychoanalysis is a hermeneutic discipline and therefore the methodological criticisms are quite simply misguided. Psychoanalysis is not at all engaged in investigating the causes of human behavior, but rather in trying to decipher its meanings. The lack of predictive power and mathematical precision as a reproach against psychoanalysis need not worry us at all. Psychoanalysis, by its very nature, is not even looking for such qualities (e.g., Schafer, 1976, p. 205).

It is, I think, an interesting fact that the most fervent hermeneuticists in psychoanalysis are authors with a considerable background in controlled research. Gill, Klein, Schafer, and Spence have all done experimental work in such fields as psychodiagnostics, perception, and hypnosis. It is likely that this fact is not entirely coincidental. A plausible explanation is that since these authors are all well acquainted with the intricacies of empirical research, they are probably apt to comprehend the seriousness of the methodological charges raised against psychoanalysis. They therefore see only one way to answer there charges, namely, to deny the assumption they are based on.

I am thus arguing that the hermeneuticist conception of psychoanalysis is the result of both concern for and sophisticated awareness of the methodological complexities involved in psychoanalytic research. As an example I quote G. S. Klein, who talks about the possibility of justifying inferences from clinical data to theoretical constructs: "The logic and dependability of inference from phenomenology crucially influence the validity of the extraphenomenological concepts. Unless these inferences are valid, the concepts refer to witches and unicorns" (G. S. Klein, 1976, p. 51). Since Klein thinks that many of the inferences made from clinical data are not valid, he arrives at the conclusion that our conception of psychoanalytic theory must be revised quite drastically if it is to stand up to criticism.

This is in marked contrast to the view of those authors who believe that psychoanalysis is to be regarded as belonging to natural sciences yet think that the epistemic credentials of the discipline are sound. Brenner (1982) provides a good example for this:

> . . . what a psychoanalyst does with the data which derive from applying the psychoanalytic method is no different from what any scientist does with his or her data. An analyst postulates the same cause-and-effect relationships with respect to psychoanalytic data as a physicist, for example, postulates with respect to the data available to him or her [p. 4].

What, then, is Brenner's defense against charges like Grünbaum's (see chap. 1 above)? All I could find was:

> . . . there are philosophers of science who are critical of psychoanalytic theories, and who mistakenly characterize psychoanalysis as speculation rather than as a branch of science. This they do despite the fact that they are themselves without experience in using the method that provides the basis for the theories they criticize [p. 4].

This is precisely the kind of statement which gives psychoanalysis the name of a "dogmatic establishment" (Gardner, 1984). First Brenner claims that psychoanalysis is to be measured by the standards of natural science and then criticizes philosophers for applying these standards to psychoanalysis! Referring to the fact that philosophers do not have experience in analytic clinical work is *not* the kind of defense a natural science methodology allows for. Instead, natural scientists (and psychologists modeling their work accordingly) include a precise description of the method used in their empirical work in every article reporting a finding. And this Brenner does not do. Grünbaum (1984, p. 189) therefore rightly criticizes Brenner for not measuring up to the very criteria he endorses himself.

The authors advocating the hermeneuticist conception of psychoanalysis thus have more, rather than less, methodological sophistication than Brenner, who simply seems to be unaware of the complexities involved in the issue. This conception relies on the idea that hermeneutic disciplines cannot follow a strict methodology. As we have seen in section a of this chapter, modern philosophical hermeneutics denies that there can be anything like a canon of rules determining the correctness of interpretations. The ultimate criterion for the validity of an interpretation must consist in the consensus of the interpretive community that a text has indeed become intelligible. This in turn means that it has become integrated into the frame of meaning within which the interpretive community lives—a frame which for reasons of principle cannot be formalized. This is quite different from what happens in natural sciences. If psychoanalysis is entirely a hermeneutic enterprise, it may be exempt from the strictures and demands of scientific method.

The question which must now be asked is: to what extent is the hermeneuticist conception of psychoanalysis an adequate interpretation and defense of psychoanalysis? The bulk of the present essay is an attempt to contribute to an answer. For reasons of space, and in order to maintain a thematic unity throughout the argument, I will limit myself to a discussion of those theses which pertain to the question of *whether the clinical theory of psychoanalysis can be validated.*

Theses 1 (that metapsychology should be discarded) and *2* (that psychoanalysis should avoid using subpersonal terminology) therefore fall outside the scope of this essay. *Thesis 1* was first expounded (and advocated) by G. S. Klein and Roy Schafer independently at the beginning of the '70s, following earlier, less systematic arguments by Holt (1965). They claimed that metapsychology was to be abandoned, both because it contained a great deal of obsolete nineteenth-century metaphysics and because it could not be validated in the context of clinical practice.

During the last 15 years quite an extensive literature has emerged around the question of what the nature of psychoanalytic theory should be (for a representative selection see Gill and Brenman, 1959). The dispute involves several subquestions: Is psychoanalysis a general or only a clinical psychology? Is the notion of mental energy useful or does it only encumber psychoanalysis with useless complications? Is it necessary for psychoanalysis to wait for neurophysiological evidence for its ultimate validation?

The recent discussion around the epistemic status of psychoanalysis has received renewed impetus and interest by Grünbaum's challenging work, which I have presented in chapter 1. Grünbaum's approach is interesting in that he only deals with the clinical theory of psychoanalysis; he refrains from discussing the epistemologically more vulnerable part of psychoanalysis, metapsychology, and claims that even the clinical theory, which is taken to be epistemically sounder, cannot be validated by clinical methods, but only through controlled research.

My goal is to investigate the extent to which the hermeneuticist conception of psychoanalysis helps to defend the methodological soundness of *the clinical theory and method of research of psychoanalysis only*. Therefore, theses 1 and 2, which relate to the question of whether psychoanalysis should be more than a clinical theory, can be safely omitted from the present discussion without risking oversimplification.

PART II

THE EPISTEMOLOGY OF CLINICAL INTERPRETATION AND RECONSTRUCTION

3

PSYCHOANALYSIS AND THE EPISTEMOLOGY OF REASON EXPLANATIONS

In the previous chapter I claimed that the hermeneuticist conception of psychoanalysis as a whole can be regarded as an epistemic defense of clinical psychoanalysis. In addition I showed that this conception can usefully be taken as stating five distinct theses. One of these is that psychoanalysis explains by giving a person's *reasons* for action, and these *are not causes* of behavior. Authors like Habermas (1968) and Schafer (1976) have taken this thesis to be crucial for the claim that the methodological status of psychoanalysis is different from that of the natural sciences.

Grünbaum (1984, pp. 69–83) has attacked the idea that reasons are not causes of behavior with very strong arguments. Since he also takes this thesis to be crucial for the epistemic defense of psychoanalysis attempted by the hermeneuticists, he thinks that if the thesis can be shown to be wrong, the whole hermeneuticist defense of psychoanalysis breaks down.

I think the thesis that reasons are not causes of behavior is indeed wrong. In section a of this chapter I will present the only systematic argument for this thesis to be found in the hermeneuticist literature on psychoanalysis (Schafer, 1976). Section b will demonstrate in some detail why these arguments are not valid.

As opposed to both Schafer and Grünbaum, I do not think,

though, that the hermeneuticist defense of psychoanalysis hinges in any way on the mistaken idea that reasons are not causes. Section c of this chapter provides an outline of the epistemology of reason explanations, showing that even if reasons *are* causes, they have epistemological properties, which make reason explanations methodologically more akin to textual interpretation than to scientific explanation.

a)   SCHAFER ON REASONS, CAUSES, AND ACTION LANGUAGE

Schafer is the psychoanalytic author who tries to give the most explicit arguments for the thesis that motives are not causes. I believe that these arguments are invalid. My general goal is to free the hermeneuticist conception of psychoanalysis from unnecessary complications.

Schafer (1976) explicitly tackles the relation between motives (or reasons) and causes in a section called "Why-Questions and the Explanations of Actions" (pp. 201–205). He begins by saying:

> In what sense have we used traditional motivation words to tell us why [an action occurred]? The answer, contrary to all appearances, is that we have not used them to designate causes. Instead, we have used them to restate psychological observations in the terms of a particular set or system of language rules. . . . The traditional motivation words . . . have enabled us to constitute data within a particular philosophical universe [p. 201].

Schafer then goes on to say that Freud formulated a set of language rules within which he tried to describe phenomena and that Freud's particular concern was to translate phenomena into the language of laboratory science of his day. Schafer emphasizes that Freud's adoption of this language is based on a choice, rather than being necessitated by the phenomena.

> Consequently, to say that we have used motivation words to tell us why, is to say that we have stated actions and their modes in terms of a physiochemical and biological system of some kind. It has merely been one (eclectic) way of going about the job of

making actions intelligible or more intelligible than they have
been.

Schafer's alternative is his action language:

> In its terms one might say, "He cheated greedily in making out
> his tax return." Now, simply stating the mode of the action,
> *greedily*, gives its reasons at least as well as the word *greed* names
> a motive or determinant. . . . Adopting these alternatives, one
> does not give up trying to understand and explain human activity
> systematically. The only question is how one is to do it, that is,
> what rules one is to follow and how [p. 202].

The crucial difference between the classical psychodynamic
language and Schafer's action language is that the former is
created around the notion of cause, while the latter uses *reasons*
to explain actions. He exemplifies his action language in the
following passage:

> S[tatement]: The boy made fun of the girl when she sat down
> to urinate.
> Q[uestion]: Why did he do that?
> A(nswer]: Upon being confronted by the genital difference
> between himself and the girl, he thought anxiously
> of his being castrated, and by ridiculing the girl as
> defective, he avoided thinking consciously, fear-
> fully and excitedly of this frightening eventuality.
> That is why [p. 203].

This way of speaking rests exclusively on reasons; in Schafer's
view, this implies that one renounces causal explanation. His
central argument for the distinction between reasons and causes
states that causes are necessary and sufficient conditions for
their effects, and

> . . . the idea of cause makes sense only with respect to the de-
> scription of antecedent conditions by *an independent, objective ob-
> server engaged in a particular project*. In contrast, in a psychology
> of action, these "causes" can exist only as the agent's reasons,
> which are features of his or her personal world of meaning and
> goals . . . it is how the person represents these "causes" . . . that
> is the decisive consideration for psychoanalytic understanding
> and explanation; in other words, what counts in psychoanalysis

are the causes as they appear in an individual's world. To seek
the causes for these representations only leads to further issues
of individual representation, so that causes forever elude one's
grasp while reasons of every kind fill one's hand [p. 205].

I have quoted this passage extensively because it contains the
only attempt I know in the psychoanalytic literature that argues
explicitly for the claim that psychoanalytic explanation is not
of a causal nature. Schafer provides one more argument for
this view, by saying that psychoanalysis can simply not ascertain
causal relations because it is unable to yield control, prediction,
and mathematical precision.

To summarize Schafer's arguments:

1. The psychoanalytic method cannot ascertain causes or
causal relations for it lacks predictive power.

2. Psychoanalysis explains in terms of reasons. Reasons are
not causes, because they concern the way a person represents
the world and are not objective.

3. Psychoanalysis should answer "why" questions by giving
adverbialized descriptions of actions rather than using nouns
referring to motives, as is done in the language of classical
psychodynamics.

4. Adopting the language of classical psychodynamics or action language is a matter of choice.

The next section will present a critique of arguments 1 and
2 because they are crucial to my topic. Theses 3 and 4 are not
directly linked to Schafer's epistemological defense of psychoanalysis and I will therefore refrain from discussing them here.
In the early 1970s Schafer began to develop his general program of changing the metaphorical structure of psychoanalysis
from a mechanistic framework into an agent-centered person
psychology. Much of this program can be formulated without
going into the details of Schafer's proposals for an action language.

In his *The Analytic Attitude* there still are references to action
language, but the emphasis has changed. This work is a sustained and brilliant attempt to reinterpret psychoanalysis in
terms of narrative action while taking into account recent developments in philosophy and literary theory. In later chapters

I will return to certain aspects of Schafer's mature views and we will see that these can safely be divorced from the theses to be discussed now.

b)   A Critique of Schafer

The first thesis mentioned can be cast into a deductive argument, which is valid, but, as we shall see, its premises are not plausible. The structure of the argument is:

1. The psychoanalytic method ascertains something.

2. The psychoanalytic method cannot ascertain causal relations.

3. Psychoanalysis deals with what it can ascertain.

4. Conclusion: Psychoanalysis does not deal with causal relations.

This is the only way I can think of to make the argument leading to the conclusion valid. The problem is that premises 1 through 3 beg the very question they are trying to answer, thus making the argument quite unconvincing.

This is easy to see if we take the thesis to be defended, namely, the conclusion, as an attempt to defend psychoanalytic clinical work as providing valid data. The claim of critics like Grünbaum is that psychoanalysis cannot ascertain causal relations through clinical data. Schafer's defense is to say that psychoanalysis does not deal with causal relations at all. He justifies this by recourse to premises 1 and 2. Another way to state the content of these premises is that psychoanalysis is epistemologically sound, i.e., that it deals only with propositions it can in fact confirm. Since Schafer accepts the critics' claim that psychoanalysis cannot ascertain causal relations, this in fact yields the conclusion that psychoanalysis does not deal with causal relations.

The problem is that premises 1 and 2 jointly state what is at issue, namely, that psychoanalysis is an epistemologically sound discipline. But, if this is so, the conclusion cannot serve as an epistemic defense of psychoanalysis since it is founded on the assumption of methodological soundness rather than providing a basis for this assumption. The first thesis can therefore only convince those who already accept that psychoanalysis has a sufficient evidential basis, which renders it quite uninterest-ing—whatever its truth value.

Let us therefore turn to the second thesis (in section a). In the lengthy quotation I gave Schafer says that "the idea of cause makes sense only with respect to the description of antecedent conditions *by an independent, objective observer engaged in a partic-ular project*" (p. 205). The phrase italicized by Schafer is ob-viously wrong as it stands, as can be seen in a simple example. If John smashes a window, either intentionally or accidentally, he can perfectly well describe the causal relation between his action (if it was intentional) or the event (if he stumbled) and the effect it produced (the breaking of the window). John is not an independent observer, though; he is involved in the very causal nexus he is describing. But this should be impossible if Schafer is right.

It may be possible to extract his intention by turning to other aspects of the passage quoted. I want to restate a part of that passage because it will clarify what Schafer's misconception is:

> . . . it is how the person represents these "causes" unconsciously, as well as preconsciously and consciously, that is the decisive consideration for psychoanalytic understanding and explanation. . . . To seek the causes of these representations only leads to further issues of individual representations, so that causes for-ever elude one's grasp while reasons of every kind fill one's hands [p. 205].

The last sentence states most clearly the confusion central to Schafer's whole thesis that reasons cannot be causes. Let me first state what exactly is meant by the thesis that reasons *are* causes: it is the way a person represents reality (including him-self and the persons he interacts with) that is causally responsible for the way he acts, thinks, and feels, i.e., *the representation itself is the cause of action.*

As opposed to that, Schafer says that it is the way the person represents these "causes" (he puts the term in quotation marks), which is relevant for psychoanalysis, and not the cause itself. But anyone who believes that reasons *are* causes (including myself) thinks that the way a person represents things has causal importance, which at first glance does not even contradict what

Schafer believes to be relevant for psychoanalysis. So why does Schafer think that psychoanalytic explanation cannot be causal?

Schafer thinks that if one claims that reasons *cause* behavior, one says that (a) the subject represents the world in this way and (b) gives an additional cause for the subject's action. The last sentence of the quotation implies that the view Schafer attacks states that, in having reasons, persons represent their own inner states, which in turn are causally responsible for their behavior, and that the representations and the causes are not identical.

If anyone were actually to think such a thing, this would indeed be terribly confused. Persons represent all kinds of things in the world when they reason about what to do, but certainly not their own brain states, as Schafer imputes. I actually do not know whom Schafer thinks of when he puts forth his argument. None of the recent authors I know who claim that reasons are causes (e.g., McGinn, 1979) fall into the muddles Schafer ascribes to this position.

There is a very straightforward account of how reasons cause behavior, which is born commonsensical and necessary if we want to understand how reasons explain behavior. This account can be exemplified by Schafer's imaginary case of the boy who makes fun of the urinating girl, which I quoted previously. The boy sees the girl's lack of a penis, which leads him to be in a mental state of thinking about the possibility of his own castration, or, to put it differently (Sandler and Rosenblatt, 1962), of representing himself as castrated. Since this induces anxiety, he ridicules the girl to defend against his own anxiety. Nothing in this example precludes us from saying that the boy's act of ridiculing the girl is the causal outcome of the representational and affective state just described.

Actually such a psychoanalytic account *necessitates* the existence of such causal relations. Let us extend Schafer's example and imagine that we ask the boy why he is ridiculing the girl. His answer is likely to be "because the way she urinates is so funny." But we think that this is not at all the real reason for his action. The real reason is that given in Schafer's account, namely, castration anxiety.

What do we mean by saying that the real reason is not what

the boy says it is? In psychoanalysis we very often want to differentiate between the *real reason* for an action and the person's *rationalization*. This distinction can be made only if (1) the action to be explained would not have occurred without the castration anxiety, while it would have occurred without the girl's looking funny; (2) the boy laughed at the girl *because* he tried to avoid thinking of his own castration as a frightening possibility and *not because* of his really thinking that the girl looked funny. Jointly this implies that the boy's castration anxiety was causally necessary and sufficient for his laughing at the girl, while the idea that the girl looked funny was not. What we generally mean by saying that p was the real reason for an action and that q was only a rationalization is precisely that p was *the cause* of the action, while q was only what the person (mistakenly) took to be the cause.

c) MEANINGS AND CAUSES IN PSYCHOANALYTIC INTERPRETATIONS

There are some complexities involved in explanation by reasons. Not all of them can be treated here in any way even approaching completeness, but those most pertinent to the issue will be mentioned.

Reason explanations basically have two functions: the first is to state the causes of actions. They do so often in a rather complex way, and I will briefly touch upon some of these complexities. They do not necessarily state the proximate cause of the action (Davidson, 1980; McGinn, 1979), as the following example shows: we may say of someone that he avoids close relations to women because in childhood he experienced his mother as unbearably intrusive. Such an explanation states no single event which is the cause of the person's present behavior. It describes a constellation in his childhood which created a disposition. This disposition in turn is productive of occurrent mental states which interact in complex ways to generate the avoidant behavior which is to be explained.

In such an explanation we do not know the precise sequence of events which led to the creation of the disposition, which in turn is causally responsible for the avoidant behavior. Neither do we know the sequence of external and internal events which is responsible for the ways in which the avoidant pattern is generated and maintained in particular cases. The proximate causes which are operative in each particular case can be various: feelings of revulsion which are experienced whenever a woman expresses the wish for a more intimate relation, which in turn leads to the desire to get away from her, which in turn leads to the intention to tell her that the relation is over and so on.

There is another complexity which must be taken into account. Generally it is assumed that the existence of a causal relation between two events A and B entails the existence of a strict, deterministic law which links events of the types A and B. Notoriously (Davidson, 1980, chaps. 1 and 11) psychology is not able to come up with such laws, and the question thus arises whether psychology can state that there are causal relations between events. Davidson's answer is that although psychology cannot give such laws, it can explain causally—and in fact for most causal explanations we do not know what the covering law is.

This holds true for examples as trivial as "the stone shattered the window." Most people would not be able to come up with a law stronger than "Glass is generally fragile, and if you throw something heavy and hard at something fragile, it will generally break." This law is by no means deterministic; the vagueness of terms like "fragile" and the proviso of "generally" are intended to make up for our ignorance in the matter. We assume that a genuine covering law exists, but it would not use terms like "fragile" and "heavy" at all. Instead it would refer to the underlying microstructure of the materials in question and put the law in quantitative terms.

Hence Davidson (1980, p. 160) concludes: causal explanation entails that there is a strict causal law which links cause and effect nomologically, but it does not presuppose that we know this law or even what it looks like. The terms in which we described the events in our original explanations need not figure in the causal law at all.

This has important repercussions on psychological explanations. Not only are we *de facto* at present not in the possession of any strictly deterministic causal laws, but there are reasons to believe that there cannot be such laws. *Prima facie* this seems to preclude the possibility of ever stating causal relations between mental events and actions or between mental events. Davidson's proposal (1980, chap. 11) for resolving this problem is the following: mental events are physical events as well—presumably events in our brain. Each individual mental event has a description in physiological terms, and it is probably on this physiological level that a strict causal law can be formulated. Hence psychological explanation invokes causal laws without either stating those laws or even presupposing that these laws are to be found on the psychological level.

The central point is as follows: the hermeneuticist understanding of psychoanalytic interpretation as primarily concerned with meaning seemed to authors like Schafer to necessitate the thesis that reason explanations do not state causes of behavior. As we saw in the last section, this leads to counterintuitive consequences. Davidson's analysis of the logical structure of psychological explanation shows that the interpretive, hermeneutic function of reason explanation is not inconsistent with its causal function.

The second, interpretive function of reason explanations is that they are supposed to make the action intelligible from within. This function is often called the rationalization of action in the philosophical literature (Pettit, 1979). I prefer not to use this term for two reasons. The first is purely terminological: in psychoanalysis the term "rationalization" is used to denote a type of defense in which a person explains his own behavior by virtue of something of which we believe that it is *not* its real reason. Hence in the present context the use of the term could create confusion. The second reason is more substantial: psychoanalysis mostly deals with actions which are in some respect not rational. It is true that one of the goals of psychoanalytic understanding is to show that from the point of view of the agent there are reasons to act the way he does, but it would not be very intuitive to say that the analyst finds out why these actions are *rational*. The term "intelligible" hits the connotation of the type of understanding aimed at better.

The function of reason explanation which has been emphasized by the hermeneuticist authors is to put actions (or patterns
of actions) into a context which makes them intelligible. And
there is also little doubt that one of the central functions of
psychoanalytic clinical interpretation is precisely the creation
of such a context. The patient describes how he felt literally
choked when a woman put some demand on him, and how all
he wanted was to get away from her. The analyst may say
something like, "You felt again as if your mother was going
intrude upon you with her demands, not leaving you any space
to live in, and you felt choked with anxiety and rage."

Such an interpretation is supposed to make the patient's actions and modes of feeling and thinking more intelligible. The
starting point of the interpretation is the *prima facie* lack of
intelligibility of what happened. Why should a grown-up man
choke when a woman puts some demand on him? Why should
he not be able to consider calmly whether the demand was
reasonable and then decide how to act?

The context of a small child who feels that his mother does
not let him grow and who has no way of defending himself,
leaving the distressing situation or even expressing his distress
coherently, makes the behavior intelligible. A boy may indeed
choke with rage and despair and even develop a psychosomatic
condition. If we try to see the adult's behavior as guided by an
inner experience similar to that of the boy, it becomes intelligible.

The more complex question is of course whether this function
of making modes of action and experience intelligible is in any
way tied up with a causal-explanatory role. Is it necessary for
a patient to have had an intrusive mother for the interpretation
to make the mode of action intelligible? Is a causal nexus between the patient's past as invoked in the interpretation necessary for the interpretation to have a curative effect?

Here the difference between Grünbaum and the hermeneuticists comes to its fullest expression. Grünbaum views the above
question as absolutely crucial to any assessment of psychoanalysis. He is primarily interested in the question whether psychoanalysis as a theory is true and what kind of data are needed
to confirm it. As he considers the theory to be causally explan-

atory, he thinks that no amount of intelligibility that a psychoanalytic interpretation confers onto an action or character trait can ascertain the causal relations the theory is talking about.

The hermeneuticists have generally stopped being interested in the truth of psychoanalytic theory either *qua* metapsychology or *qua* developmental theory. They are primarily focused on psychoanalytic clinical work. They feel that in the course of an analysis an experiential truth about the patient is emerging. As Schafer has pointed out (1983), past and present merge in the analysis to a mode of discourse which has an almost timeless quality. Descriptions of the past become metaphors of the present, and the present is used to elucidate the past. The psychoanalytic narrative as it grows during analytic work is not one of connecting past and present causally but rather a story which creates sense out of nonsense, finds meaning in chaos, and thus allows the patient to take responsibility for himself.

Hence the different versions of analytic theory cease to be seen as literal descriptions of developmental processes, and are understood as story lines which help the analyst find meaning in the disorder of the patient's broken, interrupted narratives. If this hermeneutic function of analytic interpretation is put into the foreground exclusively, it becomes rather irrelevant whether or not it is possible to know the truth about the causal relations between childhood events and present character traits.

Comforting as this may sound, the hermeneuticist's position is not as easy to defend as it may seem. One part of what makes the analytic narrative efficient is the belief common to the patient and the analyst that the narrative is true. It is only metatheoretical reflection which leads to the skeptical view of psychoanalytic developmental theory as story lines which do not trace the structure of actual development, and of individual psychoanalytic interpretations as creating order rather than telling the truth. The complexities of psychoanalytic reconstruction of the past will be dealt with in chapter 5.

d) THE METHODOLOGICAL PRINCIPLE OF HUMANITY

Interpretation of human action has epistemic properties

which are different from explanations in the natural sciences. The main difference can be put in a nutshell: in reason explanations we try to reconstruct a person's point of view *from within*. The type of intelligibility we try to create when we explain human action from within therefore incorporates an element which is not to be found in explanations of the type natural science gives: no one would even understand what it means to reconstruct a stone's or an electron's point of view from within.

The fundamental assumption of interpretation of human action is as follows (see Gadamer, 1960): If a human being is considered *qua* person—as opposed to a biological organism or a biochemical system—we do not just look at him or her as an object interacting with other objects according to causal laws. We assume that this human being has a point of view onto the world. He has beliefs, modes of perception, and understanding. His actions are to be understood as a function of his perspectives onto the world and his desires.

In other words, by explaining the reasons a person had for doing what he did we assume that the person himself or herself *interprets* the world. The object of interpreting another person's perspective is therefore in certain respects itself an interpretation. This is what the hermeneutic tradition meant by saying that *Verstehen*, understanding, is an *existentiale*, i.e., an activity constitutive of personhood (Gadamer, 1960, part II, chap. 2).

The process of interpretation is based on the assumption that the perspective of another human being (or another culture) is sufficiently close to our own to be understandable. This may sound like a tautology: interpretation assumes that its object is interpretable.

But this is in fact a very strong methodological principle which we use implicitly in every attempt to understand persons: it could be called the *principle of humanity* (Blackburn, 1984, pp. 277–281). The assumption of common humanity of the interpreter and the person to be understood is the only way to narrow down the number of possible interpretations of a human being's actions and utterances. We assume that another person is psychologically similar to us in the essential respects. We also assume that the other's belief system is sufficiently coherent to allow for interpretation at all. If the belief system would be totally chaotic, we would not be able to construct an intelligible perspective out of it.

This principle is the fundamental methodological characterization of all the disciplines which try to interpret human behavior, verbal and nonverbal, provided they do so in terms of reasons—i.e., as long as human beings are viewed as persons. This includes most of both the humanities and social sciences as well as commonsense psychology. It is quite obvious that this principle cuts a sharp boundary line between these disciplines and the natural sciences. In the latter we do not try to understand electrons, molecules, or genes from within, or imagine what it would be like to be one of these entities.

The question arises of what criterion we have to judge the acceptability of the interpretation of a person's actions and utterances. The principle of humanity implies that an interpretation is acceptable if it makes an action or utterance maximally intelligible to us. The term "maximal intelligibility" can be further elucidated. First, a good explanation should take into account all the relevant evidence available, and it should be contradicted by as little evidence as possible. Second, it should make us capable of understanding from within why a person acted, spoke, felt, or thought the way he did in the given situation.

The second requirement may seem vacuous to those who would like to assimilate the methodology of interpretation and reason explanation to that of the natural sciences. In addition, it may sound dreadfully subjective. It seems that it is completely up to the intuition of the interpreter to say when he feels that a mode of action or utterance is intelligible. There is no objectifying method to determine whether or not the right interpretation has been reached. Does this mean that interpretation is completely subjective?

It is worth returning to one of the main theses of modern philosophical hermeneutics mentioned in chapter 2, section a. Hermeneutics has come to think that there cannot be such a thing as a *method* of interpretation. To understand a text ultimately means to incorporate it into the horizon of intelligibility of the interpreter *qua* member of an interpretive community.

This can be elucidated as follows. The need for systematic

understanding arises only when the effortless understanding of ourselves and others breaks down. No one makes a conscious effort to achieve an understanding of ordinary utterances. Interpretation *qua* systematic activity is called for when effortless, unproblematic understanding has broken down or has never existed to begin with.

The question is, of course, *whose* effortless understanding has broken down. It is quite often the case that a text, action, or utterance is effortlessly intelligible to one group of persons, and not so to another. The understanding of a foreign culture is a most telling example in this respect: the anthropologist may have to make a protracted effort to understand the meaning of a ritual which is a matter of course to the natives.

The anthropologist's horizon of intelligibility (his preunderstanding of the world, see Gadamer, 1960, part II, chapter 2) does not initially allow for an effortless integration of an activity like rain dances. This is why he will have to investigate and get a view of the primitive culture's view from within until he can understand their activity. The question is when we can say that sufficient understanding has been reached. The point which has been made by Gadamer is that we understand once we have integrated the object of understanding (text, ritual, utterance, etc.) into our own preunderstanding of the world—which may be changed in the course of the understanding.

This means that the point at which we understand is primarily determined by who we are. There is no criterion beyond the intuition that the text has actually been understood conjoined with the requirement of completeness and coherence with the evidence. Hence there is certainly some truth in the idea that there is no way to objectify the process of interpretation completely, and that its criteria are relative to context and culture.

The principle of humanity states essentially the same point. We use our own humanity, our capacity to have perspective on the world, in order to understand others. It is only the fact that both the interpreter and the actor or speaker who is to be understood have a subjectivity (or common humanity) which makes it possible for human beings to understand each other. This subjectivity is not unique to each person but shared in varying degrees by members of the species *homo sapiens* which makes a *disciplined use of subjectivity*, and thus some objectivity of interpretation possible. The degree to which there is similarity of perspective between persons varies with common cultural background and experience, but this variation should not be taken to mean that interpretation is not possible. The fact is that despite the inexistence of some algorithmlike methodology determining the correctness of interpretations and reason explanations, we often agree with each other on such issues.

The principle of humanity is of crucial importance in psychoanalytic practice. It might even be said that the fundamental step which Freud took at the beginning of his career was to radicalize the principle of humanity and to apply it to phenomena which were previously exempt from it. Neurotic and psychosomatic symptoms began to be seen as humanly intelligible rather than as phenomena which were only amenable to physiological explanation.

The radicalization of the principle of humanity takes on manifold ways in the psychoanalytic situation. As Spence (1982a) has pointed out, the analyst's basic working assumption is that there is meaning to be found on every level of the patient's communications. First and foremost every analyst is educated to assume that every session has a theme. It is assumed that the patient's free associations are not random, but that the right type of listening will uncover a central, unconscious theme which guides all of the patient's associations.

As Spence has also pointed out, this working assumption is far less an empirical hypothesis than an *a priori* creed. There is no way in which this working assumption could be falsified: every analytic therapist who cannot formulate the central theme at the end of a session says, "I didn't really understand what was going on today." He will never say anything like, "There was nothing to understand in this session."

Psychoanalysis takes this principle to an extreme by always assuming that the lack of progress in an analysis is a function of failure to understand. Psychoanalysis is committed to considering human beings exclusively as persons. The assumption is that every aspect of human behavior is intelligible; i.e., behavior is seen as intentional action all the way down. Furthermore, it is assumed that by correctly understanding the meanings of actions, we help the patient to take full responsibility for who he is, and give him the freedom to change if he truly wants to.

Again: in certain aspects these assumptions are not really empirical hypotheses since they are by their nature unfalsifiable. If the patient did not get better, there is something left to be understood. Much of the development of psychoanalysis after Freud was the incorporation of new phenomena under the principle of humanity. Patients with extreme disturbances whom Freud deemed to be untreatable were taken into treatment. New story lines were added to the classic oedipal constellation in order to find meaning where previous analysts saw only illness (see chapter 4, section b).

The hermeneuticist interpretation of psychoanalysis took the developmental theories of psychoanalysis—like the theory of the Oedipus complex; oral, anal, and phallic stages of development, and the like—to be primarily story lines which help the analyst to find meaning. As such their fruitfulness was to be measured by their heuristic potency in helping to generate interpretive hypotheses in the clinical situation. Their literal truth *qua* theories of development became less important than their ability to allow further widening of the principle of humanity to include pathologies and phenomena previously not understood.

The task of the next chapters will be to show that the psychoanalytic use of the principle of humanity is not far removed from modes of reasoning to be found in other disciplines and in commonsense psychology. I will trace in some detail how the analyst establishes his object of interpretation and what it means to interpret unconscious meanings.

The part of psychoanalytic clinical reasoning easiest to defend does not concern the relation of the past to the present. In fact most actual interpretations given in psychoanalytic practice refer to the patient's present mental states without reference to the patient's past. Such interpretations are more easy and straightforward in their structure, as a brief example may show. After a vacation a patient comes back to therapy and greets his therapist happily. After sitting down his mind goes blank, he cannot think of anything to say, and he feels distinctly uncomfortable looking at his therapist. A possible interpretation would be: "You know, I felt before that you were quite happy to see me again, and your way of expression was quite affectionate. Now it looks to me that you are terribly embarrassed by your feelings—maybe because you think I feel that your feelings are ridiculous." The following chapter will deal in detail with the question of how present unconscious mental contents can be understood by the analyst, and how his reasoning can be made defensible.

4

PSYCHOANALYTIC INTERPRETATION
AND ITS JUSTIFICATION

a) GRÜNBAUM'S VIEW OF PSYCHOANALYTIC INTERPRETATION

In chapter 3, I criticized the attempt to salvage the epistemological status through the claim that psychoanalysis has no
business with causes, and then tried to show the grain of truth
in the thesis that there is something special in reason explanations which makes their epistemic properties unlike those of
natural science explanations. I now turn to Grünbaum's views
on the nature of psychoanalytic interpretation which underlie
Grünbaum's contention that psychoanalysis cannot claim any
support for its propositions from clinical material and that only
controlled extraclinical research can produce the desired evidence.

My main goal is to weaken the grounds for Grünbaum's more
extreme claims. I will show that his model of psychoanalytic
interpretation does not reflect the current theory and practice
of psychoanalysis. The modernist conception of psychoanalysis
allows for the justification of analytic interpretations by reasoning analogously to those found in other humanistic disciplines and commonsense psychology.

Grünbaum does not give an explicit account of the logical
structure of psychoanalytic interpretation, but is possible to
discern his conception on the basis of his general approach, as
well as from some more explicit remarks on this topic. It is clear
that Gruñbaum thinks that the logical structure of psychoan-

alytic claims is still essentially the same as that of the theory advanced by Breuer and Freud in their *Studies on Hysteria* (1893–95), even if the content was changed.

In *The Foundations of Psychoanalysis* (1984) Grünbaum analyzes Freud's arguments for the repression etiology of the psychoneuroses. Breuer and Freud (1893–95) claimed to have had evidence for the hypothesis that hysterical symptoms were caused by the repression of some traumatic event. The evidence was that "each individual hysterical symptom immediately and permanently disappeared when we had succeeded in bringing clearly to light the memory of the event by which it was provoked and in arousing its accompanying affect" (p. 6). Grünbaum says, after quoting this passage:

> What, then, is the evidence they give for their etiologic identification of the repressed experience of a particular traumatic event E as the pathogen—avowedly not as the mere precipitator!—of a given symptom S that first appeared at the time of E? [p. 178].

Grünbaum rightly takes the claim made by Freud and Breuer to be that a particular event is causally necessary and sufficient for the occurrence of some hysterical symptom. His discussion centers on the question whether the adduced evidence is sufficient to confirm the hypothesis. His answer is negative (see chap. 1). It is more important that Grünbaum does not say anywhere in his book that psychoanalytic propositions have changed since 1893. He thus takes the structure of analytic interpretation to be of the same basic nature as they were then. This becomes clearer when, in a different context, Grünbaum criticizes Habermas for taking the patient to be the ultimate arbiter for the correctness of analytic interpretations:

> For the possession of such access to the content of momentary mental states is a far cry indeed from being uniquely privy to the actual existence of the causal nexus between, say, certain infantile experiences and specified adult personality dispositions. Yet just such *causal* interpretations are at the heart of psychoanalytic interpretations, being central to the conjectured etiologic reconstruction of the patient's neurosis [p. 29].

Here Grünbaum is quite explicit about what he takes to be the core of psychoanalytic theory and interpretation. The stress is on the causal nexus between infantile experiences and adult neurotic symptoms.

I am in no way imputing that Gruñbaum misrepresents his sources. He mainly deals with Freud, who says in 1914: "The aim of these different techniques has, of course, remained the same. Descriptively speaking, it is to fill in gaps in memory; dynamically speaking, it is to overcome resistances due to repression" (p. 147). In this specific respect Freud's views did not change significantly from 1893 to the end of his life when, in 1937, he claimed that the analyst can quite reliably fill up the gaps in the patient's memory; i.e., Freud always thought that the reconstruction of the patient's past as it actually was had to be the centerpiece of analytic work and that therapeutic success depended on the truth of these reconstructions.

In chapter 1 I presented Grünbaum's arguments against the possibility of validating claims about causal connections between childhood events and adult symptoms in the clinical situation. As I said there, I believe Grünbaum's argument on this point to be cogent. Only a very strong empirical assumption like what Grünbaum calls the necessary condition thesis would change the situation in this matter.

The question we must ask is therefore: are psychoanalytic interpretations really causal statements of the type Grünbaum takes them to be? The answer is negative. There have been profound changes in psychoanalytic theory and practice which are highly relevant to the epistemological relation between clinical data and analytic interpretation. The brief presentation of these changes will be followed by an attempt to evaluate the possibility of justifying interpretations in the clinical situation along the line of one of the central assumptions of the hermeneuticist ideas about psychoanalysis.

b) CHANGES IN THE CONCEPTION OF PSYCHOANALYTIC INTERPRETATION

The psychoanalytic view of the nature and function of interpretation has changed considerably through the years. These changes were motivated by clinical considerations and not by methodological concerns, but they have very fortunate epistemological consequences. The content and structure of analytic interpretations are conceived of in a way which makes it far more plausible to think that their accurateness can be assessed on the basis of clinical experience.

The account that follows is restricted to pointing out some of the milestones of the developing conception of psychoanalytic technique and presents a picture of a roughly hermeneuticist view of interpretation as it emerged in recent years.

From 1893 to 1897 analytic work was directed toward the very clear-cut aim of getting the patient to recall some specific event and reexperience the accompanying affect. The turning point of 1897 was the famous letter to Fliess, in which Freud (1950, p. 215ff.) first put forward the hypothesis that his patient's apparent memories of seduction in childhood were actually wishful fantasies the patient had repressed.

Freud continued to induce the patient to remember aspects of his childhood, even if the focus turned to the patient's inner world as a child and away from external events. This is reflected by the quotation in section a in which Freud states that the goal of analysis is, descriptively speaking, to fill in the gaps in the patient's memories.

There is a second strand in Freud's clinical thought, which puts greater emphasis on the present. In his paper on the dynamics of transference Freud (1912) focuses on the fact that the therapeutic relation becomes a new edition of the patient's infantile object choices. The working through of the evolving transference neurosis comes to be the main goal of the analysis. Attention is shifted from the distant past to a process occurring in the present of the therapeutic relationship. This did not abolish Freud's emphasis on the final goal of getting the patient to remember rather than to act (whether in transference or outside of it). Transference was seen by Freud as having two aspects: it is a resistance to the central aim of the cure (remembering), and by the same token it is the major opportunity for the analyst to get direct access to the repressed past.

Schematically speaking, one could characterize the development by saying that the second strand in Freud's clinical thought gradually became more important than the first. Throughout the decades after Freud's death the work in the here-and-now of the transference moved to the center of analytic work and, as we shall see, remembering as such almost completely ceased to be a goal in itself. In any case, it was no longer seen as the *condition sine qua non* of success in analytic work.

In an attempt to sketch this development, I should say that first and foremost there was an accumulation of clinical experience which indicated that work in the here-and-now of the transference had a more immediate impact than anything else in the analytic process. This was already seen in Freud's lifetime, when Strachey (1934) came close to claiming that the *only* true mutative interpretations were those relating to transference.

Second, a significant change seems to have occurred in the patient population. It was not just that psychoanalysis gradually approached patients Freud believed to be untreatable, such as psychotics and those with narcissistic personality disorders (e.g., Fairbairn 1952). More important was the fact that analysts hardly got to see the types of psychoneuroses with clearly delineated ego-dystonic symptoms such as hysterical conversions, compulsive rituals, etc. (Cooper, 1987).

The third point is partially connected with the previous one. Since analysts see more and more patients with general character problems and personality disorders, there rarely are clearly delineated symptoms, which can be counted in the simple way Breuer and Freud described in 1893–95. Today, analysts will talk far less about disappearance of symptoms than about more general features such as structural change, creation of more adaptive patterns of cognition, emotion, and behavior.

As a consequence it has become less appropriate to talk about the emergence of a transference neurosis. If the patient has a general character problem, this will be manifested by the way he deals with the analyst from the beginning of his analysis. Correspondingly recent writers on technique (e.g., Gill, 1982) do not see any problem in interpreting the transference early in therapy. This is most clearly exemplified by the insistence of Malan (1963), Mann (1975), and other authors that even in the field of analytic short-term psychotherapy the main emphasis should be put on work with the transference.

In other words, the fact that the typical patient's problems today tend to have a rather general character has partially been responsible for certain changes in technique. Possibly, though, the causal nexus has worked the other way around as well: changes in theory and technique have allowed psychoanalysis to widen the circle of potential patients.

The next point is again connected to the previous one, though not in any simple cause-effect way. The widening of the concept of transference from the original definition of a displacement of an early object choice, and the growing centrality of work in the here-and-now is also linked to the emergence of the structural theory (Freud, 1923). The development of ego psychology in the following decades brought about a profound change in the basic interests of psychoanalysis.

During the period of 1900 to 1923 psychoanalysis was primarily concerned with the contents repressed into the system unconscious. The clinical correlate to this theoretical interest was that the analyst mainly aimed at uncovering the derivatives of repressed instinctual wishes and fantasies. Resistance was to be analyzed in order to arrive at this material.

The structural frame of reference provided the conceptual tools for a new question: what are the ego's ways of defending against threatening elements of both the internal and the external world? Anna Freud's (1936) *The Ego and the Mechanisms of Defense* was the classic work presenting this perspective explicitly. Both theoretically and clinically the ego's way of coping with conflict became more important than the uncovering of repressed material *per se*. As Anna Freud herself related much later on (Sandler and A. Freud, 1980), this was perceived by the analytic community as an innovation, which almost crossed the borders of what could still be accepted as belonging to psychoanalysis. But only a short time after this, Hartmann's (1939) *Ego Psychology and the Problem of Adaptation* appeared, a book in which the ego's adaptive functions were taken to be of crucial importance for psychoanalytic theory.

As a clinical correlate to the theoretical change, the patient was no longer primarily seen as someone whose problem was that he was not conscious of repressed wishes and fantasies. Correspondingly, the goal of the analytic process widened in scope. Remembering infantile wishes and fantasies was not enough. Its aim became to change the ego's way of adapting to the pressures of the external world, the id, and the superego. Hartmann's concept of secondary autonomy had given theoretical underpinnings to the clinically observable fact that character structures, which had evolved around infantile conflicts, could gain autonomy from their origins. Both adaptive and maladaptive character traits, capacities, and defense structures could come to lead a life of their own once they were established. Their analysis therefore became an end in itself, since structural change in the patient was one of the main objectives of the analytic process.

As indicated, these ideas also contributed to an increasing concentration on work on current problems. The functioning of the patient's ego could be observed directly in the analytic situation and be worked on somewhat independently of remembering early wishes and fantasies.

The factors that lead to an increased importance of the here-and-now of the analytic situation are the experience of the therapeutic impact of such work, the change in patient population, the realization of the wider nature of transference, and the centrality of the ego's functioning. The interrelation of these factors is quite complex and I am not implying that it occurred *en bloc*. Theoretical and technical changes tend to influence each other in rather complex ways, as Sandler (1983) has pointed out.

Before proceeding to a presentation of present-day positions on the issue of the here-and-now, I must add one more factor which contributed. At about the same period during which ego psychology developed in the United States, two other schools were very influential in Great Britain: one headed by Melanie Klein and the object relation school centered around Fairbairn (1952), Winnicott (1958, 1965), Guntrip (1968), and others. Since their work involves additional theoretical and clinical innovations, it would lead me too far afield to touch upon them here. I therefore merely mention that these strands of psychoanalysis had an important share in leading to the view I will present next.

c)   THE MODERNIST VIEW OF PSYCHOANALYSIS

All these factors, as well as others not mentioned in the previous section, led to a new conception of the nature of psychoanalytic interpretation which is not reflected by Grünbaum's view of psychoanalysis. Most major analytic authors writing on technique see the centerpiece of psychoanalytic work in the elucidation of the patient's *present* mental functioning, especially as it manifests itself in the clinical setting. The emphasis on remembering as a goal in itself has almost completely disappeared. The reconstructive aspect of analytic work is still important, but its primary function is no longer conceived as formulating the historical truth about the analysand's past. Instead, it is seen as constructing a narratively convincing truth about the patient's present, linking all relevant aspects of experience of himself in interaction with his world into an intelligible whole.

I begin with an illustrative quotation from Arnold Cooper (1987) which contrasts the older conception of transference (the historical model, as he calls it) with that emerging in the recent literature (the modernist view):

> In the first, historical view, the importance of transference interpretation lies in the opportunity it provides in the transference neurosis for the patient to reexperience and undo the partially encapsulated, one might say "toxic," neurosogenic early history. In the second, "modernist" view, the purpose of transference interpretation is to help the patient to see in the intensity of the transference, the aims, character, and mode of his current wishes and expectations as influenced by the past.
>
> The historical view is more likely to regard the infantile neurosis as a "fact" of central importance for the analytic work, to be uncovered and undone. The modernist view regards the infantile neurosis, if acknowledged at all, as an unprivileged set of current fantasies rather than historical fact. From this modernist perspective, the transference resistance *is* the core of the analysis, to be worked through primarily because of the rigidity it imposes

on the patient, not because of an important secret it conceals [p. 82].

Cooper is very explicit about the central feature of the modernist view of transference interpretation, which he considers to be the "more interesting and promising"one (p. 6). The question of the historical truth of reconstruction is central to this view. This has far-reaching consequences for the structure of the claims made by psychoanalytic interpretation from an epistemological point of view. If no particular event (or type of events) is hypothesized to have occurred in the patient's distant past, no causal nexus between such an event and some presently existing symptom is asserted. Cooper also argues that the second *relatum* of the cause-effect is not some particular symptom, and that the notion of a specific transference neurosis has become obsolete:

> Those holding the modernist view, much more influenced by object-relational ideas of development, are likely to blur the idea of a specific transference neurosis in favor of viewing all transference responses as reflecting shifting self and object representations as they are affected by the changing analytic relationship, and significant transferences may be available for interpretation very early in the analysis [p. 82].

The modernist view of transference interpretation is thus difficult to reconcile with Grünbaum's interpretation of psychoanalysis, which derives from the structure of the 1893 type of hypotheses Breuer and Freud put forth. The central role accorded to the vericality of memories of pathogenic events in the process of analytic cure is heavily deemphasized.

Furthermore, Grünbaum's logical reconstruction of analytic interpretation as involving causal claims between infantile events and present symptoms does not fit the modernist view on other grounds as well. Both the nature of the events in the patient's infancy *and* the clearly delineated symptoms have become blurred in the modernist view. As said before, no commitment to historical truth is being made. Since the present phenomena in question are not symptoms, but rather generalized ways of functioning, it is unclear how the modernist view is to be assimilated to Grünbaum's clear-cut schema.

All this does not mean that no reconstructive work is being done by analysts who have abandoned the historical view of transference and its interpretation. But the function of this reconstructive work is viewed in a new way:

> . . . the analyst must listen for the dominant current conflict that is being censored (i.e., being resisted) and interpret it in such a way that the patient experiences relief, and for this purpose he should make use of appropriate interpretations, preferably in the context of the transference, of the pain and discomfort the patient is suffering. . . . However, once the patient has been able to accept the reality of the here-and-now thoughts and feelings that occupy the second system, particularly the thoughts and fantasies that arise in the transference, and his (second censorship) resistance has fallen away in that particular context, it is appropriate to reconstruct what has happened in the past, to take a genetic perspective, in the knowledge that such reconstructions have as their main function the provision of a temporal dimension to the patient's image of himself in relation to his world, and help him to become more tolerant of the previously unacceptable aspects of the "child within himself" [Sandler and Sandler, 1983, p. 423f.].

The Sandlers make it quite clear that they do not consider the establishment of vertical memory to be the causally effective agent of change in the psychoanalytic process. In their view, the main work of analysis is done in the here-and-now without explicitly looking for the roots of the present phenomena in the past. The patient's present mental functioning—mainly in the transference—is the object of most of the analyst's attention. The Sandlers advise the analyst to start reconstructive work only *after* a considerable change has taken place in the patient.

The function of reconstruction is *not* to help bring about new knowledge for the patient and thus cure him. This presents a major departure for the aspects of Freud's clinical thought which Grünbaum makes the center of his understanding of psychoanalytic interpretation. The Sandlers see the importance of reconstruction in "the provision of a temporal dimension to the patient's image of himself in relation to his world." In this temporal dimension, the patient can integrate the aspects of his present mental functioning, as he has come to know it through the work in the transference, into a coherent biographical picture of himself. The value of this psychoanalytic biography is twofold. It fulfills the patient's need for a narrative which grounds his identity in aspects of himself, which have seemed unacceptable to him throughout his earlier life. The child within is more easily accepted if this part of the personality is biographically linked to the patient's actual childhood.

These remarks are of course not intended as an exploration of the clinical views of the Sandlers. I have not even touched upon the theoretical model they are based on. They reflect a very general feature of their conception, in which they are in accordance with other important authors in the field (e.g., Gill, 1982; Spence, 1982a; Schafer, 1983). It is the shift from the historical model of psychoanalytic theory and practice to what Cooper has called the modernist view of analytic work. This shift is of utmost importance, because it considerably changes the epistemological status of clinical propositions.

d)   THE OBJECT AND STRUCTURE OF PSYCHOANALYTIC INTERPRETATION

The skepticism of philosophers like Grünbaum about the possibility of validating analytic interpretations on the couch is in part a result of their picture of what is actually done in clinical work. I have shown that this picture is quite out of date. The modernist position weakens the basis for skepticism. If the historical conception of transference interpretation was in deep epistemological trouble, this was partially the result of the structure of its claim. The factor which was to explain symptoms was not only directly inaccessible (because unconscious), but it was temporarily remote as well. In the modernist conception, with its emphasis on the patient's present mental functioning, the inaccessibility becomes less extreme.

In this section I attempt a rational reconstruction of the mental processes through which the analyst goes in formulating interpretations. The procedure of rational reconstruction (Lakatos, 1978) is generally used in the history and philosophy of science whenever the structure of justification of propositions in some disciplines is investigated. A successful rational reconstruction is characterized by the following features: (1) it does not depart too much from the actual practice of the actual discipline (and is thus a reconstruction of the discipline); (2) it is sufficiently idealized to make the structure of justification of propositions in the discipline intelligible.

There are therefore two dangers that one risks: one is that the picture of what is actually going on in the discipline is unrealistic. This generally leads to a picture of the discipline as more rational than it really is. In the case of Grünbaum's view of psychoanalysis this is not quite true. On the one hand, he makes the structure of psychoanalytic propositions seem very lucid in their empirical content, thus countering Popper's (1963) long-standing claim that psychoanalysis is an empirically vacuous theory. On the other hand, he departs from what is actually done in clinical practice to such an extent as to leave no intelligible epistemic relation between psychoanalytic theory and practice, thus arriving at the conclusion that clinical data cannot give any support to psychoanalytic theory.

The second danger is that the model of rationality underlying the rational reconstruction is inappropriate to the particular discipline. The classical example of such a mistake is the attempt to squeeze history (as a discipline) into the nomologico-deductive model of science as developed mainly by Hempel (1965). This danger is somewhat difficult to eschew, since rational reconstruction must rely on some degree of idealization (in the sense that frictionless planes in physics are idealizations) if it is to do its job of making the discipline's proceedings intelligible. Since Popper (1959) it has become quite common to think that, especially in the context of discovery, many nonrational factors play a role in scientific work. The process of creating hypotheses is not something we have rational control over, and therefore many actually occurring processes must be disregarded in the formation of rational reconstructions.

Before I present the rational reconstruction of psychoanalytic reasoning, two words of caution are necessary. On the one hand, the clinician may be struck by the overly dry and formal

nature of the description presented here of the mental processes of the analyst. He may thus be reminded that my aim is
not to be faithful to the complexity of the actually occurring
processes with their interplay of cognitive, emotional, and intuitive components. The methodologist of science, on the other
hand, may be disappointed by the lack of formalization in the
presentation. As he will see, my arguments will be as the follows.
Psychoanalysis proceeds analogously to many other disciplines.
If the clinical reasoning of psychoanalysis is discarded, the price
of having to reject these other disciplines as well (among them
the history of science) will have to be paid. This argument may
at least give the clinical method some backing, even if it will
leave many questions unsolved.

1.   ESTABLISHING THE OBJECT OF INTERPRETATION

Critics outside of the field of psychoanalysis often seem to
think that analysts make quite strange leaps of thought (e.g.,
Popper, 1963, pp. 24–37; Grünbaum, 1984, pp. 212–215). The
patient says something and the analyst immediately infers that
this is an instance of penis envy, castration anxiety, and the like.
It thus must seem that analytic thinking is rather difficult to
justify. This impression may partially be due to the type of
vignettes often found in analytic journals. In these vignettes a
central interpretation is presented with very little clinical material around it; they do not show the process which led up to
this interpretation.

A caricatural picture emerges from such vignettes. The analyst listens for a long time, forms a hypothesis, and then formulates an in-depth interpretation consisting of telling his
patient that at the age of 5 he wanted to kill his father in order
to sleep with his mother. There is probably, I hope, no analyst
who works like this. At any rate, most recent writers on technique would consider such a proceeding to reflect extremely
bad clinical work. As we have seen, the Sandlers oppose early,
direct in-depth interpretations. But even writers with a more
traditional orientation, like Greenson (1974), have taken a
strong stand against jumping to "deep" interpretations without

careful preparatory work. They do so on purely clinical
grounds, but these clinical developments have positive epistemological consequences.

The first question, which may arise for someone not acquainted with analytic practice, may quite simply be: where do
you start? The puzzle begins by wondering what it means to
start listening for unconscious processes. Such a question is
more than justified. As Spence (1982a) has pointed out, there
is something highly misleading in the notion that the analyst
is listening without any preconceptions. Actually this holds true
for the simplest utterance of ordinary language, as philosophers
of language have often pointed out (e.g., Searle, 1979), and
therefore certainly for psychoanalytic understanding, which is
supposed to go beyond the surface level.

To make this point intuitively clearer, one might think of a
cognitive psychologist, an anthropologist, a logician, and a sociologist listening to the same text. Each of them is trying to
understand the speaker, and yet each is listening for entirely
different things. The cognitive psychologist might listen to
processes of inductive and deductive inference, the anthropologist for institutional presuppositions of the speech act, the
logician for quantificational structure, and the sociologist for
the expression of attitudes typical of the speaker's social class.
Such examples could be multiplied almost indefinitely, and the
question "what does the psychoanalyst listen for?" is thus legitimate.

The answer I want to propose is on a relatively abstract level,
as demanded by the requirements on rational reconstructions.
They must be sufficiently general to allow one to see the analogy
between analytic reasoning and other accepted types of inference. I propose to think of the analyst as listening for *subjectively
determined, idiosyncratic patterns in the patient's ways of acting, feeling,
and thinking.* The analyst does so on two levels. First, with respect
to the information the patient provides about his behavior, feelings, and thoughts in his daily life. The analyst comes to know
quite a bit about his patient's habitual ways of leading his life,
and he can scan this information for recurring indications of
relatively inflexible, subjectively determined patterns. Second,
he does the same with the patient's fantasies, feelings, expec-

tations, wishes, etc., which relate to the analyst himself. These may be voiced explicitly (and the patient is encouraged to do so), or they may be implied by the way the patient talks and relates to the analyst.

Ultimately the analyst is intent on uncovering the way unconscious mental contents and their defensive modifications influence the patient's mental functioning. The question thus arises of how such influences can be detected, since the contents sought for are not directly accessible. The simplest answer is that the influence of the unconscious will mainly manifest itself through subjectively determined patterns of action, emotion, and thought (Edelson, 1984, p. 106).

The subjective determination sought for can be characterized on an even more abstract philosophical level as implying some measure of inappropriateness or irrationality in the patient's behavior (where behavior is to be understood in the widest possible sense, including mental states). The use of the word "inappropriateness" is supposed to convey that the analyst is not busy judging the degree of rationality of his patient's behavior. Instead, the idea is that the analyst tries to see in what respects his patient's way of leading his life is in accordance with his consciously formulated goals and values, and whether he uses his potential in realizing them.

The patient presents his thoughts and actions as he is consciously aware of them. These conscious labelings may range from "trying to complete a deal," through "wanting to have an enjoyable evening with friends" to "making love to his wife," or "buying a present for his children." Each of these activities is set against the background of the patient's practical possibilities, personal relations, family status, which roughly delimit the rationally intelligible ways to do what he plans. Furthermore, there are the socially defined and humanly expectable emotional concomitants of types of activities and personal relations. It is against this background that rationality or irrationality, appropriateness and inappropriateness of the patient's behavior (in the widest sense of the word) are judged.

The analyst of course does not go through such an assessment of what the patient relates to him about his life with conscious deliberation. He uses a capacity for preconscious integration of the information, a capacity relying on implicit knowledge each member of a culture has by virtue of his own socialization. To give a simple example: we all know the norms of emotions appropriate under various circumstances in interactions with a teacher or a boss, even though we may not be able to spell out these norms and expectations. But this background enables us to judge intuitively what would count as appropriate and what is irrational in a given situation.

The relation of students to professors provides a simple example because this relation is relatively clearly defined in several respects. Within the confines of the university the professor's status is higher than the student's. This is expressed in a variety of norms. The professor has certain rights the student does not have: he has access to certain places (offices, faculty clubs, etc.); he has the authority to structure his courses; and he determines their contents, reading assignments, type of examinations, and so on. He also assesses the quality of the student's work and whether it is sufficient to fulfill the requirements of the course.

These features are officially determined; along with them go certain unwritten characteristics of the relation of students to professors. Students are expected to show a certain amount of respect and politeness toward professors. In part this respect should be based on the *prima facie* assumption of the professor's superior competence in his field of expertise. Ideally the professor's superior status should thus be founded not just on his official rights but also on his actual abilities.

It is not unreasonable to expect certain emotional concomitants. Depending on a professor's actual competence there might be some deference in the student's attitude. There should be some desire to fulfill the professor's demands, and a minimal amount of fear is justified by the professor's authority to judge the student's performance. We may expect that the student's esteem of his own academic capacities hinges to some extent on the well-founded appraisal of his work by his teachers.

This list is not intended to be complete. It is not incidental that many of the features mentioned are qualified by "a certain amount," "some" or "to some extent." By studying or teaching at a university one develops a sensorium for the appropriateness of a student's relation to his professors. It is easy to recognize when respect begins to shade into exaggerated humility on the one hand, or when aggressive assertiveness exceeds the norm on the other hand. This does not mean that we can always enumerate the expected behaviors; nor can we easily pinpoint the specific modes of action which make a student's behavior inappropriate.

The analytic therapist should have as much as possible of the sensorium relating to a wide variety of social and interpersonal situations available to him. This is a precondition for the detection of those subjectively determined, idiosyncratic modes of thought, feeling, and action which provide the starting point of interpretation. A brief example will illustrate the point.

A 26-year-old medical student in therapy quite often brought up his feelings toward his professors. He greatly admired competent doctors who in his eyes were highly self-confident, and he was very preoccupied with what they thought of him. He was particularly sensitive to the slightest criticism. If he had examined a patient and a teacher showed him that he had overlooked something, he took this to be an indication that the professor thought him incapable of becoming a good doctor. The patient could be preoccupied by such criticisms for several days: on the one hand, he wondered whether indeed he could not be relied on (although no one had said so); and on the other hand, he harbored fantasies in which he showed the professor how good he really was.

It is quite easy to identify the fragments of this patient's feelings which are not warranted by the actual situation. Part of the role of being a medical student is to be supervised, and no one expects students never to overlook something. But the patient took every criticism to be an indication of his possibly being incapable of being entrusted with the health of patients. Hence his feelings can be taken to reflect an idiosyncratic pattern of thought and emotion. In the course of therapy this pattern turned out to be rooted in a biographically very important constellation, in which the patient was repeatedly accused of his aggressive behavior toward younger siblings.

Such judgment is grounded on a higher degree of certainty, when it comes to the analytic situation itself. One of the reasons for keeping the analytic situation unstructured and for maintaining the anonymity of the analyst is to make the detection of subjectively determined feelings and beliefs in the analysand easier. The analysand's only explicitly formulated task is to say whatever comes to his mind (the "basic rule"). Therefore, every additional definition he implicitly (and usually unconsciously) introduces into the role he gives himself vis-à-vis the analyst is not warranted by the explicit definition of the situation and is thus subjectively determined. The same goes for roles he attributes to the analyst in their interaction. The analyst's role is defined by his task to listen, to understand, and to communicate his understanding to the analysand; and if the analysand attributes other roles to the analyst, this is an expression of the patient's idiosyncratic way of structuring relationships.

The analysand knows little about the analyst's actual life; he does not even see him during the session (at least in the classical analytic setting); and he has very little evidence on which to ground his beliefs about the analyst. Therefore, most of these beliefs are bound not to be rationally founded; the source of these beliefs is likely to be in the analysand's unconscious mental functioning, although he may try to rationalize them consciously. Here again an appraisal of the cogency of the reasons the analysand puts forth for what he thinks is of course important.

Incidentally, two things may be noted here: most of the definitions of "transference" which have been given in the literature (Sandler, Dare, and Holder, 1973, p. 45) include the element of the inappropriateness of the analysand's emotions and attitudes toward, and beliefs about, the analyst, which fits quite well with the formal account given here. The analyst is, of course, not as empty and unknown a figure to the patient as implied. In fact, Gill (1982) has put great emphasis on the necessity to take into account the impact of what the analyst actually does in his interaction with the patient when trying to understand the transference situation. Some of the patient's feelings and beliefs about the analyst may be realistic, and should therefore not be understood as expressions of interference of unconscious contents. This complicates the situation somewhat (at least epistemologically; clinically it is very important that the patient can feel that the analyst is genuinely empathic), but does not change it fundamentally.

The following vignette illustrates the type of reasoning by which veridical perceptions and transference distortions can be differentiated from each other. A 40-year-old woman sought therapy because of repeated attacks of tachicardia and other conversion symptoms. These turned out to cover up a persistent high level of chronic anxiety. After a few months a pattern repeated itself within the sessions. She sat down on her chair and said that she did not know what to talk about. On the basis of earlier material I linked her difficulty in talking freely to her fear that I considered her to be vulgar and uncultivated.

Instead of alleviating her fear and enabling her to probe into her difficulty to talk, my interventions caused her to attack me relentlessly. She pointed out time and again that I was younger than she, and that she did not believe that I had enough life experience and maturity to be able to help her. She caricatured gestures of mine and denied that we were doing anything worthy of being called psychotherapy. In her frantic attempts to pinpoint my weaknesses she more than once said things about me which I felt to be right.

Gradually I began to feel that indeed I was incompetent to help her and I often felt humiliated and hurt. In trying to keep composure I sometimes adopted a rigid stance and tried not to react to her attacks and denigration by anything but transference interpretations. As this went on I became incapable of relating to her in a genuine and nondefensive way.

My interpretations did not do any good, and my behavior gave her further "proof" that because of my lack of experience I resorted to techniques I had learned from books. The emotional atmosphere in which she continually denigrated me as a person and therapist was mixed. On the one hand, I sensed despair and worry in her voice. She seemed to be genuinely afraid that I could not help her. On the other hand, I felt that she also enjoyed throwing me off balance and putting me down.

After a prolonged period in which the deadlock persisted I felt that if we did not succeed in keeping the various aspects of what was going on apart, we would not get any further. As she launched into her next attack, I simply said that I felt how terribly afraid she was that I was not able to help her. I also told her that I was convinced that my failure to cope with her attacks in a reassuring manner had certainly reinforced her fears. This intervention calmed her down to a certain extent.

I think that the effect of this intervention was due to several factors. (1) It established some emotional contact again. During the period in which I had felt very hurt I had been distant from her and could not empathize with her fears. (2) I validated her perception of me as insecure to the extent they were veridical. This was very important to her as she was often afraid of going crazy. (3) I showed her that I could live with and acknowledge my weaknesses, and therefore gave her more reason to trust me.

I never thought that my actual behavior was the only or even the main reason for her fears. But, as Gill (1982) has emphasized, it is of great importance to give due weight to all the factors in the therapist's actual behavior which may explain any aspect of the patient's reaction. This cleared the way for the understanding of the transference elements not due to the actual situation.

Now that the patient was calmer, it was still very difficult for her to speak freely. Her pleasure in putting me down gave way to a sense of awkwardness. I now tried to help her to probe into her obsession with my age. It turned out that what bothered her was not my age as she estimated it, but the age difference between us. As we tried to understand more of this she became visibly distressed and ashamed. Toward the end of the session she could finally express her fear that since I was younger than she, I considered her sexual needs, fantasies, and preoccupations as both ridiculous and repulsive. Since there was no time left, I just responded by saying that if she had felt like this all along I could understand how difficult and humiliating it had been for her to be in therapy with me. In the following sessions her fear that her sexuality was repulsive led to important material, but I will stop here.

This vignette illustrates quite clearly how a patient's veridical perceptions interact with preconscious transference elements. The reasoning which enabled me to tease these elements apart was roughly as follows: I assumed that the patient's obsession with my age was primarily due to some subjective wish attached to it. But I also took into account that it is very understandable that patients wish to have experienced and mature therapists. Since the patient's aggressive and devaluating attacks had caused me to behave in a defensive manner, this strengthened the patient's fear that she could not trust me.

What could not at all be understood by the assumption that she was preoccupied with my presumed lack of experience was the pleasure she took in putting me down. I suspected that by devaluating and humiliating me she reversed the relationship as she preconsciously experienced it. And indeed it turned out that her attacks masked a fear of being disgusting. In addition, her preoccupation with my age provided her with a rationalization for not probing into the painful feeling that I was repelled by her sexuality and her very physical presence.

The analyst therefore has firsthand knowledge about some processes in the analysand. In acquiring it he uses abilities every sane human being possesses and uses effortlessly in everyday life. All of us can identify that another person is trying to seduce, attack, please, or denigrate us, that he is trying to defend himself against us, or seeking our approval. The analyst can refine these capacities and use them with greater sensitivity than we (including the analyst himself) generally do in everyday life. This is possible because the analyst is, as a therapist, exempt from the pressure of reacting directly to the patient's promptings and can thus concentrate on his perception of, and emotional reaction to, the patient. Furthermore, he is protected by his relative anonymity from being involved in the interaction to an extent which would cause him to be preoccupied with looking for immediate ways to respond to the patient.

So far I have not described anything in the analyst's cognitive ability which is not directly related to attributive and inferential processes known to each of us *qua* competent participants in ordinary human interaction. The steps which follow are also quite easy to understand. Once the analyst has identified a certain type of irrational behavior, thought, and feeling in the patient, he may form a hypothesis about its reflecting a pattern. He can follow through this hypothesis in the transference and in what he comes to know about the patient's life in general.

This corresponds to two types of interventions Greenson (1967) describes. The analyst *confronts* the patient with some pattern of behavior which the patient does not acknowledge to himself. Once the patient has accepted that there is something to be examined, the pattern in question is clarified by analyzing it more closely and following it through in its different manifestations in the patient's life, i.e., it is *clarified*.

2. INTERPRETATION

I shall next pursue the line of thought to be found in the modernist conception of psychoanalytic work. As shown in section c, the aim of interpretation is no longer seen as informing the patient about a causal nexus between events in his childhood and his present symptoms. It is rather to provide a narrative which gives intelligibility to the patient's previously inexplicable patterns of action, thought, and emotion. This conception affects the epistemological status of psychoanalytic interpretation. In particular, many of the cognitive operations of the analyst are closely analogous to those found in other disciplines as well as in commonsense psychology.

As Cooper (1987) points out, the modernist conception does not put much weight on the veridicality of the patient's childhood memories. These are rather taken to be on a par with fantasies, which ought to be analyzed. The memories brought up are thus investigated for possible defensive distortions, for wishes underlying them, and the like. Similarly, the patient's motives for bringing up memories at a particular point in a session must be understood. They can, for instance, be to please the analyst, to direct attention away from current conflicts concerning the analyst or from something in the patient's present life he is ashamed of. The fact that an early memory has come up is not given the special status it had in the historical view of psychoanalysis. The occurrence of a previously inaccessible memory is not seen as an indication that a major piece of analytic work has been completed and that the recalled event can now without further ado be used as a causal explanation of present symptoms.

Correspondingly, the narrative woven through the course of an analysis is not a series of statements of the sort "because x happened to you at age y, you now have symptom z." Neither is it necessary for the success of analysis to end up with a clear chronology of pathogenic events. The result of a full analysis is rather "the construction of multiple histories" as Schafer (1983) has called it. Different narratives are woven which intersect with each other, each highlighting other aspects of the patient's biography.

The reason why multiple histories must be told instead of one definitive biography is that in the modernist view there is not only one possible perspective on the patient's biography. It is one of the patient's problems that he is inflexible in the way he feels about his life, both past and present. He is rigidly tied to one view of himself and others, and incapable of seeing the complexity of his own motives. He comes to analysis with a story about himself, a story not necessarily consciously spelled out. By sticking to this story he refrains from facing aspects of his self both past and present, which are painful to him or which may arouse guilt, shame, and anxiety. The starting point of the analysis is, as Schafer, the Sandlers, Gill, Cooper, and others emphasize, the analytic encounter, i.e., the patient's present mental functioning. In other words, the starting point is the patient's presently rigidly adhered-to story about himself in interaction with his world.

The analyst's object of investigation is not the patient's past as such. He rather analyzes the patient's *stories about his past and present*. An analogy will elucidate this point. We can read a historian's work in order to get information about the period which is the topic of his work. But we can also read them in order to investigate the preconceptions and implicit assumptions which guide the historian's thinking and writings about the historical periods constituting his topic. We might be especially interested in those aspects of his guiding framework which we believe will lead to blind spots in his perspective and to unrealistic conclusions. We could find out that the historian has an implicit scheme, in which certain figures are heroes and others villains or that he sees a particular historical process as a tragedy, a comedy, or a romantic struggle toward a goal to be arrived at. We would then be involved in doing metahistory rather than history in the ordinary sense (White, 1973, 1978).

Applying the analogy, we can say that it is the patient as historian, as the writer of his own biography, who is the focus of the analyst's attention, rather than the actual events the patient is talking about. The shift in perspective away from the historical conception of psychoanalysis is that in the latter the past is the center of interest and the patient's present is seen as a function of that past. As opposed to this, the modernist conception focuses on the patient's present versions of his autobiography. All topics brought up by the patient are taken to be at the same level, and facts about the past do not have special explanatory status. Whatever the chronological location of the events related, it is the patient's perspective of them, more than the actual events, which matters. Correspondingly, the question of the historical truth of the patient's stories matters only insofar as very unlikely versions of purportedly actual events serve as indications of some defensive distortion; i.e., they show us the patient's biases as narrator of his own biography.

At this point it is possible to make more precise one of the core theses of the hermeneuticist conception of psychoanalysis. Grünbaum (1984, p. 54) complains that using the weasel word "meaning" often obscures the question of what analysts are looking for (and this is sometimes indeed the case). For Grünbaum the answer is very simple. Psychoanalysis looks for straightforward causes of neurotic symptoms. As we have seen in chapter 3, this is to some extent true, and the thesis that psychoanalysis does not deal with causes is misguided. But we also saw that the type of causes psychoanalysis is dealing with is of a special nature. Furthermore, I have shown that the modernist view of psychoanalysis is certainly far from seeking causes of symptoms in childhood events.

Now that we have seen that the analyst's intent is to uncover how his patient thinks and feels about his biography (his temporally extended self so to speak), we are able to elucidate how the "meanings" which cause the patient's behavior are to be conceived of. In ordinary language we actually use phrases like "this episode meant such and such for him" quite often. Let us briefly inquire into the significance of such locutions.

There is a very simple use of "meaning" in certain contexts. We can say that not every human being means the same to someone. I take this in the trivial sense that we are acquainted with some people and not with others, that not everyone is a friend or a relative. In ascribing a certain role to someone, we attach a corresponding set of attitudes, feelings, and expectations to this person. Taking someone to be a friend implies, among other things, that one has a set of obligations toward him and to expect from him to fulfill the same kind of obligations toward oneself. One generally has certain positive feelings toward a friend and expects the same from him. It is quite an intricate task to make explicit the cognitive, affective, and behavioral presuppositions, sets of expectations, and type of interactive rituals implicit in such roles (like "friend," "spouse," "teacher," "business partner"). In part, such roles are defined socially, but every person adds his personal slant to them. In addition, each dyad of interaction is influenced by the specific history of the relation and many other factors.

Every such role can be said to constitute part of the méaning persons have for each other. In other words, the meaning of one person for another consists of the various cognitive, affective, and attitudinal sets he attaches to that person. Implicit in this is, of course, that every person has a meaning for himself—what we would call his self representation (Sandler and Rosenblatt, 1962).

It is possible for such representations to be unconscious. In the present context this means nothing more than that the individual is not capable of spelling out the sets in question, although they are causally effective in the determination of his behavior, thinking, and feeling. In fact, most of these meanings are unconscious in the descriptive sense. If this were not the case, the work of anthropologically oriented sociologists like Erving Goffman (1959, 1961) could teach us nothing at all. What Goffmann has done throughout his work is to spell out implicit ways in which we organize our experience by imbuing it with frames of meaning, Goffman's main concern being the organization of social experience (for a presentation of his general theoretical frame, see Goffmann, 1974). If we were conscious of all these meanings, works such as Goffmann's could not possibly be of any significance since it would formulate knowledge available to any member of the culture described.

The work of anthropologically oriented sociologists and social psychologists like Goffmann and Garfinkel is quite often analogous to the activity of psychoanalysts. They try to make explicit aspects of the representational world not introspectively accessible to persons. Correspondingly, something similar to insight in psychoanalysis can be experienced when reading these sociological works. One is inclined to say, "That's exactly right; that's the way we behave in such situations." Part of the difference between the discipline resides in the fact that the sociologists describe frames common to all members of a given culture, whereas psychoanalysis attempts the description of frames which include a wide interpersonal variation. Besides, psychoanalysis is mostly concerned with meanings, not just descriptively but also dynamically unconscious, i.e., meanings which most of us are strongly motivated not to acknowledge. (That this can also be true in the case of the sociologists is exemplified by Goffman's famous work on mental asylums.)

Nothing said in the last pages should strike one as new or original. It is quite commonsensical, and it is meant to be so. My point is that unconscious meanings in psychoanalysis are not far removed from things known from everyday life and from other, quite respectable disciplines.

There is thus a precise sense to be attached to such typical psychoanalytic locutions as "Having sex with his wife means to him committing incest," or "Cleaning the house means to her messing around with feces." The first example can be analyzed in the following way. Committing incest is an activity associated with a particular set of attitudinal, cognitive, and affective frames and expectations. The attitude is strongly negative, the effect is one of revulsion, shame and fear, and the cognitive expectation is of disapproval and punishment. To say about a patient that having sex means to him committing incest implies that the mental set just outlined is attached to sexual contact with his wife, although he is not aware of this face about himself.

The question remains how we can justify such an ascription of unconscious mental content. There are many analogous ascriptions in commonsense psychology. A simple example will do to show the analogy: "Jim says that Sam is a good friend of his, but actually he does not like him a bit." If asked why we have to believe such a statement, we might point to such facts as: Jim avoids meeting Sam; he never does anything for Sam, even if asked for it; he never expresses any warm feelings for Sam and rather gives the impression of not trusting Sam a bit. We show that Jim's actual behavior and his direct expressions of emotion do not fit his avowed friendship for Sam, but that the actual behavior is made intelligible by the assumption that he does not like Sam at all.

Every time we say that someone is lying, we reason in this way, and we do not take the person's word as the sole authority for his mental states. Epistemologically this is not very different in cases in which we think someone is lying consciously, and in cases in which we think that the person actually believes what he is consciously saying about himself. In both cases we infer what we think to be the actual mental state indirectly from whatever behavioral (verbal and nonverbal) evidence we have. The framework we use in doing this is the one described in chapter 3 (section c), in which we intend to maximize the intelligibility of the other person's overall mental state (the principle of humanity). Incidentally, the analogy between propositions about the mental states of others and those about the unconscious has been used by Freud (1915) as the central epistemic defense of theories about the unconscious. I would like to stress, though, that in the present context I am not trying to defend the possibility of knowing that there is an unconscious. I am assuming this possibility and, on this basis, arguing that statements about particular unconscious contents can be defended by ways of reasoning known to us and acceptable in other contexts.

If we relate the points made about establishing the object of interpretation, we can summarize the rational reconstruction of the analyst's mental activity up to this point as follows: the analyst listens to the patient and tries to uncover subjectively determined, idiosyncratic patterns of action, cognition, and emotion. Establishing the existence of such patterns is done through the activities of confrontation and clarification. The analyst then tries to formulate the cognitive, attitudinal, and emotional sets (the representational world) through which the analysand is viewing himself and others. The justification of the interpretation is that it makes the patterns it is supposed to explain maximally intelligible in the same elaborated on in chapter 3. The mental states hypothesized should make it possible to see the patient's experience from within, i.e., to give us an idea of what it would be like to experience the world in this way; and to make intelligible why a person with the patient's mode of experience should act, think, and feel the way he does.

Through the course of an analysis the analyst should be capable of combining his more successful interpretations into a larger narrative. This narrative should provide an intelligible account of the general way in which the patient had to be a biased and distorting historian of his own biography, and what the motivations for maintaining these distortions have been. In this analytic biography the same meaning-structures used to explain the patient's unconscious perception of his own present should explain his conception of his past. Both the starting point and the ultimate touchstone of this analytic biography are the ways by which the account of the patient's unconscious mental life provides a coherent history of the analytic process itself. Such a story, which should unify many aspects of the patient's life into one explaining set of propositions, gains its final justification by its own coherence and parsimony.

e)   EPISTEMIC APPEAL TO ANALYSTS' SPECIAL ABILITIES

The reconstruction of the analyst's intellectual activity appears almost deceptively simple. Indeed, the account leaves out a great deal of complexity, but emphasis on the more commonsensical aspect of analytic work is important at this juncture of metatheoretical discussion of psychoanalysis. On the one hand, there is Grünbaum with his claim that without a well-confirmed background theory analysts can never have the slightest indication of the truth of their interpretations. The argument of this chapter has been that Grünbaum's skepticism is the result of a mistaken view of what analysts actually do: their main concern is with the patient's present mental func-

tioning. Hence their inferences are far more akin to many at-
tributions of mental states which we perform in ordinary life
than Grünbaum assumes.

On the other hand, there is the hermeneuticist tendency to
obscure the aspects of the analyst's train of thought which are
more easily and rationally reconstructed. The relatively indis-
criminate use of words like "meaning" and "narrative" easily
leads more hard-nosed critics like Grünbaum to suspect that
there is no intellectually defensible substance behind such locutions as, "Psychoanalysts look for the hidden intentionalities
of the patients' behavior." I have therefore emphasized the
extent to which analytic reasoning can be broken down into
thought processes which every human being performs constantly. The analyst's implicit knowledge about the appropriateness of behavior, thought, and emotion is not that far
removed from the ordinary sensibilities of mature members of
a culture. Neither does he use any mysterious faculties to identify his countertransference: he just has ordinary human reactions to a person who seduces, attacks, admires, or devalues.
The peculiarities of the analytic situation and his training help
him to make more sensitive use of these reactions, but this does
not make his capacities any more incredible than those of the
trained musician to identify the structure of a complex fugue.

This leads us to a somewhat delicate point. Analysts often
deny that someone who has no experience of analytic work can
competently criticize psychoanalysis (e.g., Brenner, 1982, p. 4).
Such a position implies ultimately that only someone trained
as an analyst can fruitfully discuss the credibility of psychoanalytic hypotheses and theories. This of course infuriates critics.
Any claim of the sort that only a particular group of people can
know something about the truth of certain propositions is
bound to evoke such reactions as calling psychoanalysis "one
of the most persistent dogmatic establishments of recent times"
(Gardner, 1984).

The point is a delicate one, because it has done much to
discredit the intellectual honesty and intellectual respectability
of psychoanalysis. One reply may be that in order to criticize
current physical theories one also needs long and arduous training. An effort must be invested to understand any intellectual

discipline, and criticizing a theory presupposes understanding it; therefore psychoanalysis is no different from other disciplines in this respect.

Such a reply does not touch upon the central problematic point: there is a great difference between acquiring the relevant knowledge about theories in physics, chemistry, or biology on the one hand and getting analytic experience on the other hand. Academic institutions only use criteria of intellectual aptitude and scholastic achievement in their selection of students and teachers. In contrast, in psychoanalysis an applicant's personal maturity is a precondition of being accepted for analytic training. Furthermore, the training analysis is generally regarded as the most important part of analytic training. This requirement goes far beyond the confines of achieving scholastic expertise: it involves the willingness to enter a process of change which has repercussions on the most intimate aspects of one's personal and emotional life. Henri Ellenberger (1970, p. 549ff.) has commented on this fact by pointing out that Freud revived the tradition of the Greco-Roman philosophical schools. These were movements in which disciplines had to prove personal commitment and the ability to shape their lives in accordance with the school's doctrine.

Ellenberger's comparison is made in a sympathetic vein, and its ramifications are worthy of more serious consideration than I can give them here. In the present context his point can serve as an elucidation of the profound difference between ordinary academic disciplines and psychoanalysis. In particular it helps to understand why critics from outside psychoanalysis often think that they are not dealing with a discipline which is akin to science, but rather with an esoteric school, adherence to which is closer to embracing a *Weltanschauung* than it is to the provisional commitment to a research program (see also Kernberg, 1987).

If analysts adhere strictly to the idea that only people who have had active analytic experience can seriously discuss and criticize psychoanalysis, the logical consequence is that only someone who has gone through the process of entering the circle of analytically trained therapists can participate in the debate about psychoanalysis. This in turn entails the prerequisites I mentioned before: the person in question would have to be a member of the analytic school. Such affiliation necessitates that one undergoes a training which touches upon the innermost characteristics of one's personal life, and only someone who is willing to accept such conditions is capable of adequately judging the epistemic credentials of psychoanalysis.

This situation is quite different from the rules of discourse in ordinary academic disciplines. Participation in critical discussion does not necessitate such deep commitment to a theory as to force one to have this theory influence one's personal life. From the perspective of sociology of science this means that psychoanalysis only allows for critics whose prior commitment to the validity of the theory is sufficient to accept arduous rites of initiation into its school. This would amount to the sociological analogue of what Popper called the immunization of theory from criticism.

Given this constellation, it is of the greatest importance to delineate exactly to what extent it is indeed necessary and legitimate to found an epistemic defense of psychoanalysis on the special skills analysts acquire through their training. I want to propose a clear criterion for legitimate recourse to these skills. Appeal to special abilities of analysts must not violate the following principle: *It must be possible to show that the claimed capacities are refinements of ordinary human capacities, and it must be made plausible why under specified circumstances such refinement can actually occur.* This can be called the *continuum principle,* because it postulates that the abilities claimed for analysts must be on a continuum with ordinary human abilities.

The continuum principle can be illustrated with an analogy from the domain of music. The trained musician is able to identify many musical structures and connections which a person of average musical gifts and without training does not notice. Many people who have heard Brahms's fourth symphony do not notice that the fourth movement consists of 31 variations on the theme of the first 8 bars. In this particular case it is rather easy to show someone of average musical gift that this is indeed the case. It is usually enough just to point out the fact (provided he knows what a variation on a theme is). In other cases musical connections are far less obvious. The analysis of more complex Bach fugues requires a rather sophisticated knowledge of musical theory, and a lot of practice in musical analysis.

The trained musician's capacities exemplify the continuum principle. It can be shown that they are refinements and extensions of abilities to be found in people with average musical gifts: the capacity to identify harmonic relations, extended musical Gestalten, rhythmical structures, and so on. It is also possible to specify the kind of theoretical knowledge and practical listening experience necessary to acquire these skills. Hence the trained musician's claims that he can identify musical structures not accessible to ordinary listeners does not violate the continuum principle.

The case of music is particularly instructive, because there exists a phenomenon which *does* exemplify a capacity which is not continuous with ordinary musical gifts, namely, absolute pitch. Normally people can identify intervals, i.e., the relation between the pitch of two tones, but they have no way to identify the absolute pitch of a tone, if not given a tone of known pitch with which they can compare the tone to be identified. It seems that there are very rare individuals who can identify absolute pitch without having a reference tone to compare it with, and the phenomenon is generally assumed not to be reducible to ordinary capacities. If we assume that absolute pitch is indeed a capacity *sui generis,* it could be said to be a capacity which violates the continuum principle. Absolute pitch is to ordinary hearing not as sharp eyesight is to weak eyesight, but as color vision is to color blindness.

Using this analogy we can clarify what the methodological continuum principle demands of an epistemological account of psychoanalysis. If such an account claims that analysts acquire special abilities in the course of their training, these abilities should be to ordinary human psychological sensitivities as the well-trained musician's capacities are to those of the musical layman, and not as absolute pitch is to ordinary hearing.

It is possible to give examples which would violate the continuum principle, although I do not know of any case in the analytic literature which violates the principle clearly. However, the invention of examples does not simply demolish a strawman.

It is meant as a thought experiment which should help us to delineate the boundary of legitimate argumentation in meta-theoretical debates on psychoanalysis. Examples would be the claim that analysts are in direct, immediate contact with their patient's feelings; or the claim that through their countertransference they can know immediately, without inferential reasoning, what their patients feel; or the claim that unconscious fantasies can directly be read from the patient's material.

These examples violate the continuum principle because there are no analogous capacities to be found in ordinary human beings. We normally assume that what is given to us immediately is a person's overt behavior and the Gestalt qualities of this observable behavior. By "Gestalt qualities" I mean expressive properties like a sad tone of voice, angry facial expression, or nervous hand movements. Darwin (1896; see also Ekman, 1980) claimed that we can identify expressive movements directly. This does not imply that through such expressive activity the other person's feeling state is directly intelligible to us, but only that the expressive quality (which may be deceptive, at least in humans) is not inferred but perceived as a single Gestalt.

Whatever we ordinarily believe about the inner states of others is based on (mostly implicit and preconscious) inference from the directly observable data. We assume that people cannot be in immediate empathic contact with other people's feelings and thoughts, if this is supposed to mean that this contact is not mediated through the other's overt expressions, verbal or nonverbal. Hence such claims could not be made for analysts without violating the continuum principle.

What then would count as a legitimate invocation of the analyst's capacity? An analyst notices that his own interventions have an almost imperceptible tendency to put the patient down. Alerted by this he devotes some more introspective attention to his feelings at that very moment and notices that he actually feels irritated by the patient. Wondering about the nature of the irritation, he considers the fact that its immediate expression was the need to put the patient down. He then conjectures that this need may be a reaction to some devaluating tendency in the patient's way of talking to him. He therefore sets out to look for such a tendency in the content or mode of the patient's material.

What the analyst does in this short sequence is that he first becomes conscious of a barely perceptible feeling within himself by noting a detail about his own behavior, e.g., a very slightly ironical tone of voice in his interventions. He then proceeds with a mixture of introspection, inferential reasoning, and observation of the patient to try to identify the nature and source of his own feeling.

This exemplifies special analytic skills because in ordinary life we do not tend to become conscious of such slight nuances of feeling states, much less to act on them. If someone irritates us or denigrates us, we feel vaguely uncomfortable or we somehow try to alleviate the discomfort, either by getting back at the person or by somehow covering up the feeling.

The analytic therapist's specific skill is to refrain from acting on his feelings. In the example above the analyst actually becomes conscious of a feature of his way of acting, i.e., he has already started to act on his feelings, but he stops this, tries to reflect on it by using a series of introspective, inferential, and interpersonal devices. This is a simple instance of using one's countertransference as a means to understand the interaction in the therapy—and ultimately the patient's mental states at a particular moment.

None of the tools used by the therapist is essentially dissimilar from cognitive processes everybody is acquainted with from everyday life. He just uses them with some more sensitivity and in a conscious, more complex manner than usual. This he can do because he is under no pressure to act. This lack of pressure is part of the definition of his role as an analyst. Moreover, his own analysis is supposed to have made him more sensitive to his own reactions—and in particular it should prevent him from taking automatic, unconscious defensive measures to fend off his own unpleasurable feelings. His experience as a therapist should have taught him to use complex cognitive operations flexibly in order to create an understanding of interpersonal and intrapsychic constellations. Yet, as everyone who has undergone training in analytic therapy knows, it takes much time and effort to arrive at a harmonious and efficient interplay of those faculties, and one is never quite immune from the traps of one's own defensive maneuvers.

The example just given focuses on the analyst's capacity to use resources available to every human being flexibly and efficiently. I suppose that it is not unrealistic to expect that this type of cognitive activity can be made intelligible to people who have not had analytic experience. For this, elaborate accounts of specific clinical examples are necessary; accounts which do not make use of psychoanalytic terminology and which link the analyst's experience to modes of experience familiar to everyone. This could serve to demystify such statements as "The analyst uses his own countertransference to understand his patient." In particular it would serve to show that this special skill can be explained in terms not violating the continuum principle.

Such work is, I think, very necessary—and not just as an exercise in public relations—to make analytic practice intellectually respectable to nonanalysts. The analytic community could gain a deeper understanding of what is really going on in the psychoanalytic encounter. Spence's (1982a) penetrating work has shown in detail to what extent analysts report clinical findings without differentiating between data and interpretation. The result of such reporting is counterproductive in two ways: first, it prevents a fresh look at the therapeutic process and often precludes progress in clinical understanding; second, it makes analytic reasoning epistemologically opaque. This second point is of great importance to the topic of this essay: if we seriously want to open the evidential foundations of clinical thought to critical discussion, Spence's demand for stricter standards for reports of clinical data must be taken seriously. In the next section I shall explore the implications of this demand.

f) On Keeping Apart Description and Genetic Speculation

A critical reader may have asked himself the following question: "It seems indeed that it is possible to make many types of analytic reasoning quite commonsensically intelligible. It is especially plausible to say that analysts can identify many aspects of their interactions with their patients through introspection and quite commonsensical reasoning. In this way an analyst can reasonably claim to have evidence for hypotheses such as the patient is hurt, the patient is angry, the patient is in love, maybe even the patient defends against his feeling of humiliation by devaluing his therapist. All these are states of mind which we are familiar with from everyday life, and it is certainly possible to assume that the analyst by virtue of the analytic situation, his experience, perhaps even his giftedness as an observer, can identify such psychological facts better than is usually possible in ordinary life.

"But psychoanalysts claim to know a lot more than that! They claim, for instance, that they know that the patient wants to merge with them, that he is afraid of being swallowed up or anally penetrated or castrated and so on. These claims are far less commonsensical. And that's exactly where it starts to become interesting. *None* of the previous examples included anything very specific to Freudian psychoanalysis. The rational reconstruction does not bring us any closer to understanding how one can know about the facts which are specific to psychoanalysis: oral-sadistic impulses, anal retentiveness, castration anxiety, the Oedipus complex, etc. Is therefore not more needed than just refined commonsense to test the hypotheses of psychoanalysis?"

This question is justified, and the answer is not simple. Let me begin by plotting out where the question is based on common misunderstandings of psychoanalytic propositions. These misunderstandings are partially due to the tendency of analysts to report clinical material without differentiating between data and genetic reconstruction.

For one thing, the layman would be surprised at the extent to which certain fantasies are explicitly expressed without previous interpretive work leading up to them. A patient fantasized for a long time that I was "zoomed" into the consulting room just before he came in and "zoomed" out a moment after he left, and that I did not exist between his sessions. This patient was not psychotic and functioned moderately well. He was aware of the unrealistic quality of his fantasies, but he emphasized that they constituted an emotional reality for him. Furthermore he became extremely panicky before the first breaks in his therapy. He lost all sense of time; the period of 10 days for which I was to be absent seemed to him literally endless. He could not imagine that I actually would continue to exist and that it was therefore possible that I would come back. All of these fears and fantasies were explicitly formulated by him without my doing much to bring this about.

This patient therefore exemplified certain hypotheses of psychoanalytic theory quite overtly. In particular the examples show that although his reality testing was on the whole intact, he had a level of mental functioning on which there were no stable object representations. Furthermore he had explicit fantasies that I was created and disappeared according to his needs. This illustrates Winnicott's theory (1958) that there is a stage of mental functioning at which objects are experienced as being undifferentiated from the subjective needs which they satisfy.

The very fact that patients are encouraged to say absolutely everything that comes to their minds often provides access to aspects of mental life which are not usually spoken about. Some manifestations of archaic mental functioning are familiar to almost everyone from fantasy life, but in ordinarily life attention is rarely focused on these aspects. The analytic setting is therefore uniquely suited to the investigation of certain aspects of human mental functioning (G. S. Klein, 1976). The relative lack of censure of expression and the trust which the patient generally has in the analyst allow for the observation of processes which are otherwise difficult to come by in persons other than oneself.

It is important to avoid a common confusion at this juncture. It is one thing to say that many processes described by psychoanalytic theory are often easily accessible in the analytic situation. It is another to claim this as direct evidence for the truth of etiologic and developmental hypotheses. The example just given illustrates a type of mental functioning, but it certainly does not immediately show that the patient's trouble originated at some specifiable point in his development. The statement that the patient exemplifies a theory formulated by Winnicott must be understood in a minimal sense. Nothing more is implied than that his observation shows that a phenomenon described by an analytic theorist can indeed be observed. It does not mean that one can also infer from the observation the developmental period from which the phenomena stem.

Hence the first part of the reply to the question posed above can be summarized as follows: many phenomena described by psychoanalytic theory can be observed in a direct manner. This occurs more often than is generally assumed by critics outside of psychoanalysis. It is often obscured by reports of analytic material which do not differentiate sufficiently between description and genetic reconstruction. Spence's demand mentioned in the previous section again proves justified. More accurate clinical records will allow for relatively unproblematic evidence for psychoanalytic theory.

Two aspects of psychoanalytic terminology must be differentiated: one is descriptive and the other is theoretical. The first concerns the description and organization of clinical phenomena, e.g., particular mental processes. Terms such as "splitting," "repression," "projecting," and "reaction formation" can be understood without presupposing much of psychoanalytic developmental theory. It is interesting that some of these terms have been introduced within a particular theoretical framework, but are now used by theorists and clinicians who do not accept the original theory. The term "projective identification" provides a good example. It was coined by Melanie Klein (1946), who used it to refer to a particular type of archaic fantasies which she thought to be typical of the paranoid-schizoid position, a developmental stage which she placed in the first three months of life. The term has found widespread acceptance, but some theorists explicitly tried to disconnect the clinical phenomenon from Kleinian theory (e.g., Ogden 1979, 1982). It is therefore possible to use "projective identification" as a tool of clinical description and explanation without accepting the Kleinian theory of the paranoid-schizoid position.

In a seemingly paradoxical way a similar constellation has arisen with respect to the concept of the oral phase of development. Freud originally introduced the notion of oral sexuality in his *Three Essays on the Theory of Sexuality* (1905). The theoretical framework within which Freud defined the notion was centered around the idea of erotogenic zones, which constitute the focus of libidinal satisfaction. The oral phase of development is characterized by the primacy of the mouth as the erotogenic zone. In recent decades important conceptions of the nature of the oral phase have emerged in which the concept of the erotogenic zone does not play a central role. Winnicott's view (1958) of the oral phase is hardly linked to libido theory in general and certainly not centered on the notion of the mouth as an erotogenic zone. It is true that Winnicott himself rarely uses the term "oral phase," but in common psychoanalytic parlance it is still possible to talk of his conception of orality.

This relative independence of terms from their original theoretical environment becomes more salient in the sphere of clinical description. Two clinicians can agree on the description of some person as having strong oral characteristics because the person shows strong dependence on others, passivity, a prevalence of incorporative modes of fantasies and symbiotic types of object relations. This description does not imply an etiologic hypothesis about the roots of such a personality structure. An extreme, but quite possible case would be that of a clinician who is completely agnostic with respect to the psychoanalytic theory of development, but finds the term "oral personality" useful as a tool to designate a cluster of personality traits which can often be observed clinically. Such a combination of *complete* agnosticism and the use of typically psychoanalytic terms is of course not the norm, but clinicians corresponding quite closely to this description can be found. Hence clinicians who do not share many theoretical convictions can in principle agree on quite a number of descriptive facts about a patient. They may use a common vocabulary derived from psychoanalytic theory to describe ego functions such as adaptive style, prevalent defenses, and level of frustration tolerance, as well as the quality and degree of maturity of object relations, superego development, and stability of sexual identity.

The use of many terms of the clinical vocabulary of psychoanalysis does not entail the acceptance of particular developmental hypotheses. This logical state of affairs is a precondition for theorists of different persuasions discussing the etiologic explanation of certain clinical pictures. Such discussion presupposes that there be at least some common ground in the description of the phenomena, and hence some common clinical vocabulary. This does not imply that there is an observation language which is absolutely theory neutral. This positivistic ideal has been found to be illusory for all disciplines—even for the archetype of a respectable science: physics (Kuhn, 1962). In chapter 6 I shall explore the consequences of the lack of such a neutral language, but I must emphasize that there is *some* degree of independence of theory and description.

This is important if we are concerned with the question to what extent certain mental processes described by psychoanalytic theory are accessible to relatively immediate observation in the analytic setting. Only if terms like "incorporation fantasy," "splitting," "incomplete individuation," "phallic defense," and "oedipal rivalry" have a descriptive core *independent of genetic speculation* can we claim to have good evidence at least for the existence of the clinical phenomena which these terms denote.

The modernist conception of psychoanalysis described at the outset of this chapter derives part of its appeal precisely from the fact that it weakens the link between clinical description and genetic speculation. As we saw recent authors tend to emphasize the aspect of analytic work which is centered on the present. The reconstruction of the historical truth about the patient's past and the establishment of causal links between the past and the patient's present problems have lost their centrality in the modernist's conception of what the analyst does.

This conception therefore entails the desideratum formulated. The modernists think that a great deal of analytic work can be done without etiologic speculation. My insistence on the necessity to isolate the purely descriptive aspect of the psychoanalytic vocabulary is well in tune with what many theorists and clinicians think about how clinical work should be performed. I think that *only if this differentiation between the directly accessible aspect of psychoanalytic clinical thought and the speculative genetic aspect is taken seriously can the epistemological value of clinical material be defended.* In addition I concur with Spence's (1982a) claim that such methodological soundness is a necessary condition for the advancement of the knowledge of what actually happens in the analytic situation.

There is therefore a sense in which the opening question points to a real problem in psychoanalytic thought. Since most psychoanalytic terminology originates in certain developmental theories, analysts often conflate clinical description and genetic speculation. To the extent that they do, they claim to know more than is reasonably warranted.

I have argued that even if we restrict knowledge claims to the directly accessible aspects of clinical description, much of what is unique and typical to psychoanalysis is preserved. This thesis has remained on a programmatical level. *It is an important task for psychoanalysis to work out in detail the directly observable contents of psychoanalytic theory.* Such work would enable us to assess more clearly how much we really *know* about the analytic process, and how much still has the status of unproven speculation (Eagle and Wolitzky, 1986). Some first steps have been made in this direction (e.g., Malan, 1976), but most of this task remains to be carried out in the near future.

The thrust of my argument has been slightly positivist, in the degree to which separability of data and interpretation was assumed. Now it is necessary to point to the limits of this independence. In section dl of this chapter I asked what the analyst listens for. We saw that this question is legitimate, since there is no such thing as listening without preconception, especially if the meanings sought for are not easily perceptible. Hence the analyst is not free of theoretical preconceptions. Even when an analyst criticizes others for understanding in a stereotyped way—e.g., always in terms of oedipal conflict—it generally turns out that he has his own predilections, such as interpreting in terms of early traumas (Eagle and Wolitzky, 1986).

The very decision to treat patients by listening to them and trying to understand the unconscious meanings of their verbal and nonverbal behavior is a function of a particular theory. This is especially obvious if one considers how many alternative psychotherapeutic approaches exist. Raymond Corsini's anthology *Current Psychotherapies* (1984) includes presentations of 12 approaches, all of which have considerable following all over the world. In addition there are the 250 less established forms of psychotherapy listed in Corsini's *Handbook of Innovative Psychotherapies* (1981). It is therefore certainly not a matter of course that patients with psychological problems should be treated in a manner even remotely close to the psychoanalytic method.

Even if we restrict ourselves to well-established psychotherapeutic methods which aim at giving the patient insight of some form, this includes several schools who claim to have evidence for their theories in their clinical material. Theoretical preconceptions therefore certainly influence what a therapist comes to see and understand in his patient.

5

THE FUNCTION AND VALIDATION OF PSYCHOANALYTIC RECONSTRUCTION

a)   A CASE ILLUSTRATION: THE MAN WITH THE ABSENT MOTHER

The account of psychoanalytic reasoning given has strongly emphasized the analysis of the patient's present mental functioning. Yet there is no doubt that reconstruction plays a crucial role in psychoanalytic work. I have quoted the Sandlers as saying that reconstruction should be attempted only after a particular motif has been worked on in the present of the transference. They see reconstruction as the summing up of such work in order to give the patient a temporarily extended view of his own self. Other authors put the reconstructive work more into the center of ongoing work. Schafer (1983) sees the analytic process as a constant to and fro between past and present. Ultimately a well-conducted analysis for Schafer "becomes a condensed, coordinated, and timeless version of past and present" (p. 197).

Hence at least some authors who are distinct modernists (to use Cooper's term) see reconstruction as an integral part of *all* aspects of analytic work. In fact clinical material presented by A.-M. Sandler (1985) shows that they as well do not necessarily use reconstruction at the end of an interpretive sequence, but move quite freely between present and past. Their emphasis on the here-and-now is primarily a warning not to let the analytic work glide into intellectual speculation detached from the patient's immediate affective concerns. As long as this principle is not violated they would probably not object to reconstructive formulations at any stage of the therapeutic process.

Prima facie the importance of reconstruction seems to force upon us Grünbaum's epistemological query: How can you ever *know* that a particular reconstructive account is *true?* How can you ever know that the aspect of the past you talk about is indeed causally relevant to the present?

The question is whether reconstructive work must be seen as providing the patient (and the therapist) with knowledge about the causal links between the past and the present. We must therefore have a closer look at the function of reconstruction in analytic work. I will try to show that the primary function of reconstruction is not simply the acquisition of knowledge about causal links. Along with a different view of the function of reconstruction a new perspective on the question of how reconstruction can be validated will emerge. As a starting point for the discussion I will use an extensive vignette from one of my patients, whom I will call the Man with the Absent Mother.

This patient was a 25-year-old man doing his doctoral dissertation in one of the sciences. He sought therapy because of chronic, profound depressions which were often accompanied by suicidal ideation. When some event particularly distressed him, he used to take a razor and cut his forearms very slightly, but he had never actually attempted suicide. I took him into treatment under the following condition: he had to promise me to call me at any time of the day if he felt that the suicidal impulse was overwhelming him. Despite the severe pathology I felt sufficiently sure of his integrity to rely on this promise.

As treatment began, his depression took on an anxious and agitated character. Soon it became clear that he was afraid that if he did not suffer terribly, I would discontinue treatment immediately. In addition he felt guilty about his suffering. He thought that I expected him to become better within a few sessions, and that I considered him to be profoundly ungrateful because he did not improve quickly. My reaction was to reemphasize my willingness to treat him and to have him restate his promise that he would not attempt suicide without calling me first.

This initial period was accompanied by a series of dreams about me and much material from his biography which revealed the emergence of a highly idealizing transference. He experienced me as an infinitely reassuring, soothing, understanding, and accepting figure. He often came into the session in a panic, his face white and tense. Within minutes he began to calm down; his features became more relaxed and his face slightly flushed.

During this period we came to understand one of the main functions of his suicide fantasies: he did not think of suicide as leading to death, a state of nonbeing. Instead, in his fantasy suicide meant to go to a place where there was no suffering, no frustration, but only uninterrupted well-being and satisfaction. Very reluctantly he also started to tell me about an elaborate fantasy world he had built for himself over the years. In this world he did not have his actual parents. Instead his father was an immensely rich and powerful tycoon, and his mother a highly attractive and artistically inclined woman. He himself was a brilliant writer to whom everybody was attracted. He experienced this fantasy world as a place to which he turned; his daydreaming was very intense and provided an escape from his daily suffering.

Within a few months both the suicidal impulses and the fantasizing ceased almost completely. My understanding of this process was that the therapeutic relation had taken over the function of both of them: the therapy had become the "place," the space he could enter to find comfort, soothing, and where he could be held and fed. The metaphor of feeding was felt to be appropriate, because he often said that he lived from session to session; he felt that he had to get enough out of the session in order to live on it until the next one.

This holding environment, as he experienced it, provided the setting for a gradual unfolding of his biography. His parents had tried to be very conscientious, but they obviously had very little ability to react to his needs. Two episodes illustrate this. He was born with a rather severe eye defect; he could not adapt his focus at all. Once he could walk this expressed itself by his constantly bumping into furniture, by difficulty in orienting himself, and by great trouble in grasping things. The parents, however, discovered this defect only when he was almost 4 years old. Until then they ascribed the child's difficulties to his clumsiness.

The other episode occurred early in his life. The patient became very fat, and as an adolescent he was about 20 kilos overweight. At age 16 his parents convinced him to enter a weight watchers program, and he lost most of his overweight rather quickly. Those who had done well could participate in a public distribution of awards. The patient dreaded the idea, but not only did his parents insist he go, but they also invited the local press, and gave special interviews concerning their son's successful diet. The patient did not dare deprive them of the pleasure and underwent the whole procedure. When he told the episode, he was flooded with feelings of dreadful humiliation and helpless rage. I myself found the story and the quality and intensity of the patient's feelings very difficult to bear.

At the beginning of the treatment he had said that his greatest fear was that it might turn out that he had not really loved his parents. The correlate of this fear was a constant tendency to accuse himself of all the bad things that had happened to him and an incapacity to have any negative feelings for his parents. Instead he often incurred the corresponding affects in me, and I tried to communicate them to him through showing him other possible perspectives on what he told me about his past. Sometimes this was quite easy; for instance, he would accuse himself for not explaining to his parents that he needed a certain type of empathy when telling me about constellations at home when he was 4 years old. I then pointed out to him that he was relating to his childhood self in a completely unrealistic way, thus legitimizing his gradual coming to understand the profound failures of his parents. The concomitant changes were that he could gradually reexperience many aspects and scenes of his childhood and adolescence with an appropriate affect. He could feel rage at their failures and the anxiety of feeling utterly alone. At the same time his depression gradually weakened.

There was one area, though, in which no progress occurred.

The patient experienced himself as utterly disgusting and re-pellent. In his fantasy many people had a gravitational field which attracted others to them, whereas he intrinsically repelled people. One expression of his self representation was a fantasy in which he saw himself as an octopuslike monster sitting in the kitchen, emptying the refrigerator and gorging himself with all the food he could get. Although he was rather slim at the time, he continued to feel fat, and he felt guilty and revolted by himself every time he ate something like ice cream. He also felt that his liking for records and books was an expression of in-satiable greed, although he did not spend much money on these hobbies.

His experience of himself was of course reflected in his in-terpersonal relations: he felt inadequate, boring, and clumsy. He was unable to understand how a woman could possibly be attracted to someone as repellent as himself. His rare sexual experiences had been quite traumatic for him: he felt like a dead weight on the woman. He thought they were just passively undergoing the sexual act for him to achieve satisfaction, wait-ing to get rid of his weight on them.

In the transference this had repercussions as well. On the whole the idealizing transference persisted during that initial period. He continued to experience me as an all-understanding and perfect therapist. Any attempt on my side to analyze his unrealistic view of myself and to allow him to experience some-thing other than the blind idealization met with confusion and anxiety. Within this overall transference he had recurring bouts of fear that I would experience him as utterly repellent and draining and that he could not possibly understand what sat-isfaction I could derive from treating him. The quality of these bouts was not annoying. They did not have a passive-aggressive or masochist quality. What came across was a mixture of im-mense pain at not being able to feel that he had anything good to give and a great fear that I might get enough of him at some point.

The typical session began by his relating a specific problem to me—generally concerning his daily life. It was very easy for him to use this starting point for associations ranging widely over all kinds of material, but the specific problem of the beginning of the session remained a constant feature. He was aware of this, and it bothered him. He told me more than once that he actually prepared that problem. He took this to be an indication of his lack of spontaneity and creativity, and he was afraid that he could not have anything to say otherwise.

Then after a year of treatment there came a session in which he did not start by talking about a particular problem. I noticed this since it was highly unusual, but could not see anything in the material relating to this point. At the next session the patient arrived in an extremely panicky state. He himself related this to the fact that he had not brought a specific problem to the previous session, but he was incapable of making any more sense of this link. It was very difficult for him to associate freely, since he felt frantic anxiety. I first tried to understand this by relating to familiar ground: his fear that if he did not have problems, he had no right to therapy and I would discontinue treatment abruptly if he did not suffer enormously, as well as his fears of boring and repelling me. His frantic panic persisted, and all he could connect it to was his inability to come up with a specific problem during the previous session.

At this point I let myself drift in order to allow room for associations in myself. What came to my mind was a persistent feeling of mine that I had no sense whatsoever of who the patient's mother was and what she was like, whereas I did have a sense of his father's personality. I had actually once asked him to describe her to me, but the only clear picture I had was of her being dressed in old clothes at home, clothes which for some reason I pictured to be greyish. I felt that all I could say about my picture of his mother was that she had remained an absence for me. I then wondered whether his panic had something to do with his feeling of absence of his mother which he had transmitted to me. His not having brought up a particular problem might mean that he was about to loose contact with me completely—even though I was physically here and was not going to throw him out.

I therefore asked him what he and his mother generally talked about. He was puzzled for a moment, and thought about the question. Gradually he came to the conclusion that all he could remember about his interaction with his mother was centered around practical issues. She often asked what he wanted to have for lunch, or whether lunch had been fine. He only remembered turning to her about practicalities like things he needed and problems that had to be solved. He could not remember ever just being with her, playing with her, going out with her except for shopping. He did remember that when he was particularly afraid of a school exam the following day, his mother would sit at his bedside for some minutes holding his hand. He described a feeling of being utterly alone in the presence of his family in the house.

I then said that I thought his panic was related to the possibility of loosing contact with me altogether. He had always felt that the only way to be with his mother was to have a practical issue, and the lack of a "presenting problem" for him meant that he was completely alone and would lose my presence. This interpretation immediately calmed him down. Later in the session I told him about my feeling of his mother being an absence rather than a presence and that we should try to understand more about what had happened in this respect.

During the following months a somewhat clearer picture gradually emerged. The patient could remember very few instances of physical contact with his mother. In his memory whenever there was physical contact, it was initiated by him; for instance, by climbing up on his mother's lap trying to elicit a response, but he would not really get one. He also recalled that he liked sitting on her and sucking the skin of her arm.

His aunt had told him about one of the pictures to which he returned quite often. He was 18 months old sitting in the garden and crying. He had a cookie in his hand and asked for another one for the second hand. It turned out that every time he cried he was fed—in particular, with sweets. As a result he was quite fat even in early childhood. In his schoolyears his overweight combined with a certain visual deficit which had remained after he had undergone surgery on his eyes. It had made him quite clumsy, which in turn made him the laughing stock at school. He tried to overcompensate by bringing to school attractive toys which his parents bought for him in great quantities. His greed at the time was therefore transferred to toys on which he felt his capacity to attract friends depended.

Gradually the following reconstruction emerged. His mother seemed to have interpreted every sign of distress in her baby as hunger. The result was that he himself learned to misinterpret every tension and frustration as hunger and later as greed. But the greatest source of his distress was a chronic lack of responsive, joyful interaction with his mother. Apparently she did not have the ability to relate to him on a level other than a feeding one and the later substitutes for oral gratifications.

The situation was complicated by the fact that the child had suffered from a severe eye defect. This made it very difficult for him to build stable object representations. The patient brought dreams and fantasies which indicated that objects emerged and disappeared in inexplicable ways, and he showed extreme separation anxiety when I took vacations. The infant probably did not relate easily to his environment, thus reinforcing the mother's difficulty in forming a strong, affectionate tie to her child. A dream illustrates the patient's feelings about himself: He hurries in an ambulance to a house in his hometown. He comes to rescue a baby who lies on a bed half dead, with only one monstrous eye staring into empty space.

The fact that the mother seemed to have felt no joy in holding the patient as a baby and playing with him was added to his other difficulties in building up representations of stable objects and a cohesive sense of self. His basic feeling from early on was that he physically repelled his mother. He quite often said, "My essence is greediness and nastiness; my essence is to be bad; to repel people." This greed I understood as the result of his not having developed a capacity to differentiate between different needs—in particular, he could not identify his yearning for responsive, joyful interaction with his mother and instead channeled all tension into a frantic drive for oral satisfaction.

During the months in which this work was done the interaction in the sessions was typically as follows: the patient came with rather undifferentiated states of distress and suffering which he could not really identify. He often restated that we might be able to alleviate part of his problems, but he always ran against his feeling about himself as a repellent, greedy, ugly monster. I always felt that he was showing me a formless bundle of distress and that my task was to unpack it and slowly teach him the names of all the ingredients which had been squeezed into this bundle. Its only name had been, "I feel bad, tense, repellent, and depressed." In other words, I felt that I was helping him gradually to learn to differentiate between different self states he had never learned to identify. My main role was one of providing the empathic, echoing, and at the same time structuring object he had never had.

The main result of this period of work was that this basic feeling of self began to change gradually. His hatred and disgust of himself started to give way to other feelings: as he gained a more complex understanding of his present feelings and a richer picture of his past, he began to see that it was not his "bad essence" which had been responsible for his suffering. Despite much anxiety he could gradually recognize his parents', particularly his mother's, failures. Rage and despair appeared and gradually changed into a profound feeling of sadness about all that had gone wrong in his life.

b)   Skeptical Remarks on the Relation Between Therapeutic Effect and Reconstructive Truth

I have chosen this vignette because reconstruction is central to it. In the particular session to which the patient arrived in a state of panic, I started from a reconstructive hypothesis which I linked to the transference. In the months following this session much reconstructive work was done. The immediate effect of the single interpretation and the work done afterward were quite remarkable. Does this mean that the reconstruction is true?

Grünbaum as well as psychoanalytic authors (e.g., Eagle, 1980; Spence, 1982a; Eagle and Wolitzky, 1986) have warned against the fallacy to be found so often in the psychoanalytic literature: if an interpretation is therapeutically successful and makes sense of the material, it must be true. They have pointed out that this inference is invalid. Let me restate the alternative possibilities.

1. The reconstruction may be historically wrong, i.e., refer to an event or constellation which has not occurred. *Eo ipso*

neither the therapeutic effect nor the sense-giving function of the reconstruction can be due to the truth of the reconstruction.

2. The reconstruction may be historically correct, i.e., it refers to something which has actually occurred. Yet the event or state of affairs referred to is not causally connected to the present symptom, state of mind, or whatever is being interpreted by the reconstruction. Presumably neither the therapeutic effect nor the organizing quality of the interpretation is then due to the historical truth of the reconstruction.

3. The reconstruction may be historically correct *and* the event reconstructed is causally connected to the interpreted symptom, state of mind, or whatever is being interpreted. Even this does not entail that the therapeutic effect and the sense-making quality of the interpretation are in any way related to the historical truth. The therapeutic effect may be due to the therapist's empathic manner of stating it, the sense of conviction with which it is uttered, or whatever other factors may be operative in the therapeutic interaction.

In short, the therapeutic effectiveness of a reconstruction is by no means a logically sufficient condition for either its truth value or (in case it is true) for the relevance of its truth. Applying this principle to my vignette one might well say the following. The interpretation I gave in the session in which the patient was panicky may have calmed him down without being true. For example, it may only have convinced him that there was nothing to be afraid of. I told him that his panic was due to the distant past, and it may have been this aspect of what I said which made the panic subside.

As for the reconstructive work in the months following that particular session, a not implausible argument might run as follows. The patient had been convinced for a long time that he was a disgusting, repellent, greedy, and worthless person. I consistently related this feeling to partially remembered, partially hypothetical aspects of his childhood and adolescence. This gradually led him to believe that his feelings about himself were not justified. Again this need not have anything to do with the truth of the interpretations. Warmth and empathy and my constant refusal to take his view of himself at face value may have been the factors responsible for his changing feelings about himself.

This point of view has actually been introduced into the psychonanalytic literature by Kohut. In his posthumously published *How Does Analysis Cure?* (Kohut, 1984) he quotes a clinical episode related to him by a South American analyst. The analyst had told a patient that she had to cancel an appointment in the near future. In the next session the patient was silent and withdrawn until the analyst interpreted her silence along Kleinian lines. She said that her announcement about being away had turned the analyst from a good, warm feeding breast into the bad, cold, nonfeeding one. The patient's silence was a defense against her intense sadistic rage in which she wanted to tear the analyst *qua* bad breast apart. The patient was reported to have responded very favorably to the interpretation. Not only did she talk freely afterward, but she verbalized a number of "biting" fantasies and other material supported the interpretation (p. 92).

Because of his general theoretical outlook Kohut did not believe in the literal truth of the interpretation. He was therefore faced with the question why the analyst's intervention had such a favorable effect. His explanation should be quoted:

> To my mind the interpretation was right in its essential message to the patient. Its specific content was actually of negligible importance and should be understood as being the nonspecific carrier of the essential meaning that was transmitted. And what was this meaning? The message that was transmitted to the patient was easy to understand. Independent of the mode in which the message was expressed, as far as the patient was concerned the analyst had said no more than this: you are deeply upset about the fact that one of your appointments was canceled. It is this simple but, I believe profoundly human message, expressed with human warmth, that the patient heard—never mind the transference revival of the archaic experience of the bad breast, the transference repetition of a catastrophic damming-up of libidinal impulses resulting in the transference or the profound loss of self-esteem that followed the abrupt loss of the mirroring self-object that had sustained her self. And I am convinced, furthermore—to make my point from the opposite direction—that the analyst could have spoken the same words without the patient's wholesome response to the interpretation if she had failed

to transmit her correct empathic perception of the patient's dev-
astated state via her choice of words, the tone of her voice, and
probably many other still poorly understood means of commu-
nication including bodily movements, subtle body odors, and the
like [p. 94].

It would be quite interesting to analyze Kohut's whole argument around this case example closely, but this would lead
us too far afield. I will say only so much: Kohut explicitly says
that he is not a nihilist with respect to experience-distant reconstructions. This is not surprising since he spent almost two
decades in formulating an important new theoretical framework of his own, which—at least since 1977—he considered as
explicitly opposed to classic ego psychology. But in the quoted
passage he comes dangerously close to espousing a profoundly
skeptical position with respect to *all* genetic speculation. I find
it particularly remarkable that he includes his own self-psycho-
logical approach in the list of possible genetic-dynamic interpretations of the patient's state of mind which he deems *not* to
be essential to the therapeutically operative message to the patient.

Kohut singles out two factors as essential to the therapeutic
impact of the Kleinian analyst's interpretation: (1) the content
referring to the simple fact that the patient is upset about the
cancellation of the appointment; and (2) the empathic warmth
of the way Kohut assumes this "profoundly human" message
to have been transmitted. It is quite clear that these two factors
are not very characteristic of a psychoanalytic way of understanding the patient. A warmly uttered "You are deeply upset
about the fact that one of your appointments was canceled"
could easily occur in a Jungian, Adlerian, existentialist, or Gestalt therapy, although taken in isolation it is most reminiscent
of the Rogerian approach.

My intention is not to show that Kohut is inconsistent by
stating both that he is not a nihilist with respect to reconstructive, *and* that ultimately therapeutic impact is not due to the
truth of reconstruction. Nor do I want to argue that Kohut had
ended up being un-psychoanalytic. I think that the tension in
his view is characteristic of the intellectual predicament of pres-

ent-day analysts who are not dogmatically sure of the truth of their beliefs.

Let me exemplify this with my own case report of the previous section. I have refrained from using specifically psychoanalytic terminology as far as possible, and I have done so on purpose. My understanding of the case can easily be characterized as an amalgam of Kohutian and Winnicottian lines of thought despite my restraint in the use of their terminology. One of the reasons for this restraint is that I think that vignettes should not derive their persuasive power from triggering associations of the sort "aha, self-object failure" or "aha, holding function of the therapist." Yet I have no illusion about an analytic case history *not* evoking such associations to *some* extent. But reports should rely as little as possible on the effect of the recognition of well-entrenched story lines. Ideally a case history should convince someone who has no knowledge of psychoanalytic theory. This would minimize the danger pointed out by a critic outside of, but not unsympathetic to, psychoanalysis that analysts accept explanations just because they reduce material to familiar theoretical concepts (McIntire, 1971).

Do I believe in the historical truth of the reconstruction of the origins of my patient's suffering? Reflecting on this question, I remain strangely indecisive. I must emphasize that the vignette isolates one—albeit crucial—story line among several others which emerged in this therapy. With this proviso I can say that during the therapy both the patient and I had a strong sense of verisimilitude with respect to the emerging story. This was particularly true because aspects of the story centered around the patient's direct memories, which he relived in an intense, affectively colored way. Hence I rarely felt that I was speculating, but rather that I was just helping to organize material which easily fell into place by itself.

I am of course aware that this feeling of just making a story explicit which was really there before is quite illusory. In fact I can still pinpoint junctions in the course of this therapy at which I was making quite conscious choices between alternative interpretive lines. For example, the patient once saw me with a woman. In the session following this event he talked about how he had felt. On the one hand, he had been curious about whom I was with, and what exactly my relationship to her was. But he had felt that his curiosity was utterly disgusting and perverse, and so he had not even dared to look any closer.

There exist several possibilities: one association which came to my mind at that point was that the patient had repeatedly expressed a fear of being sexually perverse, possibly homosexual. Hence one way of looking at the episode was in terms of an inverted Oedipus complex: his refraining from looking at us more closely might have been a defense against a wish to disturb and separate us because of his underlying wish to have me for himself. Another alternative was to look at the event in straight oedipal terms; he might have defended against a wish to compete with me. Something along these lines would have been plausible for someone thinking in ego-psychological terms.

I waited for more material, and was most impressed by his conviction that his very wish to know anything about me was despicable and disgusting. The quality of the accompanying effect was mainly painful. I could not detect any sign of defensive modifications to be expected on the ego-psychological hypotheses mentioned above; neither was there an indication of the typical neurotic anxiety accompanying unacceptable wishes. I felt that the patient was afraid of my being repelled by the very fact that he wanted to know anything about me. Hence I decided not to take the line looking for underlying conflict of one sort or other. I related to the patient's expectation of how I would feel about his curiosity and to his own attitude toward his wish to know about me. I said that I was struck by how certain he was that his wish to know about me could only be seen as perverse and disgusting and not, for example, as healthy and normal curiosity. This comment first puzzled the patient. He could not think about his curiosity as something normal; and he related similar feelings about other instances where he felt that his desire to know was ugly, perverse, and intrusive. The session ended on a note of sadness, because the patient understood how he was unable to take any motivation of his at face value, as legitimate and good.

This episode can certainly be seen in several ways. One of them is that I may have been right in focusing on the patient's self-perception as disgusting and perverse at that particular point in the therapy. Any attempt to probe more deeply into underlying conflicts may just have been a blow to the patient's unstable self. Instead of leading to insight such probing would have increased the patient's hatred and disgust of himself. Yet, it might be said, this does not mean that on a deeper level one might not have found different motivations, maybe along the ego-psychological lines mentioned above.

I am not unwilling to consider such a view of the episode just related. In fact at later stages of the therapy I sometimes did interpret along ego-psychological lines. At one point the patient became suicidal again when a woman he was interested in started to go out with someone else, who had actually asked the patient whether he would approve of this. The patient had said he did not mind, but then reverted to his self-depreciating feelings, his conviction that he could not be loved, and suicidal thoughts. I then pointed out to him that he did not allow himself to feel any anger either against the man or against the woman, and that his explicit approval of their dating perpetuated his avoidance of any competition. His reawakened suicidal thoughts I interpreted as aggression turned against the self, an interpretation which turned out to be useful.

I am aware that strictly ego-psychology oriented therapists or Kleinians would have handled the case differently from the very beginning. A Kleinian would have taken the patient's idealizing transference as a defense against wishes to empty me of all the good things inside me, particularly since the patient did see himself as greedy. An ego psychologist would not have taken the vacuousness—as I did—as an indication of an actual maternal deprivation in the parent's childhood.

Where does all this leave us then? The "man with the absent mother" is a case in which both the patient and I had a strong feeling that we were uncovering the truth about the genesis of his sufferings. Yet even the cursory glance I have given the case has allowed for a great deal of alternative hypotheses and explanations of the processes which have occurred. As I said at the beginning of this section, the reconstructive work was important in this case, and I have presented the reconstructive work as crucial to the therapeutic process. Yet we cannot get around the question whether we should not embrace the more skeptical norm of Kohut's dilemma: even though there are many reconstructive hypotheses, should we not embrace the parsimonious hypothesis about the nature of the therapeutic action? Is it not the simplest hypothesis that the patient was helped by the combination of a warm, empathic relationship and my firm determination to take his feelings about himself to be a reflection of his psychic reality, but not as giving the whole truth about who he was?

I am inclined to accept this parsimonious hypothesis to a certain extent. There is much evidence for the idea that the type of human relationship between the patient and the therapist and the therapist's attitude and personality are crucial to therapeutic outcome (for a review of this research, see Garfield and Bergin, 1978). There is too much evidence to maintain the classic psychoanalytic view that the only agent of true therapeutic change is insight into the roots of the patient's psychopathology. In classic analysis this point has been made indirectly through Greenson's (1965) emphasis on the importance of the working relationship between patient and analyst and Stone's (1961) work on the analytic situation. But it was Winnicott (1954) who saw early that, at least in certain cases, the real aspects of the therapeutic relation were not just preconditions for therapeutic work, but actual therapeutic agents. In Kohut's work this aspect of analytic influence has become central to a whole theory of the nature of psychoanalytic cure.

Hence even within psychoanalytic theory insight is no longer considered the only therapeutic agent. This entails the conclusion which Grünbaum arrived at from a different perspective, namely, that therapeutic effect cannot be taken as a criterion for the truth of an interpretation. This is particularly problematic since the psychoanalytic literature is replete with reasoning using this criterion implicitly or explicitly: the interpretation was helpful, *ergo* it must be true. Grünbaum concludes that without the tight link between therapeutic effect and truth (the necessary condition thesis) there is no way we can ever know about the truth of reconstructions on the basis of clinical material.

I think that this conclusion is not warranted to the degree Grünbaum believes. In what follows I shall present an epistemological model of psychoanalytic reconstruction which is not linked to the criterion of therapeutic effect. My argument will be that careful analytic reconstruction is similar to reasoning in history and related disciplines. I am of course aware that the comparison between psychoanalysis and history is not new. Novey (1968), Sherwood (1969), and many others have thought along these lines. Yet I hope that the particular model I am about to offer will introduce further clarification into this confusing and problematic area.

c)   THE ANALYST AS CRITICAL METAHISTORIAN

Do my reflections entail total skepticism with respect to reconstruction? One must distinguish between several aspects of this issue. The first concerns the classic position taken by Freud, that only true reconstruction can be therapeutically effective (what Grünbaum calls the necessary condition thesis). This strong position, we have seen, is untenable in the face of the empirical evidence. Too many other forms of therapy are successful, and too many other factors have turned out to be important in the therapeutic process to maintain the necessary condition thesis.

As mentioned, Grünbaum thinks that *only* the necessary condition thesis guarantees that the clinical method can *ascertain* the truth of clinical propositions in psychoanalysis. I have exemplified that even in cases where the reconstructive work was both successful and convincing to patient and therapist, explanations other than the truth of the reconstruction can be given for both the therapeutic effect and the sense of conviction engendered.

I therefore believe that with the present state of knowledge, no particular version of psychoanalytic theories of the etiology of neuroses can claim conclusive evidence. In this I concur with Grünbaum, but I do not think that no evidence *whatsoever* for psychoanalysis *is* available from clinical data. (I will return to this point, and will argue that Grünbaum sees the issue too much as an all or *nothing* affair with respect to psychoanalysis as a whole.)

At present, however, I am not dealing with psychoanalysis as a general clinical theory; rather I am concerned with hypotheses about particular patients. My approach has been to ask whether individual clinical accounts can be rationally justified. By "rationally justified" I do not mean "ascertained beyond any doubt," but I believe that there are good reasons to accept a case history as presented by a psychoanalyst. Contrary to Grünbaum, I do not think that the justifiability of single case accounts presupposes a well-established, general, clinical theory. If particular explanations always were to presuppose knowledge of established general laws, disciplines like history and law would not be possible (see section e below).

My view of the epistemology of reconstruction can be put in a nutshell: every patient comes to therapy with a stock of memories of his past. This stock of memories can be called his chronicle of his life. He also has a narrative of his history. This I will call his autobiography. The psychoanalytic reconstruction of his development is a critically retold history based on the patient's chronicle of his life and the patient's present mental functioning as manifested in the therapeutic interaction. The criteria for the acceptability of the analytic reconstruction are the same as for any historical account: the reconstruction must explain as many as possible of the available data; it should be inconsistent with as little as possible of the data; it should be coherent, elegant, and contain as few as possible assumptions inconsistent with accepted background knowledge. With regard to the chronicle, a historian bases his work on data which have survived into the present. These include documents of all sorts: eye witness accounts, correspondences, legal contracts, chronicles, works of art, and so on. The historian has a huge amount of implicit and explicit presuppositions of how these documents are related to the events, persons, and processes he is about to describe. He also has heuristic rules to deal with conflicting data, e.g., inconsistent accounts of the same event. This does *not* mean that he has a full-fledged general theory about how documents are related to the historical reality they reflect. Such a theory would have to be a general theory of human behavior and social processes, something which nobody has or ever is likely to have.

The analogy to the historian's documents is what I called the patient's chronicle. By this I mean his stock of more or less distinct direct memories of events in his life, his memories of what he has been told about himself, and his beliefs about his past grounded on a variety of sources such as photographs, letters, and medical records.

The distinction I am making between the patient's chronicle and his autobiography is not one that is to be found in reality—at least not neatly. The patient's autobiography is his historical account of his own biography. It includes his interpretation of what he believes to be true of his past and the causal links he constructs between different events, constellations, and processes in his life. Moreover, he attributes significance to the developments in his life. By this I mean he organizes his life into meaningful stories: successes, failures, comedies, tragedies, absurdities, never-ending struggles. In this the patient is no different from any historian. As Hayden White (1978) argued, the historian does not just establish facts: he links them into humanly meaningful sequences or modes of emplotments. White indeed sees the central function of the historian as organizing historical data meaningfully. In this function lies the difference between the chronicler and the historian. Where the chronicler records facts in a more or less disconnected way, the historian organizes. In this White concurs with other major historians like Carr (1961) and Elton (1967).

In the patient's mental reality the chronicle and the autobiography are of course not distinct. He does not have a store of uninterpreted memories on the one hand and narrative organization on the other hand. In this the situation is precisely analogous to that of the historian's sources. The documents available to the historian are in themselves both records and interpretations of the historical reality they reflect. But if necessary the historian will distinguish between the facts recorded and the interpretation imposed by the recorder.

On what basis can the historian do this? Ultimately because of his own interpretation of the same facts, events, and processes. In particular he will do so if he assumes that the eyewitness, chronicler, or other historian he relies on is biased in his way of looking at things. Such an assumption can also be based on heuristic principles of all kinds; for instance, that persons who were themselves involved in certain events try to exculpate themselves in their own accounts of these events, or that writers with a strong ideological commitment try to support their ideology in their historical accounts. A list of such examples of heuristics would be endless. What distinguishes the good historian from the bad one is his capacity not to rely on hard and fast rules, but instead to be guided by a sense of relevance and his ability to judge the logic of situations from case to case.

The analyst often needs to distinguish between his patient's chronicle and his autobiography. He does so in ways very analogous to the historian by using heuristic principles and specific knowledge about the patient. His principles include familiar propositions of psychoanalysis: that persons try to refrain from thinking about aspects of their past and present which evoke anxiety, guilt, shame, embarrassment, and humiliation; that persons try to avoid internal and external conflict by falsifying their perceptions of themselves and others. A continuation of this list would amount to an account of the psychoanalytic theory of motivation, defense, and mental functioning under conditions of conflict.

It must be emphasized, though, that in the present context I do not look at the propositions of psychoanalytic theory as an established body of knowledge. Instead I take it to be a set of heuristics guiding the analyst in his search for bias in the patient's autobiography (his history of his own life). In this respect it is on a par with many assumptions of commonsense psychology which function as heuristics for the analyst no less than they do for the historian. These hypotheses can be viewed as being more or less useful rather than as laws about human mental life which amount to a strong theory.

The analyst is thus presented with the patient's autobiography as the patient tells it. He tries to find the biases, the rigidities, idiosyncrasies, and blind spots of the patient *qua* autobiographer, by using the heuristics of commonsense psychology and psychoanalytic clinical wisdom.

The analyst has another invaluable source of information about the idiosyncrasies of his patient's ways of constructing his past reality. In the previous chapter we have seen that the analyst listens for subjectively determined, idiosyncratic patterns of the patient's thought, emotion, and actions. He does so particularly with respect to the patient's way of functioning in the analytic situation, that is, within the transference. The analyst is intent on finding the patterns which the patient uses to organize his autobiographical account. His knowledge about the patient's way of experiencing his *present* reality is of course an invaluable source of information for this project.

Hence the analyst does not jump from the patient's present mental functioning (his symptoms, character traits, etc.) directly to conclusions about the patient's past. His starting point is an existing biography of the patient, namely, his autobiography. This autobiography is gradually amended, enriched, and made more complex. The analyst does this *via* the gradual formulation of the motivated distortions he uncovers in his patient *qua* historian. Hence (as said previously) the analyst acts first as a metahistorian, and on the basis of his analysis of the patient *qua* historian he helps the patient to arrive at a less distorted autobiography, the analytic reconstruction.

An important element is still missing in this logical analysis of the analyst's activity as metahistorian and historian. The analyst is guided by another important set of heuristics: the whole range of assumptions—specifically psychoanalytic and commonsensical—which the analyst has about human development and human life. The analyst assumes, for example, that there is no life without culturally unacceptable sexual wishes (both in childhood and adulthood), without anger and rage, without humiliation and shame, without anxiety and guilt. He assumes that every human being has needs for dependence and autonomy, stability and change, love and acknowledgment.

Hence the analyst assumes that his patient must have had his share of all the aspects of the normal range of emotions, wishes, needs, and thoughts which are parts of the analyst's conception of the *condition humaine*. If he sees that some such aspect is absent, either completely or partially, in the patient's account of his past and present, this constitutes a reason for the analyst to wonder what has happened to this aspect of the patient's mental life. He thinks that there must be a bias in the patient's view of himself, and he looks for a motivation for this subjective bias. In this search he is guided by the heuristics provided by commonsense psychology and the psychoanalytic theory of motivation, defense, and functioning under conditions of conflict previously mentioned.

Let me illustrate this somewhat abstract line of thought by returning to the case of the "man with the absent mother." The patient's autobiography was crucially formed by a central theme: all his suffering and depression were the result of the intrinsic essence of his self, which he saw as repulsive, disgusting, bad, and greedy. As a metahistorian I saw this theme as an indication of an idiosyncrasy of the patient's way of organizing his biography rather than taking it to be the simple truth about the patient's past and present. In doing this I was guided by several heuristics. For one thing I was directly acquainted with the patient, and the human being I knew was not repellent, bad, and greedy. Also the patient's account was too monolithic, too simple to fit into my own scheme of things.

Hence I was faced with the question why the patient had become and remained such a biased autobiographer, especially since his view of himself was so self-destructive. One motive for this bias which he had mentioned at the beginning of the therapy was his terrible fear that he might not really have loved his parents. Yet in his fantasy world he had parents other than those he actually had. His activity of fantasizing was linked to profound feelings of shame and guilt. The motivation for the distortion therefore could be that the patient felt profoundly guilty and ashamed about his wish to accuse his parents, especially his mother, of any failure. This for him meant being nasty and ungrateful. On a more hypothetical level his fantasy could be seen as the symbolic expression of killing his parents and substituting them with others. This hypothesis was substantiated by the patient's later, horrified realization that he was a murderer, and his difficulty in understanding clearly that the murder was only committed in fantasy. So a further motivation for sticking to his view of himself was that any accusation of his parents would have activated his dread of actually having murdered them.

These fantasies and murderous wishes were in fact operative

in several respects. Not only were they a central motivation for not seeing his parents' part in the genesis of his problems, but they themselves were an unconscious source for his thinking that his essence was bad. Thus the gradual uncovering of his motivations for distortion opened the way for reviewing his autobiography. Instead of looking at all the facts known under the perspective of how his disgusting, bad self had been responsible for all his suffering, a more balanced and realistic picture could emerge. The analysis of the patient *qua* historian led to a different history, more in tune with the richer conception of human reality which guided my attempt to understand the patient's past and present.

This leads me to an important point of a more general nature. In the last decades psychoanalysis put great emphasis on very early developmental stages, of which no patient can have conscious memories. I am not concerned here with the general developmental theory, but rather with particular reconstructions. With respect to individual reconstructions I have emphasized that the analyst's starting point is the patient's version of his own history. Does this not conflict with the idea underlying many important schools in psychoanalysis that the earliest stages of development are the focus of analytic work?

At least one aspect of my reconstruction of the patient's childhood dealt with his early infancy. How does this fit the logical analysis of the analyst's reconstructive activity? Carrying the analogy to history further, one might say: the reconstruction of such very early developmental periods of which there are no conscious memories relates to reconstruction of later stages as prehistory relates to the history of periods about which there are contemporary written records. The prehistorian and archeologist must try to build a picture based only on whatever mute remainders of prehistorical cultures there are. Such work must of necessity be more speculative and less certain than historical work which is based on written records as well. If, as I claimed, no particular psychoanalytic theory of the etiology of psychopathologies is sufficiently established, then the reconstruction of the earliest stages is more speculative than reconstruction of later stages.

This note of caution must be extended to all psychoanalytic

reconstruction to a certain extent. All too often psychoanalytic work has been guided by imagined certainties, such as that the root of *all* neurosis *must* be the Oedipus complex, or that the goal of *all* analysis *must* be the working through of the depressive position.

Analytic work relies on the central idea that the analyst brings to his therapeutic work a conception of the *condition humaine* which is *richer* than the patient's. If an analyst has a highly monolithic picture of human development, both normal and pathological, his only justification for adhering to this could be that he has a strong, well-established, general theory of development and etiology. Such a theory, however, does not in fact exist.

Acknowledging the lack of such a theory raises a somewhat surprising question. What special competence does a psychoanalyst have which entitles him to the claim that he is a specialist in the construction of analytic biographies? The force of this question is based on the fact that we have a cultural prototype for the specialist, namely, the natural scientist. He is supposed to have mastered a set of well-established, formalized theories and more or less specified techniques for their application to certain domains. This picture applies, in various degrees, to the physicist and chemist, computer scientist, biologist, engineer, and medical doctor.

This picture of the natural scientist does not apply to the psychoanalyst, but our culture knows other forms of expertise as well. Examples are the historian, the art dealer, the professor of literature, and the financial counselor. These professions are not based on strong, formalized theories with predictive power on which the expert can ground his theories and judgment. Yet there is no doubt that their expertise in these domains can be developed. Moreover, there is generally a consensus within these disciplines on who the authorities in the field are.

What constitutes the expertise of a historian, for example? No cut and dried answer is possible. But from a work like Elton's *The Practice of History* (1967, especially part II), a fair impression of the professional historian's skills can be gained. They involve mastery of the relevant languages, skills in the handling of primary sources, mastery of the established academic channels of information gathering, and the like. In addition to these more technical skills, he is expected to have wide knowledge of history concerning his own field of specialization and, in a less circumscribed manner, general cultural knowledge. All of this will of course not yet make a good historian. To be good, he needs gifts like a capacity for synthesis, the peculiar quality of historical imagination, a sense of relevance, a good grasp of human affairs, and a talent for narrative writing.

None of these requirements can be formalized, and only some of them can be taught in a formal sense of the word. Yet historians have a clear sense of what good history and bad history are. Section e will briefly delineate the general philosophical view which makes such a fact seem surprising. The domains of the sciences certainly do not exhaust all the rationally grounded intellectual disciplines.

The psychoanalytic therapist's competence does not reside in the mastery of a formal, well-established theory. The list of qualities which makes someone into an analyst cannot be easily defined. This is due to many factors, one of which is that many of these qualities are personality characteristics like maturity, objectivity, flexibility, and empathy. The mastery of psychoanalytic theory is to a certain extent a prerequisite. But, as Waelder (1962) pointed out, there are excellent clinicians who do not know much about the more abstract parts of psychoanalytic theory.

The making of an analyst involves the acquisition of certain specifiable skills: the capacity to organize clinical material in ways prescribed by the psychoanalytic model of man; the ability to listen carefully to other human beings; the ability to empathize (i.e., to experience another's emotional life from within without identifying with the other); a developed sense for the humanly appropriate and expectable; a keen eye for significant *leitmotivs* in human lives; a synthetic capacity to integrate disparate bits of information of a wide variety into meaningful structures, etc.

What *method* does the analyst use? Not unlike the good historian, the good analyst does not rely on hard and fast rules. He may have rules of thumb like Freud's advice that if the patient suddenly shuts up, one should wonder whether a thought about the therapist has crossed his mind. Only the insecure beginner will rigidly stick to such rules. What rules does the expert follow then? As Hubert and Stuart Dreyfus (1986), have emphasized, both psychological evidence and conceptual considerations lead to the conclusion that experts generally do not apply rules. Instead their previous experience brings them to the point where the material or problem they are faced with organizes itself into meaningful structures without their consciously or unconsciously applying any formalizable rules.

It must be pointed out that their model applies to experts in every field, even domains like physics and chess, and is not peculiar to the less formalizable disciplines. To borrow an old distinction of the philosophy of science; the difference between the more and the less formal domains lies not so much in the context of discovery but in the context of justification. Even in mathematics there are generally no algorithms for the invention of proofs, but once a proof is given, there are formal ways of checking whether the proof is valid. In the humanities, the human power of judgment plays a great role, not only in the creation of a historical narrative, for instance, but also in the assessment of its plausibility.

The necessary power of judgment is itself a function of expertise, and this expertise, as mentioned, is not formalizable. It is a matter of experience, knowledge, and talent. Hence, in the humanities, and no less so in psychoanalysis, the attainment of expertise is strongly correlated with the amount of experience and thus with age. Unlike mathematicians and theoretical physicists, historians, literary critics, philosophers, and psychoanalysts can hardly attain their peaks of creativity before the age of 30.

These are truisms. The reason I mention them is that they are intimately related to the question of how psychoanalytic reconstruction can be validated. The plausibility of a reconstruction is a matter of degree ranging from implausible to a very convincing, but never approaching certainty. The better the fit with the data and the less the account is based on theoretical propositions which are not well grounded, the higher the degree of plausibility of the account.

The epistemology of psychoanalytic reconstruction proposed entails some practical consequences: the expertise of the analyst does not consist in the mastery of a well-established theory with strong predictive and retrodictive power but rather in the richness of the analyst's view of the *condition humaine*, the nuances and varieties of human emotional life, and a keen sensitivity for human affairs in general. If this is true, then certain types of inferences to be found all too often in the analytic literature are illegitimate. I refer to the way of reasoning Peterfreund (1983) has called the *stereotyped approach*.

A general characterization of the stereotyped approach is that it legitimizes clinical inference on the basis of little evidence by using certain theoretical propositions *as if* they were well-established laws of strong predictive and retrodictive power. Peterfreund provided extensive documentation of this approach. One often quoted and criticized example is that of Hanna Segal (1967) who, in expounding Kleinian technique, argues in favor of early deep interpretation. As an illustration she mentions the very first session of analysis with a candidate, who began the session by expressing his determination to qualify and to get as much analysis as possible in a short time (p. 202f.). In different contexts he spoke of cows and his digestive problems. Segal does not provide more material, but she concludes that the patient thus far had presented a clear picture of his transference fantasy, and so she could immediately arrive at the following interpretation: she herself was the cow, like the mother who had nursed him, and he was going to empty her greedily, and as fast as possible, of all her analysis-milk.

This vignette has been criticized severely by both Greenson (1974) and Kernberg (1980, chap. 3) on purely clinical grounds. Both argue that irrespective of the truth or falsity of the interpretation, such technique cannot lead to genuine insight in the patient, but at best to indoctrination (Kernberg) and at worst to massive feelings of guilt and total confusion (Greenson). Both do not touch upon the question whether Segal indeed had any good reason to see this interpretation as plausible. I think that the questions of therapeutic efficiency and verisimilitude can to some extent be separated. A false interpretation could very well have a therapeutic impact (Segal claims this to have been the case in her example), and a true one might not do anything to the patient.

It seems that Hanna Segal believed that the material she mentions does indeed constitute good evidence for her interpretation. I think it does so only in conjunction with a law of the following kind: "If in a session there are hints of wanting to get something out of the analysis or analyst, and cows, breasts, digestion, or other 'oral' material is mentioned, then the patient has strong oral wishes toward the analyst." Segal probably relies on this type of law implicitly, given her orthodox Kleinian position. She does not mention though that she uses any law and seems to think that the material itself provides evidence for her interpretation. Hence her vignette fits the characterization of the stereotyped approach described above.

Any interpretation which relies on such laws (implicitly or explicitly) is epistemologically acceptable only if there is prior, *independent* evidence for the truth of the laws. I do not know of any research by Kleinians which provides such independent evidence. Clinical evidence is not acceptable if it relies on such laws, because the interpretation would both rely on the law and provide evidence for it. Such reasoning is circular and unacceptable.

"But does this not disqualify *all* clinical data as evidence? Do not *all* psychoanalytic interpretation and reconstruction make such implicit and explicit use of law? And are not most of the laws of psychoanalysis devoid of strong independent evidence?" This question is to be expected and would reflect Grünbaum's position.

While not being able to offer a foolproof answer which would satisfy a hardheaded philosopher of science like Grünbaum, I do not think that the situation is quite as hopeless as the question implies. Previously I distinguished between the reliance on psychoanalytic propositions and commonsense psychology as heuristics and the acceptance of them as established, strong laws. There is no clear cut-off point defining the difference between the two, but I would characterize the difference as follows. A rule is used as a heuristic rather than a law if knowledge of the rule is useful but not necessary for the assessment of the plausibility of an account using it.

In other words, psychoanalytic case histories are of course always linked to psychoanalytic theory in some way, but there are differences in the strengths of these links. In some cases (especially in the stereotyped approach) only acceptance of some aspect of psychoanalytic theory as well established can make the clinical account plausible. In other cases even someone knowing very little of psychoanalysis could come to the conclusion that the psychoanalytic history given in the account is plausible. Such an account can be called *undogmatic*. The assessment of such a case history could proceed along the same lines as the critique of any historical account. I have sketched this way of reasoning above and argued that they rely on rules only as heuristics and not as strong laws.

Do such undogmatic accounts exist? I can mention some examples which seem paradigmatic to me: Freud's account of the Rat Man (1909b) and of Little Hans (1909a); Greenson's case history of Lance, the transsexual boy (1966); Kernberg's vignettes in chapters 6 and 7 of *Object Relations Theory and Clinical Psychoanalysis* (1976); Kohut's "The Two Analyses of Mr. Z" (1979), and Anne-Marie Sandler's vignette in "The Structure of Transference Interpretations in Clinical Practice" (1985).

The interpretations these authors give of their cases are not necessarily *true*. I am referring to the way they present their case histories. One reason for choosing these particular examples is that no two of these authors have exactly the same theoretical orientation. Undogmatic presentation is not bound up with theoretical orientation at all.

It is not easy to give a positive characterization of an undogmatic presentation. The negative characteristic mentioned before was that undogmatic clinical presentations do not rely on unproven rules as established laws to make their interpretations plausible. This is a *conditio sine qua non* for lack of dogmatism. A positive virtue that can be mentioned is a literary one: undogmatic case histories read more like biographies or novella-like stories than technical papers. They are not replete with technical terms used in a semidescriptive and semiexplanatory way. They flow without the hindrance of inferential jumps which the reader feels he must accept *ex cathedra*. Instead the reader gets a strong sense of who the patient is and how he became what he is.

These are characteristics of good narrative writing in general and good historical works in particular. Once again I must emphasize that these qualities do not guarantee the truth of a case history. Many of the problems Spence (1982a) has so masterly exposed in his *Narrative Truth and Historical Truth* remain. Every presentation of material which is not verbatim includes an unwitting element of interpretation, a selection according to the analyst's theoretical bias. To some extent this is true of every historical account. Fact and interpretation can never be kept apart completely, but there are varying degrees to which the reader is given evidence for interpretations which range from dogmatic assertion to careful exposition.

Critical discussion of analytic case histories can take different forms. If it is a microdiscussion, then it should preferably rely on verbatim transcripts of sessions or ideally on video recordings. Spence (1982a, p. 192f.) has pointed out that even tape recordings miss much of what goes on in analytic sessions. This is of course true, but one need not draw very skeptical conclusions from this fact. In ordinary historical and biographical research, not even the verbatim material is given, and historians still think that they can responsibly discuss the intentions, plans, motivations, and beliefs of historical figures. If it is true that one could always have more precise data, it is not impossible to work on less than complete (whatever "complete" may mean) data.

Discussions on a microlevel will generally deal with a particular interaction between patient and analyst, or with a particular small excerpt of text by patient or analyst. The research of Hartvig Dahl (1983) and his associates has shown how various new research methods can be used in this field.

The microresearch should go hand in hand with discussion on a more global level. The old hermeneutic maxima, that a text must be understood through its parts and yet the parts can only be understood within the context of the whole, applies to psychoanalytic case histories as it does to any historical period, institution, or person. Discussion of overall interpretations of case histories do not necessarily rely on detailed transcripts. If this is the case, the participants in the discussion find themselves flooded with an indigestible quantity of material. This too is not particular to psychoanalysis. Historical works, for instance, can deal with both very narrow subject matters and with whole historical periods. Large-scale works generally rely on more specific research which has been done, but they also often provide the context and inspiration for specific research. Hence the dialectic between whole and part is essential to any attempt at understanding human phenomena, psychoanalytic and other. The extent to which detailed data are needed depends on the type of discussion attempted.

I have pushed the analogy between psychoanalytic reconstruction and historical research quite far, and have claimed that if historical research can be done responsibly, psychoanalytic reconstruction should be a rationally assessable activity as well. An inevitable question arises at this point: if my guarded optimism is justified, why is it that psychoanalysts often cannot reach agreement on the interpretation of cases? Does this not show that psychoanalytic reconstruction is ultimately pure speculation?

The fact that analysts often disagree—especially if they belong to different schools—is, I am afraid, incontrovertible. One major reason for this is that the stereotyped and the undogmatic attitudes are not only to be found in the writers of case histories but also in the discussants. The analyst who listens to the work of others has several possibilities. He can listen to the material itself, wait for patterns to emerge, and judge the extent to which data and interpretation form a coherent whole. But he can also look for the meanings and structures which he "knows" in advance to be there. If he listens in the latter, stereotyped way, he is most likely to find what he is certain he will find. As Spence (1982a) has pointed out, soft pattern matches can always be found in clinical material. If we are determined to find certain themes and correspondences between our theory and the material, we will invariably find them.

Hence discussion between analysts who have a stereotyped approach is quite unlikely to be fruitful. If they belong to the same school, they will easily agree on the basic features of the case. They might disagree on details, but they will feel safe in agreeing that the patient's problem is indeed centered on a certain conflict or trauma. If they belong to different schools, they will have trouble taking each other's positions very seriously, and this again will preclude a fruitful dialogue.

Let me now correct an oversimplification I have been guilty of: I have spoken of stereotyped versus undogmatic approaches as if analysts can be classified neatly as belonging to either of the two categories. It is probably far more accurate to say that every clinician has his more stereotyped and his more undogmatic and flexible moments. There may be instances in which one is eager to find quickly what one is looking for. This can happen both in therapeutic sessions and in discussions of case material. And there are moments in which one is more capable of maintaining openness to what is actually being said, by patients and colleagues alike.

In any case I am sure that the stereotyped approach is pernicious to the possibility of rational, open discussion. And in psychoanalysis, as everywhere else, stereotyped thinking is the result of the avoidance of uncertainty and complexity. It is quite human to want to feel that one knows even if all one has is belief. But the future of psychoanalysis depends on the realization that we know far less than the optimistic founding fathers of the discipline thought. Their optimism and sometimes cavalier attitude to soundness of argumentation was essential during the conquest of yet untrodden ground. Three generations later we cannot claim the same prerogatives. Even though we may mourn the loss of the heroic period of the beginning, we must acquiesce in the role assigned to us by the historical point at which psychoanalysis has arrived.

d)   An Inconclusive Coda on Truth and Cure

The model presented in the previous section has dealt exclusively with the extent to which psychoanalytic reconstructions can be rationally assessed. I concluded that such reconstructive work is quite similar to work done in history. If history and related disciplines are rationally grounded, psychoanalytic reconstruction is based on defensible modes of reasoning as well.

There is still a question to be answered which I have left open at the end of section b of this chapter. Is there any connection between the therapeutic efficiency of an interpretation and its truth value? No use has been made of therapeutic efficiency as an indicator of truth in the epistemological model presented above. I am afraid that at the present state of knowledge any general claim about a connection between truth and therapeutic effect of interpretations is bound to be hazardous, to say the least. All I have to contribute to the topic are therefore some clarifying, but unsystematic remarks.

One thing seems quite clear: the existing evidence in psychotherapy research as documented in the standard work on the topic (Bergin and Lambert, 1978) leads to a conclusion which is worth quoting:

> 1. Psychoanalysis/insight therapies, humanistic or client-centered psychotherapy, many behavioral therapy techniques and, to a lesser degree, cognitive therapies, rest on a reasonable empirical base. They do achieve results that are superior to no-treatment and to various placebo treatment procedures.
> 2. Generally, the above schools of therapy have been found to be about equally effective with the broad spectrum of outpatients to whom they are typically applied [p. 170].

The relevant point is that psychoanalytic therapies have never been shown to be superior in outcome to other forms of psychotherapy. This fact has already preoccupied us in chapter 1 in the context of Grünbaum's claim that only the necessary condition thesis can really ascertain that the clinical material can be used as evidence for psychoanalytic theory. This thesis states basically that only insight into the genesis of the patient's neurosis as predicted by psychoanalytic theory can lead to a cure of neurotic symptoms. Bergin and Lambert's conclusion provides an empirical falsification of the necessary condition thesis.

Is it possible to maintain that psychoanalytic reconstruction is either necessary or sufficient as a condition for success in psychotherapy? The obvious answer seems to be negative. Indeed I see no way to prevent this conclusion with respect to the general question of cure in psychotherapy. Does this mean that psychoanalytic reconstruction has no therapeutic importance whatsoever? Is it nothing but a luxurious addition to those aspects of psychoanalytic work which actually do have therapeutic impact?

It is worth quoting Bergin and Lambert again:

> . . . however, we still face the problem of never having adequately measured the subtle intrapsychic changes that appear to occur in verbal psychotherapies. It is conceivable that sophisticated criteria of affective and cognitive changes would reveal differential consequences of different interventions; but, thus far, this has not been tested [p. 170].

Bergin and Lambert give expression to what many analytic psychotherapists have been claiming—or at least hoping—for a long time. Although it may be true that as far as symptom removal is concerned psychoanalysis has not turned out to be superior to other established psychotherapeutic approaches, psychoanalysis is superior in respects which are far more difficult to measure. It might be expected, for example, that patients who have successfully completed analysis have become more mature, more subtle and differentiated in their personality structure, object relations, structure of interests, and emotional lives than their counterparts who have had their symptoms removed in more directive therapies.

The vast majority of patients seeking help are probably not interested in this kind of change. They are troubled by some particular problem and want to solve it. This is of course nothing but a statement of the old clinical wisdom that psychoanalysis is only suitable for certain kinds of patients; those who are sufficiently intelligent, verbal, and introspective to profit from the type of help offered by psychoanalysis.

The consequence of these facts for the question of the link between reconstructive truth and therapeutic effect seems to be the following. The relation between these two properties of interpretation is certainly not as clear-cut as Freud took it to be. Reconstructive truth is neither a necessary nor a sufficient condition for therapeutic efficiency. Yet it is possible that something like the following is true: for a certain type of patient some of the desired outcomes of psychotherapy are linked to reconstructive work. Admittedly this is a terribly vague statement, and I will try to give it some more substance.

One of the aims of an analysis is to give the patient an understanding of the workings of his mind. He comes to know the ways in which he defends against thoughts, wishes, and emotions which evoke psychic pain in him; he comes to understand how he colors and interprets situations in his own, idiosyncratic manner; he comes to understand how he uses fantasy to compensate for pain, humiliation, and anxiety. Freud thought that this was the only way to cure neurosis. We have seen that this is not true. Yet we might say that this insight into one's own character becomes an aim in itself for psychoanalysis.

Is this insight nothing but a luxury? It might be taken as such if one sticks to the model of neurosis as ego-dystonic, relatively isolated symptoms. Freud himself was mostly faced with such problems, at least at the beginning of his career. As I noted in chapter 4, the situation has very much changed since then. The typical patient turning to analysis mostly does not suffer from some clearly delineated symptoms. His complaints are vaguer, his problems mostly characterological. Hence the criterion for cure becomes far more difficult to state. If someone comes to therapy complaining of a persistent incapacity to form satisfying relations with men, it is difficult to operationalize the conditions under which one could say that she has been cured. Prima facie it might seem that no objective definition can be given at all.

Psychoanalysis has often been reproached for being intolerably vague in its criteria for cure. Terms like "more mature object relationships," "less rigid defensive structures," "greater capacity for sublimation," "increased anxiety tolerance," and the like are taken not to be sufficiently operationalized. Hence psychoanalysis is taken not to be willing to subject itself to the rigor of truly scientific testing by being evasive about what will count as a success of the therapeutic process.

There is certainly some truth to this reproach, but it also misses an important problem. If a patient comes with a circumscribed complaint abut a crippling symptom, it is quite clear that this symptom should be made to disappear, especially when it is clearly ego-dystonic. These are the type of cases behavior therapy is treating so successfully (although even here other perspectives are possible; see chapter 6, section e below). If a patient's complaint is one of general dissatisfaction with life or personal relationships, or a feeling that he or she is not able to find vocational fulfillment, it becomes far more difficult to say *a priori* what "cure" consists in.

Assume that a patient complaining of a lack of meaningful personal relationships is very introverted, somewhat shy, but has a rich and differentiated inner life. What should the goal of therapy be then? To turn her into a gregarious, extrovert and easygoing woman? Or should one help her to seek rich personal relationships more in tune with her present personality? I am not addressing the very important question about the limits of psychotherapeutic change here; the problem is not pragmatic. The point is one of principle: there are many questions which no therapist can answer at the beginning of therapy without imposing his own predilections and values onto the patient. It might well be that the introvert patient comes to a therapist who is extrovert and who happens to prefer people who are gregarious and easygoing. No one would say that this could constitute a sufficient reason for the therapist to try to change the patient in this direction.

How, then, should the goal of the therapy be determined? A simple answer seems to be: ask the patient what she wants to be like. It is not necessary to show in detail why this is not a particularly feasible answer. The patient may often simply not have an answer to this question. One of the reasons for her coming to therapy may be her lack of direction, her incapacity to conceive of a better way of life. Alternately the patient may have an answer, but the answer may be no more than a wishful fantasy, as is often the case with patients who have narcissistic character traits. The patient may not be able to think of anything but a grandiose picture of self as a bearable identity. In this case the goal of the therapy is more likely to help the patient to change her ideal picture of herself than helping her to realize it (which may not be feasible anyway).

The psychoanalytic answer is likely to be: in the course of the analysis the patient should acquire sufficient inner freedom to formulate for herself goals and ideals which are both realistic and derive from the patient's true self, i.e., which are not imposed on her from outside. "But what is the patient's true self?" one might ask. The answer sounds circular: whatever the patient becomes after overcoming her inhibitions, neurotic distortions, infantile anxieties, and wishes. It is in a sense a vacuous answer, since the analyst can really not specify in advance what solutions, values, and projects the patient should finally adopt for herself. Most analysts would probably accept that not only *do* they not know what the patient should be like at the end of the analysis, but that it would be a mistake if they should *want* to know it. They would only encourage the patient's tendency to look for answers outside herself, to cling to parental figures, and to disclaim responsibility for who she is.

Psychoanalytic answers to the goals of therapy often take a negative form. The patient should not be under the aegis of repressed infantile wishes, she should not distort her perception of self and others defensively, she should not be ridden by excessive anxieties, and so on. This negative way of formulating goals fits well with the general outlook formulated in the previous paragraph. The patient is not directed toward goals, but he is helped to formulate his goals on a more mature basis.

How does all this link up to the question of the therapeutic function of reconstruction? The psychoanalytic view of mental health is essentially developmental. The patient who has characterological problems is taken not to have resolved some basic developmental task optimally. Psychoanalysis, when faced with a suffering individual, asks: how has she become what she is now? Why was she not capable to find better, more constructive ways to live her life? The answer is not just to be found for the sake of satisfying the analyst's curiosity. The patient must come to know the answer: once she will know it, the reasons which have prevented her from creating more constructive solutions to her problems will cease to be operative (at least we hope so: one of the major theoretical problems Freud struggled with in the latter part of his career was the nature of the manifold resistances against cure).

The answer must thus be a story, the critically retold autobiography of the patient, as we have seen in the previous section. We can now see a rationale for this proceeding: if indeed the analyst refrains from formulating the goals of the analysis (except in the very general, mostly negative way delineated above), all he can do is to help the patient understand why she could not be someone other than who she has become. The very same reasons for her having become what she is are operative in her perpetuating her damaged identity. By making these reasons inoperative, she should acquire the freedom to change and restructure her life.

In this brief sketch of the clinical rationale of reconstruction I have not claimed that insight into the genesis and the dynamics of the patient's trouble are necessary conditions for therapeutic effect. There are many other ways to help people change. The specifically psychoanalytic way of doing so is characterized by its extreme nondirectiveness. The goal is to increase freedom, and psychoanalysis takes inner freedom to be closely linked with self-knowledge. Hence much of the rationale for the psychoanalytic approach to psychotherapy is ultimately of an ethical nature. It may be unique in that it considers the patient's autonomy and truthfulness to be supreme values. Ultimately the psychoanalytic view of psychopathology is one which equates mental health with truthfulness and inner freedom, and illness with self-deception and inner drivenness.

At this juncture two questions arise: the first is again methodological: "All you say sounds quite nice; there may be something edifying in talking about weighty ethical issues in psychotherapy once in a while and to get one's mind off the daily practical and methodological questions. But you promised to say something about a question which is methodological in nature, namely, whether the truth of reconstructions is linked to therapeutic effect. What you gave us here is a very general outline of the theory why reconstructive truth is supposed to matter therapeutically. This does not help: what is in question is precisely whether this theory is *true*. A restatement of the theory is of no value in dealing with this point."

This question is justified, and yet it misses something: I did not just restate the psychoanalytic theory of cure. I also argued that a psychotherapy which puts central emphasis on inner freedom and the patient's capacity to take responsibility for who she is must ultimately rely on self-knowledge as the central agent of change. Every directive approach necessarily curtails the extent to which the patient determines her goals, values, and the means by which she achieves them herself, from within. Hence my argument was essentially that one of the most important rationales for the psychoanalytic method is connected to a *Weltanschauung*, a philosophical view of human nature and existence. The idea is that not all issues in choice of method in psychotherapy are of a purely pragmatic nature. The tendency in psychotherapy research is to assume that the goals of psychotherapy are given, and that we just have to find out which are the best means to achieve these ends. My argument runs counter to this view.

Unfortunately this does not settle the methodological query which might be continued as follows: "Fine, let us assume that indeed you have given some kind of *a priori* argument why a *Weltanschauung* centered on autonomy and responsibility necessarily leads to a type of psychotherapy which is centered on self-knowledge. This still leaves you with two things to prove: (1) that self-knowledge is indeed a therapeutic agent. Your argument shows why this is desirable, given certain values. But, as you should know, not all that is desirable is real! (2) Assuming that the answer to the first question is positive, you still owe us a criterion to distinguish between *real, true* self-knowledge and mistaken belief about oneself. And this brings us back full circle to where we started from: how can we know whether a reconstruction is true, and how can we know whether the truth of a reconstruction is in any way related to its therapeutic effect?"

Indeed there is a sense in which we have come round full circle; I do not have the required argument showing the link between reconstructive truth and therapeutic effect. Was the way leading to this point in vain? I hope that T. S. Eliot's lines hold true for my undertaking as well: "We shall not cease from Exploration/ And the end of all our exploring/ Will be to arrive where we started/ And know the place for the first time."

I hope to have made explicit one point which seems crucial to me: since Freud psychoanalysts have always thought that even though there may be other forms of psychotherapy, psychoanalysis is in some way special. This special nature is not to be sought in some unique capacity to cure. The present state of research does not allow for this possibility. Psychoanalysis is not just a descriptive theory; it also embodies a philosophical view of man. The strong feeling of practitioners and theorists of psychoanalysis that it contains some truth which may be difficult to capture through scientific research seems to me due to this fact.

This statement is not meant to deny the fact that there are many theoretical hypotheses in psychoanalysis which are not substantiated by objective, controlled research and which need such confirmation. Yet it directs attention to the fact that the field of psychotherapy, more than many other domains, is characterized by a complex interplay of issues: there are purely empirical questions mainly to be settled by research, but there are also many questions which are of a more fundamental, philosophical nature, and they cannot be settled on purely empirical grounds. What follows is intended to probe more deeply into the complex interplay between the empirical and the conceptual. I will explore which of the problems of psychoanalysis are issues of pragmatic efficiency of therapeutic procedure, and which belong to the domain of basic perspectives on human nature and existence.

e)   THE RATIONALITY OF THE CLINICAL METHOD

A succinct summary of the content of the last two chapters has argued that because the currently most accepted view of psychoanalysis is that analytic work focused mainly on the patient's present mental states and not on causal relations between the patient's past and his present symptoms, the clinical method of investigation has some degree of epistemological soundness. My approach has not been to inquire whether the general propositions of psychoanalytic theory are substantiated by clinical material. Instead the focus was exclusively on the question whether single interpretations or interpretative chains can be given a reasonably sound evidential foundation on clinical material. It has been shown that the analyst's reasoning is akin to forms of perception and inference to be found in commonsense psychology.

The probable objection of critics of scientific temperament

is that this is not sufficient to defend the clinical method of investigation. Science does not rest content with commonsense justifications. It proceeds further to test its theories with a standard stricter than common sense. Hence my defense of the clinical method can establish at most that psychoanalytic propositions have some plausibility.

The response to such an objection touches upon the general philosophical question whether rationality coincides with the scientific method, and whether there is something like a general scientific method at all. A thorough treatment of these questions is beyond the scope of this essay. All I can do is to state without argument what my position on the topic is.

The outcome of the philosophical debate on the nature of scientific knowledge combined with developments in the historiography of science have led to the following results: (1) If by "scientific method" one means an algorithmlike, timeless decision procedure for the confirmation of scientific theories, then there is no such thing (e.g., Goodman, 1954, 1972, part VIII; Putnam, 1978, 1981, 1983). This does not mean that there are no standards for the assessment of knowledge claims which are accepted by the wide majority of people working in particular fields. It only means that these standards cannot be put into a general, formal framework valid at all times and for all disciplines. (2) I speak of intellectual disciplines instead of science in the singular or even scientific disciplines in the plural. The reason for this is that along with Putnam (1981) and others I do not think that rationality and science are coextensive. Science is a particularly impressive form of rational activity, a form which has played a crucial role in the development of Western culture during the last three centuries. But it is detrimental to take science—or more exactly physics—as the paradigm for rationality in general. Among other things, this has led to the tendency to regard all intellectual and other activities significantly dissimilar to physics as nonrational and subjective.

The result of this positivist frame of mind was quite disastrous with respect to topics like ethics and political philosophy. In ethics, it led to the theory that moral judgments did not allow for any justification. They were supposed to be no more than attempts to induce particular emotive responses toward particular types of actions. This emotivist theory of ethics ultimately saw ethical judgments as on a par to saying "phew!" to a child, when he does something nasty. Needless to say that this view left little room for the idea that there are more or less rational or more or less defensible ethical convictions. It seemed that there was as little point in discussing values as there is in discussing the relative merits of preference for vanilla and chocolate ice cream (Stevenson, 1944).

Such conclusions are inevitable if rationality is taken to be coextensive with the scientific method of current research in physics. The works of the philosophers mentioned under point (1) and the studies in the history of physics by authors like Kuhn (1962), Feyerabend (1974), and others started to change this picture. They showed that the actual proceedings of scientists did not follow any of the normative models developed by philosophers. The history of science falsified all existing methodologies of science, in particular the inductivist view perfected by logical positivism and Popper's falsificationist philosophy of science (Lakatos, 1978).

This ultimately led to the conclusion that there is no formalizable, timeless methodology of science. This weakened the position that science constitutes the only paradigm of rationality, and that all other activities aspiring to be rational must strive to become sciences.

Some philosophers have swung the pendulum too far in the opposite direction. Paul Feyerabend concluded from his studies (e.g., 1974) that "anything goes," i.e., that there are no methodological constraints whatsoever in science. On the basis of his brilliant reconstruction of the history of analytic philosophy, Richard Rorty (1980) arrived at the relativist conclusion that there is no more to rationality than the consensus of whatever cultural community one happens to belong to. Then there are the fashionable "deconstructionists" led by Jacques Derrida (1976), who preach total relativism in interpretation.

In a paradoxical way these extreme positions hinge on the hard-nosed absolutist position which believes in the existence of a timeless epistemology; then complete relativism is the unavoidable conclusion. The difference between absolutism and relativism lies in their reaction to this conclusion. Whereas for the absolutist relativism is the specter which haunts his worst dreams, the relativist embraces it joyfully. It makes legitimate a more playful and less oppressive pursuit of his interest.

In recent years the middle ground between these extremes has been occupied by a group of philosophers the most important of whom I consider to be Hilary Putnam (1978, 1981, 1983). They have worked out a view which explicitly takes into account the historicity of reason fruitlessly denied by the absolutist, without embracing relativist conclusions. The middle ground opened by Putnam, Goodman (1978), Bernstein (1984), and others will serve as a guideline to answer the scientistic objection which opened this section. The objection was that the reconstruction of the analyst's reasoning offered in this chapter does not correspond to scientific method and is too close to commonsense reasoning to count as a successful epistemic defense of the clinical method.

To a certain extent this reconstruction endorses Grünbaum's position that the clinical method is not scientific.

The question is what conclusions one is to draw from this—to my mind incontrovertible—fact? Is it that the clinical method is not scientific? If this means that it is very dissimilar to physics, I agree that it is not scientific. Since the word "science" has a honorific connotation which derives from the prestige of the natural sciences, Putnam's (1978) suggestion to speak about social *studies* instead of social *sciences* is quite sensible.

The argument for the rationality of disciplines which are not akin to the natural sciences is very simple: if the only rationally defensible way to ground empirical claims is the experimental method, most of the social sciences and humanities as well as law are nonrational disciplines, and their claims are without any evidential foundations. This conclusion constitutes a *reductio ad absurdum* of its premise that only science provides evidence for empirical claims.

The second part of my answer to the scientistic objection is from analogy: historians and biographers as well as legal judges infer motives and beliefs of other human beings on the basis of indirect evidence. They do not only rely on explicit verbal utterances acknowledging the mental states in question. This is particularly clear in the case of penal law: a judge can convict someone who claims not to have done something on purpose, despite the defendant's denial of his having acted on purpose. In section c of chapter 3 I have argued that such reasoning (there I used the example of detectives) is in many respects dissimilar from what we know from the natural sciences, since it is based on the methodological principle of humanity. As citizens we accept the judge's inferences to be sufficiently well grounded to warrant life imprisonment or even capital punishment. But the judge does not have to prove scientifically that all human beings (or a relevant subclass) act purposively under the circumstances of the given case. If only scientific evidence were sufficient for the ascription of mental states for which we do not have direct evidence, our legal systems would be paralyzed!

Historians do not always have direct evidence for the mental states of the historical figures they deal with. Yet we often accept their conclusions as being reasonably well-grounded, even though they do not give scientific evidence for any implicit generalizations they may use (for a good discussion see Mc-Cullagh, 1984). In fact such examples could be multiplied almost indefinitely, ranging from law through the social sciences to the humanities. In view of Grünbaum's (justified) insistence that psychoanalysis gives causal explanations, it should be emphasized that many of these disciplines (e.g., history) explain events and states of affairs causally.

It would be preposterous to claim that all these disciplines are not rational because they do not conform to statistical hypothesis testing or some other attempt to codify causal inference. And the claim that there *must* be some such canon, even if we do not know it yet, is grounded on nothing but the fear that if there is none, rationality will perish. Instead it seems that we must learn to live with the idea that rationality is not a monolithic, ahistorical and formalizable structure. Philosophy has for a long time worked with the assumption that a single theory of rationality is possible, but the results of recent years make this assumption implausible.

How, then, can we determine whether a knowledge claim is acceptable or not? It seems that no general answer is possible. If we want to know how good historical writing is done, we should not look up textbook in epistemology. We should even less inquire how physicists work and try to measure the work of historians by the methods of physics. (Indeed the studies quoted above have made it implausible to think that there is such a thing as an ahistorical method even in physics.) The best we can do is to look at what good historians do.

Method fetishists will shy away from this conclusion. Does this not mean that there are no constraints? This is the nightmare of those science-oriented methodologists who see only two alternatives: either there is a formalizable method, or pure anarchy will reign. But this dichotomy does not exhaust the alternatives. Human power of judgment goes beyond any formalizable methodology. With respect to any such methodology we can always ask whether it reflects our intuitions about rightness and rationality. And as a matter of brute fact Western culture has made enormous progress in many fields without such a methodology.

I am not pleading epistemological anarchism, total relativism, and least of all inexact, sloppy, and irresponsible thinking. The last two chapters have emphasized time and again that standards of reasoning and reporting data in psychoanalysis are often unsatisfying. Psychoanalysis, like any other discipline, can be practiced in a responsible and in an irresponsible manner.

Let me end this chapter by pointing to the change in perspective implied in this essay. I have not asked whether psychoanalysis is a science, or whether it is scientifically respectable. Instead I have asked whether its claims can be rationally assessed. Underlying this shift is the emerging insight of philosophy that science does not constitute all of rationality, and that not every rational proceeding must be modeled on the most successful of sciences, physics.

The three chapters of this part have dealt exclusively with the rational assessibility of *particular psychoanalytic interpretation and reconstructions*. The general line of argument was that these activities are sufficiently similar to other disciplines and activities (history, law, commonsense psychology) which I deem to be rational, to warrant the conclusion that psychoanalytic reasoning is rational as well. But we have also seen where the standards of present-day analytic theory and practice are too lax, and in chapter 7 I will return to the need for extraclinical evidence.

It may be disappointing that we have not arrived at a more clear-cut conclusion. It is much more reassuring to say something like: "Psychoanalysis is a scientific discipline, and it should look like physics." The point is that all the monolithic positions to be found in the literature today seem defective to me. This certainly holds true for the careless optimism of authors like Brenner (1982, p. 4), but also for the more differentiated positions of the hermeneuticists and Grünbaum. Whereas the hermeneuticists do not see any reason for controlled scientific research, Grünbaum does not see any value in clinical data as they have been pursued traditionally.

I hope that my attempt to make the structure of clinical psychoanalytic reasoning more explicit has shown that it is basically sound. The degree of certainty it can achieve is more akin to that of historical research and legal proceeding than to the precision of the natural sciences. This may at times be less than satisfying. But Aristotle's exhortation is no less valid today than it was more than two millenia ago: "it is a mark of the trained mind never to expect more precision in the treatment of any subject than the nature of that subject permits; for demanding logical demonstrations from a teacher of rhetoric is clearly about as reasonable as accepting mere plausibility from a mathematician" (*Nicomachean Ethics*, 1955).

PART III

PSYCHOANALYSIS AS A *WELTANSCHAUUNG* AND RESEARCH PROGRAM

6

PSYCHOANALYSIS AND PLURALISM

a) THE PROBLEM OF THE MULTIPLICITY OF ANALYTIC SCHOOLS

There can be no doubt that the modernist view of psychoanalytic interpretation outlined in the last chapters eases the epistemic burden on the clinical situation. The archeological model saw psychoanalysis as concerned with establishing facts which are not accessible to the analyst as a matter of principle, since they concern the patient's remote past. Furthermore, insight was seen as pertaining to causal relations between temporally removed events and present symptoms. Grünbaum's arguments against the possibility of confirming such interpretations on the couch are cogent and probably quite impossible to rebut.

In the modernist conception the patient's present intrapsychic life becomes the factor explaining his character traits and symptoms. In chapter 4 I have tried to indicate why it is not implausible to think that interpretations concerning present mental contents can be tested in the clinical situation.

Several authors (Farrell, 1981; Spence, 1982a; Grünbaum, 1984) have argued that even this more modest claim is quite difficult to maintain. Instead of dealing with their particular methodological views, I want to examine the implications of a well-established empirical fact which presents a major problem for anyone who would like to rest quietly on the optimistic conclusion that the changes in psychoanalytic theory and prac-

155

tice sketched in the previous chapter have freed psychoanalysis from its epistemological troubles.

This empirical fact is the multiplicity of insight-oriented psychotherapeutic schools. Any optimism with respect to the possibility of validating psychoanalytic interpretations and theory is bound to suffer a major blow through the simple fact that therapists of different orientations tend to come to vastly different conclusions about the mental contents of their patients. As a matter of fact, the spectrum of schools to be found both within and outside of the boundaries of the International Psychoanalytic Association has not diminished but has become wider and more colorful: American ego psychology, object relation theory, Kleinian theory, Kohutian self psychology, and a variety of mixed models, are all examples taken from within the framework of the International Psychoanalytic Association. To this must be added a variety of insight-oriented schools largely independent of Freudian thought, like Adlerians and Jungians.

Each of these schools claims therapeutic successes. All of them claim that their success in removing symptoms, empathizing with their patients, and coming to an understanding of the etiology of their patients' problems hinges on the truth of their theoretical frameworks. What must be conceded without detailed empirical investigation is that therapists from all schools are capable of giving their patients a feeling of being understood. Otherwise it would be difficult to understand why tens of thousands of patients stay in therapy for considerable durations of time. In addition there is another fact acknowledged by some important authors (Spence, 1982a; Schafer, 1983) who state that there is considerable variation of interpretive approach even within each school.

This multiplicity of therapeutic approaches (and I have limited myself to insight-oriented schools), all claiming about equal success rates, gives strong support to Grünbaum's contention that psychoanalysis has no proof whatsoever that its therapeutic results are not due to a placebo effect, i.e., independent of the truth of the interpretation given to the patients. Furthermore, it strengthens his suspicion that the seeming confirmation of particular interpretations and of the theoretical constructs guiding them could be due to suggestive influence.

What intellectual alternatives are open in the face of this situation? The first is dogmatism, which I mention only to discard it on the spot. Saying "my approach is right and all others must be wrong, as I can see from my clinical practice" is intellectually untenable. Given that there are rather great numbers of therapists working within the tradition of each of the schools (Corsini, 1984), it would be irresponsible to claim that they must all be stupid, dogmatic, and/or insensitive.

Skepticism is the alternative chosen by authors both from within psychoanalysis (Spence) and from outside (Grünbaum). Skepticism is the position which asserts that given the data available, there is no way to decide whether a particular theory is true or not. Grünbaum's conclusion is that only extraclinical, controlled research can bring light into the current darkness, whereas Spence proposes obtaining more reliable data about what is really going on in clinical work. What they agree on is that, given the state of the art, we do not know where the truth can be found, if at all.

There may be more than a grain of truth in this position, but it is an uncomfortable one to be in. Year by year literally millions of hours of psychotherapy are being conducted. The practicing therapist cannot allow himself the philosophical option of skeptical withholding of judgment until some well-grounded theory of psychopathology and psychotherapy emerges. The psychotherapist must do something, and one of the few things known about curative factors in psychotherapy is that the therapist should believe in what he is doing, which means that a choice must be made.

The second reason not simply to acquiesce in skepticism is embodied in an experience common to most insight-oriented therapists, an experience which is one of the promptings of this essay. There is often a distinct sense of arriving at important truths about one's patients in the therapies one conducts, and about oneself in one's personal analysis. To discard this experience without further ado is difficult to accept. The question is whether there is an additional, intellectually viable alternative to dogmatism and skepticism, which would account both for the experience of significant truth and for the multiplicity of therapeutic approaches to be found.

b) A NOTE ON SKEPTICISM, RELATIVISM, AND PLURALISM

Some clarifying remarks on a topic in which confusion too often reigns are needed. This is important because I am going to argue for a pluralist position, stating that it makes no sense to say that there is only one possible description of the world, and more particularly of human beings who suffer from psychological problems. The clarification is intended to prevent the identification of the position advocated here with others which are in part incoherent.

I begin by restating what it means to be skeptical about a particular theory, or set of theories. In order to be a skeptic you first have to assume that there is a truth to be found about the domain in question. Then, you must think that it makes sense to talk about theories being supported or disconfirmed by empirical data. On the basis of these assumptions you become a skeptic, if given some set of data, you think that it is not possible to decide which of several competing theories is true. Skepticism, therefore, allows of degrees; someone may think that the truth of a given theory cannot be ascertained on the currently accessible data. This is the position taken by Spence, since he says that our present data about processes occurring in the clinical situation are insufficient to support any particular theory. His skepticism is not radical, though, because he thinks that more controlled data about the analytic process will enable us to know more about the truth of psychoanalytic theory (Spence, 1982a).

Grünbaum goes one step further in his skepticism. He thinks that no matter how much information we gather about the analytic process, this will not suffice to determine the truth of psychoanalytic theory. This means that Grünbaum is a skeptic with respect to the possibility of confirming (or falsifying) psychoanalysis, not only with currently available data, but also with future clinical data. He is not a total skeptic with respect to psychoanalysis, however, as he thinks that extraclinical research can determine the truth value of psychoanalysis.

Both these positions are perfectly coherent as opposed to relativism which is not endorsed explicitly by anyone, although the wording of some authors comes dangerously close to it (Schafer, 1983; Goldberg, 1984). Relativism, in its extreme version, states that contradicting theories can be equally true. A somewhat different version of relativism states that truth hinges on standards of rationality. Since there are different standards, contradictory theories can be true or false, depending on which standard one endorses.

Relativism is incoherent because it is self-refuting. If every statement can be both true and false, so can the propositions stating relativism itself. Moreover, any position which allows contradictory propositions to be true ultimately ends up hovering close to the brink of unintelligibility (for a good discussion, see Putnam, 1981).

Beyond its incoherence, relativism carries with it a further danger. It tends to go along with a relaxation of rigorous standards and to be used as a defense for inexact thinking. The reasoning underlying such carelessness is roughly that if everything can be both true and false, there is no point in investing energy to defend one's own position carefully. Therefore, playfulness may as well replace seriousness and rhetoric is as good as careful argumentation.

As has been shown quite stringently (Putnam, 1981; Eagleton, 1983), relativism tends to hinge on an absolute conception of truth in a paradoxical way. Its underlying assumption is that if there is any truth at all to be found, this truth must be *one*. If it is not possible to find the one true description of the world or some particular domain, this means that there is no truth to be found at all. This is also the point where relativism differs from skepticism, since skepticism says that there is a truth to be found but that a certain type of data cannot be used to determine this truth.

For my purposes, it is of utmost importance to find a position allowing for a multiplicity of right versions of the world, which avoids the pitfalls of relativism. Such a view has indeed been formulated and defended very carefully in recent philosophical writings (Goodman, 1978; Putnam, 1981, 1983) and I want to sketch its main point briefly.

The central thesis of *pluralism* is, in Goodman's words, "that many different world versions are of independent interest and importance, without any requirement or presumption of reducibility to a single base" (p. 4). The pluralist insists that we have many interests guiding us in the description of various aspects and domains of the world. These interests incorporate standards of rightness, which cannot be reduced to each other. Correspondingly, the versions of the world based on these systems of depiction are incommensurable (Kuhn, 1962).

Pluralism is *not* identical with relativism, though. The relativist says that the same proposition can be both true and false, depending on how you look at it. The pluralist shows that the interests and standards of rightness associated with different versions can neither be reduced to each other nor meaningfully be taken to compete. The pluralist does not believe that the same proposition can be both true and false; he assumes that certain theories are incommensurable, i.e., not comparable with each other.

An example relating directly to this topic is that a Freudian will investigate the patient's mental functioning by asking how repressed infantile wishes and fantasies influence and undermine the patient's adult autonomy, while a Rogerian will focus on his client's capacity to full organismic experience. The interests guiding the two therapists are different. Any attempt to claim that if one of these two perspectives is "true" the other must be "false" is misguided. Perspectives are not true or false, but they can be more or less useful or more or less rich and encompassing. Correspondingly, theories based on such outlooks need not contradict each other.

The comparison between alternative theories and practices of psychotherapy is therefore more complicated than a non-pluralist might assume. It involves different types of intellectual operations. One of them can of course be the empirical investigation of the relative therapeutic efficiency of the approaches. Even here, however, an added complexity comes into play. Given that the forms of therapy may be guided by different perspectives, it may not be possible to translate their terminologies on standards of mental health into each other. Direct empirical comparison must therefore be preceded by careful conceptual investigation into the question of the points on which the approaches are commensurable. The pluralist position implies that the result of such an investigation can be quite frustrating, and it is even possible that no common ground for comparison can be found.

c)   SCHAFER ON PLURALISM

I want to approach the position of pluralism as an intellectual alternative through a close reading of some passages in Schafer's *The Analytic Attitude* (1983). This book is possibly the most sustained attempt in recent years to come to grips with the metatheoretical problems with which psychoanalysis is faced today. It is not a purely metatheoretical book though: clinical views and epistemological concerns are woven together in all of its chapters, which makes the book both interesting to read and difficult to assess. I will try to tease out its point of view by arranging some of its passages in the order dictated by the guiding question which is how we can escape dogmatism and skepticism given the multiplicity of therapeutic approaches.

In the chapter called "The Psychoanalyst's Empathic Activity" Schafer argues against the idea that empathy is an unmediated being-in-touch with the analysand's feelings. Empathy, Schafer claims, is dependent on and guided by the analyst's conceptual model of the analysand. Such a model in turn is not to be read off one's clinical experience in accordance with a positivist conception of "experience," but must be actively constructed. From this starting point Schafer comes to say: "not only is there considerable variation in the type of models that tend to be constructed by members of different schools of analysis, there is as well great variation in the models constructed by the members of one school" (p. 40).

One might wonder whether, at least as far as the difference to be found *between* schools is concerned, the constellation of psychoanalysis is similar to what can be found in other disciplines at certain times. There can be competing theories con-

cerning some domain of phenomena, and the discipline's task
is to find out which of the proposed theories is best. In some
cases it may take quite a long time until a consensus is arrived
at. Such periods have been called periods of crisis by Thomas
Kuhn (1962) who has shown them to occur in disciplines as
respectable as theoretical physics.

At first glance it is thus the variations *within* schools of psychotherapy which are more problematic. Schafer says that this
variation "reflects in large part differences in personality type
and working style of the analyst and analysand considered as
a pair. It also reflects differences among analysts in intelligence,
wit, training, professional identifications and clinical as well as
other life experience" (p. 40).

Yet there may be a way to avoid taking this fact to be a fatal
undermining of the possibility of objective validation of analytic
work. One might say that in every discipline there are both
differences in quality and style of work between the members
of the profession. What matters is the existence of objective
criteria to determine who is right in a given debate. But it is
exactly the existence of such criteria that Schafer seems to be
denying: "The consequence of all this variability is that there
are numerous, perhaps countless models of any one analysand
that may be constructed, *all* more or less justified by 'data' and
by reports of beneficial effects on emphasizing and the analytic
process" (p. 40).

Should anyone try to say that this might be due to the fact
that different analysts tend to work with different types of patients, Schafer blocks this way out as well: "Thus it is that, on
the one hand, many analysts of different sorts of persuasions
may empathize well with a similar group of analysands, and,
on the other hand, a second analyst may empathize with an
analysand better than a first even though both analysts belong
to the same school of analytic thought" (p. 40).

This is a puzzling (and somewhat disturbing) situation, and
we should dwell on its implications for a moment. Schafer implies that different models of one and the same patient may be
equally successful in guiding the analyst's empathic activity. If
so, does the truth value of these models matter to the success
of the analyst's empathic activity? Schafer's statement that

"there are numerous, perhaps countless models . . . *all* more or less justified by 'data' " implies a negative answer. If we can vary the theory (the "mental model"), we have of a patient without losing either credibility or efficiency, the model's truth value seems not to matter at all.

Incidentally, it should be noted that an instrumentalist move will not help us much here. Instrumentalism is the position stating that the truth value of a theory's claims with respect to unobservable states and processes does not matter. Theories must be assessed only by their efficiency in organizing data, providing predictions, and the possibility of control (Nagel, 1961). An instrumentalist position in psychoanalysis would state that the truth of hypotheses about unobservable unconscious processes is unimportant, and that the theory's therapeutic efficiency is the only important criterion for assessing the theory. But if Schafer is right, then different models are not differentiated by varying degrees of therapeutic efficiency, thus robbing the instrumentalist criterion of its usefulness in this problem.

Until now it sounds as if Schafer is an extreme skeptic, but it turns out that he is not. There are several places in the book which imply that the data do not support all models to the same extent:

> It does not follow from these remarks [about the interdependence of theory and analytic reconstruction] that all strategies of interpretation, whether Freudian or non-Freudian, have an equal claim to our attention and respect, for I believe that it can be shown (though it would take extended discussion to make this demonstration) that some of these strategies are more penetrating, coherent and comprehensive and mutative than others [p. 203].

Schafer uses the term "demonstration" which is rather strong in this context. If it were indeed possible to *demonstrate* the superiority of one theoretical approach over others, it would be to great advantage, to say the least, if someone would do it. It is probably not accidental that there is no major attempt to be found anywhere to compare and evaluate different versions of insight-oriented therapies. How could one demonstrate that

one approach is more mutative than another without extensive
controlled studies comparing outcomes of analyses of different
schools—studies which to my knowledge do not exist? It is thus
not quite clear to me how Schafer would go about fulfilling the
promise of the paragraph just quoted, but at any rate we can
see that he is not as much of a skeptic as we might have believed
on the basis of the previous quotations.

The question is why Schafer is so sure that alternative approaches can be compared with each other. In the chapter
entitled "The Construction of Multiple Histories" he develops
the point of view that "the highest priority goes to arriving at
the fullest possible understanding of the psychoanalytic encounter itself" (p. 208). The analytic biography constructed in
the course of a treatment hinges on the history of the treatment
itself. The priority of the encounter over the historical statements is partially epistemological:

> It is not plausible that the analysts is directly experiencing the
> analysand as simply an infant or young child, who is reliving
> ancient events and the reactions they evoked. The analyst gains
> whatever empathic confidence he or she does from what happens
> in the analytic sessions, most of all with the analysand's resisting
> and forming transference and getting to understand and modify
> them. Looking at these events from the unique and analytic per-
> spective, the analyst knows *first hand* just what the analysand
> endures and achieves in the course of working analytically [p.
> 205f.].

The term "first hand" italicized by Schafer shows that he
definitely thinks that the analyst can have degrees of certainty
about his constructions. Even if we do not reify data positivist-
ically, it is necessary to distinguish between hypotheses which
are closer to the data ("first hand" knowledge) and those farther
away from them (see chapter 4, section f). If one can be more
or less certain, this means that not every position is equally
justified or unjustified. Schafer is therefore not an unrestrained
skeptic.

Yet we must try to understand how the more skeptical passages quoted fit together with the more optimistic ones. This
effort may be worthwhile, as the tensions to be found in *The*

Analytic Attitude are indicative of a problem besetting psychoanalysis at its present stage of self-reflection.

The contradiction which seems to emerge in Schafer's position is characteristic of almost everyone working in psychoanalysis who arrives at a minimal level of reflexive methodological self-awareness. On the one hand, we have the clear feeling that in our clinical work we are coming closer to some truth abut a patient. Order emerges from chaos, clarity from confusion, and there is a distinct sense of moving toward an understanding of who the patient really is. The experience of psychoanalysis is not one of creative mythmaking, it is one of a search for truth. On the other hand, we are faced with the uncomfortable fact that the others work with the same confidence toward conclusions different from our own. In addition, it is very difficult to show the superiority of our own framework to others (this was the starting point of this chapter). So if the truth is one and the interpretations are many, it follows that all except (perhaps) one of the proposed versions must be false.

It is on the basis of this dilemma that the idea emerges to abolish one of the antecedents in the argument of the last sentence. If the truth is not one, but rather there are many truths, the conclusion that most of the frameworks of clinical work must be wrong does not follow, even if there is disagreement between different approaches. This is, indeed, the line taken by Schafer.

His way of tackling the problem is quite radical. In a nutshell, his position is that the truths are many because every analyst literally *creates* the phenomena he sets out to understand. The main factor influencing his own creation, i.e., the theoretical framework of the analyst, leads him to act and interpret in a certain way, which in turn brings the patient to direct his associations and behavior accordingly. This makes the correspondence between the patient's material and the analyst's interpretations very likely.

Schafer's approach is doubly interesting. Not only does he not shy away from acknowledging the analyst's influence on his patient's material, but he makes this fact the cornerstone of his defense of psychoanalysis. This approach is quite intriguing. One of the central objections raised against psychoanalysis throughout its history is that the clinical data were the result of suggestion, and that they could therefore not yield confirmation for psychoanalytic theory (see chap. 1). Schafer takes the bull of the suggestion charge by its horns and tries to make it an integral part of his account of psychoanalysis. The question is whether he succeeds in this operation of apparently squaring the circle. His own words are:

> In connection with analysts' models of specific analysands, two sets of factors must be discussed here. One of these sets comprises . . . the influences exerted by the analyst's theoretical orientation. For example, a Freudian analyst does and should construct Freudian models. With the help of these models, Freudian analysts do more than establish and order phenomena into some kind of coherent and intelligible account of the analysand. They also help to create further analytic phenomena in the contexts of associating, dreaming, remembering, fantasizing, etc. These phenomena necessarily reflect the impact of the analyst's Freudian way of making sense in terms of infantile psychosexuality and other familiar variables. It is no joke—it is, in fact, an epistemological necessity—that Freudian analysts get Freudian material from their analysands while Jungians and others get other material, material not altogether different, to be sure, but different enough to require much careful reflection before one attempts to pass judgment on the superiority of one school over another simply on the basis of what the "facts" are [p. 40f.].

d)   PLURALISM AND THE SUGGESTION PROBLEM

The conclusion of the previous section, stated bluntly, is that analysts of different persuasions get different results because they work on different data. The advantage gained by this position is the escape from the total skepticism we seemed to have been forced into because of the multiplicity of analytic schools. This apparently led to the conclusion that the data put no constraints on the number of possible interpretations. Now we can say that the support for diverging models is the result of the difference in data created by the approach of different analysts.

But it seems that Schafer has only succeeded in maneuvering

us from the frying pan into the fire. Previously, we at least believed that there was a set of replicable data to be gathered from clinical work and that the problem was how to interpret them. Now it seems that even the minimal requirement of objectivity is not met by the clinical situation. If the material obtained from the patient is the artifact of the therapist's theoretical preconceptions, this material cannot possibly serve as a touchstone for any particular interpretive hypothesis—and *a fortiori* not for the theory guiding the interpretation.

This can be put in terms closer to the jargon of experimental methodology. We have a hypothesis about a connection between an independent variable (the patient's hypothetically assumed unconscious mental state) and a dependent variable (his overt verbal and nonverbal behavior). What is claimed to be operative in the clinical situation is the hypothetical independent variable, which is not directly observable. We would have reason to think so, if we can assume that there is no significant factor causally involved in the clinical situation. But going along with Schafer means to acknowledge the central role of the analyst's influence. This implies the existence of a confounding factor operating in the direction of our hypothesis, which questions the validity of the data. In simple terms, there is no way to know that all the data are not due to suggestion.

Prima facie this is the end of the story. Schafer's point plays into the hands of those who for more than 80 years have claimed that the evidential basis of psychoanalysis might rest on suggestion, and that its clinical method is incapable of furnishing knowledge about the unconscious.

Schafer does not address this issue directly. Given that his explicitly stated program is to elucidate "the structure and logical justification of interpretation" (p. ix), this lack of concern for the suggestion problem is somewhat difficult to understand. He is certainly not unaware of it, because he acknowledges the centrality of suggestive influence. This is unusual, since the generally taken line of defense is to minimize the importance of this factor (e.g., Edelson, 1984).

I want to attempt an outline of a way of dealing with the suggestion charge, which starts off from the explicit acknowledgment of the importance of the analyst's influence. I do not know whether Schafer would subscribe to my proposal, but it is certainly consistent with the aspect of his position which I have reconstructed.

My assumption is that the therapist's theoretical orientation crucially influences the patient's material. The analyst chooses to highlight certain aspects of association over other aspects; he directs the patient's attention to the facts which are salient to him on the basis of his conceptual framework. The course of a session can be crucially determined by the moments at which the analyst says something—even if it is just "What comes to your mind around this point?"

I also want to direct attention to a fact which may sound trivial but which has not been taken into account by those who have time and again brought up the suggestion charge. When the analyst says, "What comes to your mind?" at a specific point, this certainly influences what the patient will say—if only because it gives the last association a special weight. But now it is up to the patient to say something. His associations to some topic, word, or image must be drawn from his own store of memories (whether veridical or not), fantasies, feelings, reflections, or whatever. If the patient has nothing to say—or at least nothing which leads any further—then the analyst's intervention (question, hint, interpretation, etc.) may turn out to be a pointer leading to a dead end. Even the best analyst will say many things in the course of an analysis which will prove barren. They will not initiate any significant development and fade away. These interventions are never to be found in clinical vignettes, and it is therefore easy to forget that the interpretive lines are distilled out of a mixture containing many ingredients discarded along the way.

There is thus a limit to the suggestive power of the analyst. He can emphasize, elicit, and also thwart and suppress aspects of the content and functioning of his patient's mind. But, necessarily, all influence must be related to whatever material the patient is capable of providing. The patient cannot bring any associations he does not have. Even if he picks up a lead given to him by the analyst, he must do so using his own resources.

This does not deny the possibility that there may be analysts sufficiently dogmatic and insensitive to pursue their own preconceived ideas with little concern for the patient's actual material. However, even the patient's yielding to his analyst's suggestive pressure will still be the reflection of some aspect of the patient's personality.

This point should be related to the more general issues taken up in sections a and b of this chapter. A pluralistic position states that human experience and behavior can be described in many different ways. Actually there are as many ways as there are conceptual frameworks which can bring order into the facets of human existence. Furthermore, there is no necessity—and very little likelihood—that there be one such framework which is basic in the sense that all others must be reducible to it. Such is essentially the position of philosophers like Nelson Goodman and Hilary Putnam, mentioned above. A consequence of this irreducibility is that these frameworks need not be reducible to one another and that they are to some extent incommensurable in Thomas Kuhn's (1962) sense, that there is no direct way to compare them with each other.

Lest this be misunderstood, it must be emphasized that this is not a statement about the richness of human individuality; it is much more a general point about the relation between description and reality. The same applies to the description of an object as simple (or complex) as a table. Think about how differently a physicist, a chemist, a biologist, an engineer, a carpenter, a designer, a housewife, a child, a painter, etc., would speak about a table. The basic vocabulary of each of them would be as different as the interests guiding their discourse. This vocabulary can contain such terms as "electron," "fiber structure," "Louis quinze style," "difficulty to clean," depending on who is speaking. There is no sense to be attached to a claim that any of these descriptive frames is "truer" than the others. At most, one could talk about degrees of usefulness given a context of action and interest.

The same holds true for human beings—only more so. The number of perspectives which are actually taken on human personality in Western culture alone is enormous. This may become intuitively clear by just considering the numbers of disciplines to be found in the humanities, social sciences, and medicine, all of which represent different viewpoints on man.

Add to this the fact that in most of these disciplines there are several competing approaches to be found which are often incommensurable themselves.

I propose to view the conceptual frameworks to be found in present-day clinical psychology (the number of which is in itself quite impressive) as different perspectives on man. Every therapist is forced to choose some aspect under which he will think about his patients and also get them to think and feel about themselves. His choice will of course affect the material his patient will present, ranging from precise schedules concerning his smoking habits (behavior therapy) over detailed descriptions of his immediate experiential field (Gestalt therapy), to his earliest memories about sexual fantasies (Freudian psychoanalysis). Correspondingly the course of treatment and change will be quite different. The pluralist point of view implies that the coexistence of such frames does not necessitate that at least all but one must be false—no more than the coexistence of physics, biology, and economics invalidates either of these three disciplines.

This can be translated back into the context of the suggestion charge against psychoanalysis. The charge is that if the analyst's theoretical orientation influences the patient's material, the method of clinical investigation cannot ensure that interpretations "tally with what is real in the patient" (see chap. 1). The data might then be nothing but an artifact of the analyst's previous convictions and thus not indicate anything about the patient's mental functioning.

The answer I suggest is: the suggestion charge in its most general form rests on a naïve picture of the relation between theory, practice, and the world. The theory *always* guides the practice (whether experimental, clinical, or other) and thus determines what kind of data will be obtained.

This point can be clarified by using the analogy of the table. A physicist experimenting on a table elicits physical data ranging from atomic structure to coefficients of elasticity. The data a biologist collects about the structure of the wood will be quite different because of his different interests. A designer, in turn, focuses on completely different properties of the table: neither the physical nor the biological characteristics are of direct importance to him. His method of observation will include very different activities. He may have people sit as different models to check how comfortable they are to work on. He may combine them with chairs to assess their aesthetic and stylistic properties, and so on.

As for human beings in the context of clinical psychology: we can choose to investigate persons from the perspective of how they manage their sexual and aggressive drives, with jealousy or envy. Another perspective is to find out how they try to maintain a coherent sense of self. Moving away from roughly Freudian views, one may focus on how people balance their different mental functions; and Jungians will talk of thinking, feeling, intuiting, and sensing as basic functions, although other taxonomies are also possible. Other perspectives may include dealing with feelings of inferiority (Adler) or the capacity for full emotional experience (Rogers).

There is nothing in each of these perspectives intrinsically excluding the others. This may sound somewhat surprising, given the heated debates between psychotherapeutic schools. To give just one example: Corsini's (1984) anthology on current forms of psychotherapies asked each of the contributors to relate his own standpoint to others. The tendency of most of the authors was to dismiss the other approaches, and often they did so quite sharply. Theorists in clinical psychology seem to view different approaches as mutually exclusive.

The position I advocate here is that psychotherapeutic approaches and the personality theories associated with them are not necessarily competing theories about the same subject matter. Instead I propose to regard them as conceptual frames which organize phenomena in different ways. Although this formulation implies that these frames deal with the same phenomena, this is not quite true. A radically pluralistic position must recognize that there is no neutral substratum which all theories deal with. Since the methods of observation of therapeutic schools are different, they work on different data.

This brings me back to the starting point of this chapter. It seemed at the onset that the brute fact of the multiplicity of psychotherapeutic schools and the long-standing incapacity to resolve the disputes between them left no alternatives except dogmatism and skepticism, neither of which are quite palatable. The pluralistic position (which is not identical with relativism) has a major advantage. Not only is it intellectually more satisfying than dogmatism and skepticism, it is also capable of explaining the difficulty in achieving a fruitful dialogue between different schools of psychotherapy. The conceptual frames of these schools are often incommensurable, since they deal with different aspects of human mental functioning and behavior.

Furthermore, therapists of each school tend to see only data which confirm their own theories. I have stressed that the method of observation a therapist uses is not independent of the theory he is working with, and that this is not specific to clinical psychology but rather characteristic of all systematic investigations into any domain. The problem is that this very easily leads to the kind of dogmatic attitude which is unwilling to admit that there may be other perspectives not akin to one's own.

It is important to see that pluralism is *not* identical with eclecticism. As Messer and Winokur (1980) have shown in the case of psychoanalytic and behavior therapy, there are limits to the extent different approaches can be combined. Their paper shows in some detail that these limits are not due to rivaling empirical hypotheses, but rather the result of profoundly opposed perspectives on human reality (see also Schafer, 1976, chap. 3). Their argument could thus be taken to be a good exemplification of what I have called the incommensurability of conceptual frames, a topic to be taken up in the next section.

One of the results of these considerations is that the global version of the suggestion change is invalid. It is undeniable that the analyst's interventions guide and influence the patient's associations. But we have seen that the very idea that this might not be the case is incoherent: every approach to patients selects and organizes the material. Hence there is a sense in which we can gladly accept that suggestions influence patients, without being afraid that this in itself invalidates the data. This does not render the suggestion change harmless, though: it only means that its most general version is mistaken. There still remains a host of specific problems, e.g., whether the therapeutic effect of analytic therapy is due to suggestion.

e) THE ROLE OF *WELTANSCHAUUNG* IN DETERMINING
THERAPEUTIC APPROACH

The simplest view of the relation between alternative approaches to psychotherapy, psychopathology, and theories of personality is that such approaches are simply incompatible, competing theories. Where one claims that the cause of neuroses is intrapsychic conflict around sex and aggression, others claim that the cause is empathic failure of self-objects, faulty beliefs about oneself, a particular learning history, or whatever other theories in the field assume. This simple view—we can call it positivist—is simplistic and misleading.

An assessment of psychoanalysis as a theory and therapy can only be fruitful if we succeed in disentangling the levels and aspects in which different approaches to psychotherapy differ. It must become clearer where the differences are conceptual, pertain to values underlying the approaches, where they are a matter of *Weltanschauung,* and where they are more straightforwardly empirical. And let me emphasize that my critique of the positivist view does not at all entail that empirical knowledge does not matter. It does so very much, and psychoanalysis is in desperate need of more than we currently have. The point is to know what can and what cannot be resolved by empirical research.

It may be useful to show more precisely how differences in conceptualization and *Weltanschauung* express themselves in the disputes between different schools of psychotherapy (Strenger, 1989). The positivist view may dismiss such differences as marginal appendices to empirical content, which is what really matters. I do not think this is true anywhere in science, but it is certainly least true in the field of psychotherapy. Even if as therapists we are mostly faced with instrumental questions in everyday practice, we are all guided by some implicit model of what constitutes mental health. Such a model is necessarily a fusion of the descriptive and the normative, the empirical and the conceptual, and every therapist has moments in which he is forced to think about such matters of principle. If he does not do so by himself, patients will push him: e.g., the suicidal patient who asks in all seriousness why he should continue to live; or the narcissistic-hysterical patient who, at the crossroad of her therapy, asks why she should exchange her façade for more genuineness.

Freud's model of man has been discussed endlessly, and the following remarks are not meant as a contribution to the huge literature on the subject. The goal is to highlight some points which pertain to the issue of this chapter. There is a theme which runs through Freud's writings starting with the "Project for a Scientific Psychology" (1895) and ending with the post-humously published *An Outline of Psycho-analysis* (1940). It is the dichotomy between the pleasure principle and the reality principle. It would be possible to organize much of Freud's thought—metapsychological and clinical—around this central dichotomy, which is reflected in many other conceptual polarities in his writings: primary vs. secondary process, id and ego, symptom formation vs. sublimation, fixation vs. renunciation, and ultimately neuroses vs. mental health.

The neurotic, for Freud, is governed by the pleasure principle. He has not been able to renounce infantile wishes, and where he cannot satisfy them in reality, he seeks substitutions in fantasy, neurotic symptoms, and character traits. Ultimately even the motives for defense, and not just the instinctual wishes, are rooted in the pleasure principle. Instead of facing inner and outer reality without distortion, the neurotic activates defenses which prevent him from experiencing anxiety, guilt, shame, and other unpleasurable affects.

Both in his attitude to the individual patient and to whole cultural phenomena Freud takes the side of reason as opposed to the instinctual and infantile. In analysis the patient wants to enact his wishes, but Freud requires him to understand and verbalize instead. Where the patient wants to leave insight as an intellectual, one-time event, Freud patiently forces him to work through the manifold manifestations of his infantile fantasies. Where whole cultures want to perpetuate illusions, Freud exhorts them to achieve maturity and renounce the comforting distortions of reality.

Ultimately the whole setting of classic psychoanalysis is an expression of this attitude. The patient lies down and hence cannot discharge tension through motility. He must say everything which comes to his mind, but no wish—except wanting to be understood—should be gratified by the analyst. Nothing but the truth can cure, since the essence of neurosis is the avoidance of reality. Freud tried to show to his patients and to his disbelieving contemporaries that this reality was more complex and less reassuring than they wanted to acknowledge.

Freud's ethic is stoic: for him the class between man's instinctual nature and the demands of reality is unavoidable. Culture is and will always be founded on renunciation of instinctual aims, and hence man should better learn how to master his inner nature. Whatever the degree of mastery of external nature, conflict and the demand for renunication will remain essential to the *condition humaine*.

This cultural pessimism is combined with a passionate belief in the possibility of human autonomy. Freud denies his patients everything except insight by which they will come to know the truth about themselves. He thinks that this will be enough to cure them. Notwithstanding his deterministic credo, Freud ultimately sees the responsible agent, the person, at the center of character traits and symptoms. This is why he believes that change can only come from within, by changing the cause of the neurosis, and not from without by manipulating the environment.

This sketch serves as a background for consideration of how *Weltanschauung* affects the approach to the individual patient. It must be pointed out that Freud's austere ethic may not represent current psychoanalysis completely. Winnicott and Kohut in particular have introduced additional viewpoints which have implications for the psychoanalytic view of man. By way of contrast I now turn to some remarks on the philosophy underlying the therapeutic approach most remote from psychoanalysis, namely, behavior therapy.

Behavior therapy generally does not state a broad view of human nature. Paradoxically one might say that this relative lack of a theory of personality *is* the behavior therapist's theory of personality. In accordance with Mischel's (1968) general approach, the idea of underlying personality structures responsible for a wide variety of a person's behavior is suspect to behavior therapists (e.g., Wilson, 1984). Instead the emphasis is placed on situational variables as explaining factors. The explained phenomena in turn are not personality traits but individual, clearly delineated behaviors restricted to particular types of situations.

Skinner (1971, 1974) certainly is one of the central influences on behavior therapy. It is not unproblematic to apply his general views to behavior therapy, but for the present purpose it will do. Skinner has a strongly empiricist view of man, and assumes that complete knowledge of a person's reinforcement history would allow for complete predictability of his behavior. Hence behavior which appears to us to be unconditioned, "free," just seems to be so because of our ignorance of its functional dependence on earlier reinforcement contingencies (Skinner, 1971).

The emphasis is not on Skinner's determinism (Freud was no less of a determinist) but on the general view of man presented by him. There are for him no values intrinsic to human nature except the unconditioned stimuli man intrinsically values. All the rest is a matter of reinforcement contingencies; human beings can be reinforced to value almost everything. Hence the policy of reinforcements should be directed by pragmatic, mainly technological, considerations.

The diagnostic approach of behavior therapists which follows from this view is defined by the assumption that there can basically be two states of affairs: either there is too much or too little of a particular type of behavior. And the resulting therapeutic approach is that excess behavior must be unlearned, and deficit behavior must be learned. Both processes follow clearly defined laws of learning, based on operant and classic conditioning.

Skinner's extreme behaviorism (1974) is not shared by all behavior therapists. Some of them pay particularly close attention to inner behavior, like affects and imagery (e.g., Lazarus, 1984). But the basic model of man remains the same. Therapy is therefore preferably called "behavior change," and is achieved by manipulating, or helping the client to manipulate, relevant variables. Man is seen as reacting to environmental influences, which in themselves are in part a function of the particular person's behavior.

There is no doubt that the difference in empirical content between psychoanalysis and behavior therapy is enormous. And yet it is very difficult to find a clear-cut empirical decision about the superiority of either of the two approaches. There is one exception: it is quite certain that with clearly delineated functional disorders like sexual dysfunctions, phobias, and compulsions, behavior therapy is superior to any other approach (Bergin and Lambert, 1978).

The exception is in itself indicative. The disorders in question fit into the conceptual framework of behavior therapy extremely well: they are clearly delineated behaviors occurring in well-defined situations. Hence the criteria of therapeutic success fit very well with the behavioral approach. Either the excess behavior is still there or it is not; the deficit behavior occurs or it does not.

In these clearly defined disturbances the *aim* of psychotherapy seems to be quite clear. It is simply to cure the symptoms; and it is also relatively easy to define what a cure consists of: if the patient is not compelled to act in ways he does not really want to act, when he loses his irrational fears and the concomitant inhibitions or when his sexual functioning is back to normal, then we can say that the therapy has achieved its aim. Hence the behavioral approach with its clear diagnostic categories and criteria for success is highly adequate. In such disturbances the patient has a very precise idea of what he wants the therapy to achieve. His definition of the goals and that of the therapist coincide easily, thus eliminating the problem of discrepancies between assessment of outcome by therapist and patient.

But even in these simple cases, a closer look introduces unsuspected complexities. A psychoanalytically oriented therapist may probe further into the details of the sexual experience of a patient whose presenting complaint is a particular dysfunction, e.g., vaginism. He may discover that the woman in question does not feel any closeness to sexual partners, and that her experience of the sexual encounter is one of intense loneliness. He may then give attention to her interpersonal relations in general, and find out that she tends to keep others at an emotional distance in nonsexual relations as well. Further investigation may lead him to the conclusion that she experiences every attempt of others to come close to her as an unbearable attempt to rob her of her individuality and to force alien contents into her.

He may therefore see the presenting complaint of vaginism as just one manifestation of her general problem in establishing object relations. The question of how to approach her treatment now arises. The behavioral therapist's model of man is that the person is the sum total of his specific responses to specific situations. Correspondingly he will argue that the vaginism must be approached as a distinct problem, and be treated as such. He may not object to the psychoanalyst's observation that the patient has other problems as well, both in sexual and in general interpersonal relations. But he will see these as distinct from the vaginism. He may say that if the patient wants to have these problems treated as well, one can try to help her in addition to treating the vaginism, but he will not see any intrinsic connection between the issues.

At this juncture a more positivist approach may see the dispute between the behavior therapist and the psychoanalyst as a purely empirical one: each of the disputants claims that he has a more efficient way to treat the presenting complaint of the vaginism. The analyst predicts that curing the vaginism will result in the production of another symptom, since the underlying conflict has not been resolved.

The issue is more complicated than this. The psychoanalyst need not claim that the behavior therapist cannot cure the vaginism, and he need not predict symptom substitution in the case of behavior cure. Instead he may argue that the woman developed her symptom in order to express a more profound distress. A purely symptomatic approach to her problem will constitute a message to her that she should dismiss the subjective distress inherent in her interpersonal relations. She will succeed in performing adequately in sexual relations, and superficially enjoy them, such as in the achievement of orgasm. But the analyst will conclude that her sexual experience will be alienated. This will then reinforce her tendency to live with a false self to protect herself from what she experiences as an unbearable intrusion into her true self.

The issue is therefore not only one of competing claims about therapeutic efficacy. Instead it is one of profoundly opposed perspectives on human reality. The behavior therapist sees man and life as composed of a multitude of discrete response forms to specific situations. The notion of an underlying self which is expressed in these behaviors is alien to him. In his view, if you change the behaviors, you have changed whatever there is to change. If it turns out, for example, that the patient with the vaginism is actually quite depressed, the behavior therapist will understand this as the feeling of helplessness which results from the patient's inability to achieve desired goals like sexual satisfaction (Seligman, 1975). He will conclude that the patient must be instructed in ways to achieve satisfaction—e.g., by treating her vaginism—and that the depression will then be dealt with.

The psychoanalytic therapist's model of man focuses on the subjective world of the patient as the source of overt behavior. He will refuse to see the subjective distress only as the result of failure to attain particular satisfactions. He may point to the fact that overtly the patient's interpersonal relationships are "successful"; for instance, she is desired by many men and her depression is therefore not due to the lack of skills for attaining satisfactions. Rather she is unable to feel that any of her successes *really* satisfy her. Underlying all she does is a profound feeling of emptiness, because she cannot experience any of her activities as being fully hers. They remain at the level of her false self.

This hypothetical discussion could be continued endlessly. It would be very difficult to arrive at a satisfying conclusion, because of the profoundly diverging basic models of man underlying the disputants' particular arguments. Where the behavior therapist sees particular sequences of behavior (internal and external), the psychoanalyst sees expression of a subjective reality underlying all of them. Messer and Winokur (1980) have traced the implications of such differing outlooks in some detail, showing how in a particular case each phenomenon is regarded quite differently by therapists of different persuasions. The result is that their respective decisions in the therapeutic process are often diametrically opposed.

Where the behavior therapist sees painful affects, he thinks of ways to extinguish them. The analyst instead tries to trace the affect and its underlying meanings as precisely as he can, in order to discover their origins. The behavior therapist tries to persuade the patient to stop irrational cognition and emotion; the analyst attempts to help the patient to integrate them into his image of himself. The behavior therapist tries to provide efficient ways to resolve conflict; the analyst attempts to help the patient to live with complexities and the pain and guilt of human existence which psychoanalysis sees as inevitably conflict ridden.

The difference in outlook also has a profound *ethical* aspect: for the behavior therapist the good life is that in which problems are not created artificially, and instead avoided or resolved efficiently. For the analyst the mature person is capable of bearing the complexities and tragic conflicts of human existence with little or no distortion. The analyst and the behavior therapist do not share much of a common ground of values. Superficially both might agree that they think human beings should be happy. But their conceptions of happiness do not coincide. They may agree that happiness is not consistent with much suffering, but they will disagree about what type of suffering is essential to the *condition humaine*.

The more atomistic outlook of the behaviorist tends to a conception of happiness quite close to that of Jeremy Bentham, the founder of modern utilitarianism. Bentham (1789) is deeply steeped in the tradition of English empiricism, which is the historical precursor of modern behaviorism (Taylor, 1964). He viewed mental life as a sequence of not intrinsically connected mental contents. Their connection is established by laws of associations which work independently of the contents of ideas. Important constituents of mental life are the sensations of pleasure and pain. These can be associated to any activity just by a matter of association by continuity. Happiness is a function of the quantitative relation between pleasure and pain. How a preponderance of pleasure over pain is achieved is irrelevant to happiness as such. This is expressed in Bentham's famous dictum that "prejudice aside, the game of pushpin is of equal value with the arts and sciences of music and of poetry" (quoted and discussed in Putnam, 1981, p. 151ff.).

The psychoanalytic view of happiness is more akin to the notion of *eudaimonia* in Greek, particularly stoic, philosophy. For the stoics the end of life is happiness, and they see the essence of happiness in *virtue* which in turn is defined as the life according to nature (Copleston, 1946). For the stoic, man's inner nature is reason. Virtue ultimately consists in the capacity of man to master his passions, and to lead his life according to his understanding of both internal and external nature. The emphasis of the stoic ethics is therefore far more on the formation of man's inner nature than on the conquest of external nature. Both aspects of reality are regarded as having a relatively immutable essence and hence happiness can only be of such understanding as that the virtuous man acknowledges the inescapable complexities of life and accepts them.

As Messer and Winokur (1980) point out, the behavioral approach is characterized by a comic vision of reality. Problems and unhappiness are the result of circumstances, which are not necessary as such. They can be changed and happiness is achieved through changing them, hence the behavior therapist's emphasis on behavior change. The psychoanalytic vision of reality, on the other hand, is primarily tragic: conflicts and tensions are essential to the *condition humaine,* hence happiness cannot consist in trying to change the inevitable, but in being able to live with it. Their characterization concords well with my view of the behaviorist ethic as utilitarian and the psychoanalytic ethic as stoic.

For the sake of clarity I have emphasized the difference between these two schools of psychotherapy. Of course there is some common ground, and Messer and Winokur took care to show the points of agreement as well. At this juncture it is important to see where the differences in *Weltanschauung* enter the disputes between these two major therapeutic schools.

What does the emphasis on diverging metaphysical and ethical foundations of psychotherapy entail? It certainly does not mean that the choice of psychotherapeutic methods is a purely subjective affair. In section e of the previous chapter I have warned against the view that whatever cannot be ascertained by scientific decision procedures is a matter of whim like the preference for vanilla as opposed to chocolate ice cream. Rationality is wider than any particular scientific testing method.

It does entail that comparative studies of therapy outcome will not completely settle the issue between different forms of psychotherapy. Any quantifiable measure of success will be bound to miss much of what is essential to the debate. As indicated, even a relatively simple presenting complaint such as vaginism can be linked to questions ranging far beyond the problem of how to cure vaginism as quickly as possible. Questions of value and differential emphasis of aspects of the patient's functioning and personality often make the decision concerning therapeutic procedures more complex than it seems at first sight.

Comparative studies of therapy outcome *are* of course of great relevance, and I am not claiming that no empirical questions whatsoever are involved. By and large I think, for example, that in monosymptomatic functional disturbances behavior therapy is the method of choice. If such a disturbance is superimposed on more general problems, one should try to treat the specific disturbance (phobia, compulsion, sexual dysfunction) first and independently of more general therapy, if this is possible. The example given above was only meant to show that even in such cases there may be good reasons for refraining from doing so.

Psychoanalysis, however, is in desperate need of thorough empirical investigation of the curative factors in analytic treatment. Despite my defense of the clinical method in chapters 4 and 5, Grünbaum's (1984) query about the possibility of placebo effects cannot be dismissed easily. Even authors sympathetic to psychoanalysis like Strupp (1975) have repeatedly pointed out that it is far from clear whether therapeutic success hinges on the correctness of interpretations, and have adduced reasons for believing that this is not the case.

It may seem that my emphasis on questions of *Weltanschauung* precludes the possibility of dialogue. This appearance is deceptive, and hinges on the scientistic preconception that rational discussion is exhausted by scientific procedures. I have previously tried to show that there are analogies between reasoning in disciplines like history and law on the one hand and psychoanalysis on the other. Another analogy will serve to elucidate the type of dialogue I believe to be both possible and important between different schools of therapy. It is essential to democracy that it allows for the coexistence of differing views on social reality and the nature of justice. Political discussion between different conceptions has been going on for a long time and has not yet come to an end. In fact, we have witnessed powerful restatements of conceptions of social justice more centered on the value of equality (Rawls, 1971) versus views for which liberty is the central value (Nozick, 1974).

In politics and political theory the facts are that the discussion has been going on for quite some time without a definitive conclusion; and that the dialogue continues as a dialogue, that is, not simply as passionate polemic. It is the essence of democracy to assume that civilized and rational dialogue between opposing views is possible, although there may be no way to arrive at a resolution of the disputes. We are all perfectly capable of distinguishing between good political argument and empty rhetoric. The fact that we do not have an algorithmic decision procedure does not make all arguments equally nonrational.

The fact that ultimate agreement is not being achieved hinges in part on insufficient knowledge about the enormous complexity of social reality. But there are also differing conceptions of the good life and of social justice involved. Hence the situation is in certain respects analogous to that of the discussion between rivaling schools of psychotherapy. The issues are composed of an intricate mixture of the empirical, the conceptual, and the domain of values. In fact it is not at all clear where exactly the boundary between those different domains are. It is certainly not as clear-cut as the positivist conception of the logical gap between fact and value assumes.

Does this mean that no progress can be made in the discussion? I do not think so. In fact we now certainly have a better grip on the issue between the egalitarian and the liberalist conception in economic and political theory than we had before (e.g., Friedman, 1962; Galbraith, 1974). The same goes for questions of the epistemic soundness of psychoanalysis and the relation between different therapeutic schools, as the ongoing discussion involving Grünbaum, Spence, Schafer, Edelson, and other authors shows.

The analogy to politics elucidates an important aspect of the psychotherapist's predicament. He must take a position on both ethical and pragmatic issues despite his relative lack of precise knowledge about central points. He cannot allow himself not to act. Hence he needs some firmness of character and determination. If he has no beliefs to back his actions, he will not be able to help. And yet he must keep these beliefs open to constant scrutiny. The existence of alternative approaches should be seen as a blessing and not as a curse. In politics the lack of opposition leads to petrification of the existing system. In the domain of psychotherapy the monopoly of the approach would lead to dogmatism and unwarranted self-satisfaction. Psychoanalysis must take the challenge of competing approaches as an occasion to rethink and assess its own foundations.

7

CONCLUSIONS, PROBLEMS, AND PROSPECTS: LIMITATIONS OF THE HERMENEUTICIST CONCEPTIONS OF PSYCHOANALYSIS

I have tried to provide formulations of theses of the hermeneuticist conception of psychoanalysis which I believe to be fruitful. My goal was to show that the clinical method of investigation is less vitiated than Grünbaum has argued. I have tried to show in which respects it is possible to extract from the hermeneuticist literature a picture of clinical work which makes it plausible that analytic interpretations can be reasonably well grounded.

I shall now take a wider perspective and ask whether the hermeneuticist conception of psychoanalysis is sufficient as a complete epistemic account and defense of the structure of confirmation in psychoanalysis. Section a will discuss Grünbaum's critique of the hermeneuticist idea that the narrative coherence psychoanalytic interpretations impose on the patient's material is an indication of their acceptability. Grünbaum's insistence on the insufficiency of this criterion is justified, and I will therefore propose to supplement the hermeneuticist account of the confirmation of psychoanalysis by adding considerations of the coherence of psychoanalytic theory with accepted knowledge from outside psychoanalysis.

In section b I will propose a perspective on psychoanalytic theory as the core of a research program in the sense put forward by the philosopher of science, Imre Lakatos (1978). This proposal is meant to serve as an alternative to Grünbaum's demand for a direct confirmation of basic psychoanalytic principles—a demand I do not think can be met. Instead, I believe that psychoanalysis should be assessed according to its overall fruitfulness in stimulating research and as a form of therapy. Such a perspective is a major departure from the hermeneuticist view as it occurs in the literature, since it implies that clinical material alone is insufficient as a *sole* evidential basis for psychoanalysis. Psychoanalysis as a research program is better off than Grünbaum states in his final verdict.

In the last section I want to turn to completely different considerations: I will argue that psychoanalysis is a *Weltanschauung* no less than an empirical theory. Correspondingly, the choice of psychoanalysis as a frame of reference for therapy and research is more than just a pragmatic decision. I will work out briefly what I take to be some of the central tenets of the psychoanalytic view of human reality, and finally I want to link this point to the pluralist position by arguing that some choices of frames of reference can indeed not be regulated by scientific methods, as the critics of psychoanalysis demand.

a)   WHY NARRATIVE COHERENCE IS NOT ENOUGH

One shortcoming of the hermeneuticist view of the validation of psychoanalytic interpretation concerns the status of the concept of narrative coherence. Most of the authors with hermeneuticist leanings think that the ultimate test for the acceptability of analytic interpretations and reconstructions is their inner coherence (Sherwood, 1969, pp. 244–258; G. S. Klein, 1973; Spence, 1982a; Schafer, 1983, pp. 206, 236). It is not possible to extract from these writings a more precise specification of what narrative coherence consists in. This notion need not be rejected because of its vagueness. The idea of coherence is central to our thinking about all intellectual disciplines, and present-day philosophical epistemology has acquiesced with regard to the fact that this concept eschews formalization (Putnam, 1983).

An intuitive understanding of the notion of narrative coherence can be relied on because nothing of what is to come hinges on the internal structure of this notion. Let us therefore say that a coherent narrative should take into account all relevant data (i.e., be as complete as possible), that it should not be contradicted by any of them (i.e., be adequate), and it should unify them into an intelligible structure (which is ultimately the same as saying that it should be coherent).

The problem with narrative coherence as a necessary and sufficient condition for the acceptability of analytic interpretations has been formulated very succinctly by Grünbaum (1984), and I want to quote the relevant passage fully:

> Suppose that the thought-fragmentation and cackling exhibited by a certain class of schizophrenic women were taken to betoken the witchcraft cunningly practiced by them and/or their unawareness of being satanically possessed. Those claiming to have acceptable grounds for such an attribution would, of course, consider themselves justified when summoning a shaman or an exorcist. By supposedly conjuring up the possessing spirits or the like, this therapist would then fathom hermeneutically the conjectured "hidden meaning" of the babble from these unfortunate women. But the rest of us will be forgiven for telling the shaman exorcists that we deem their hermeneutic quest and ensuing revelations to be ill conceived. For they have conspicuously failed to validate cogently the bizarre causal imputations on which their "clinical investigation" of meaning and their therapy are predicated [p. 54].

Grünbaum's charge can be restated as follows: there cannot be a guarantee that highly coherent narratives woven around the symptoms of patients will nevertheless be completely unacceptable to any member of Western culture. The advantage of Grünbaum's odd thought experiment is that it provides a clear-cut example of such a case.

In chapter 6 I have argued for a pluralist stance toward the study of man, thus leaving open the possibility of diverging perspectives on phenomena of clinical psychology and psychiatry. Grünbaum's case of a shaman urges us to look for constraints upon the conceptual frameworks we are willing to accept. I want to emphasize that the possibility of highly coherent yet unacceptable narratives is not just the product of a philosopher's overwrought imagination. In fact, such views of the world have existed (e.g., Greek mythology), and exist even today. There are belief systems, like monotheistic religions, which are endorsed by some members of our culture (among them very respected scientists) and which seem utterly irrational to others. The question which arises is whether this does not make the pluralism defended above untenable.

It is necessary to recall the distinction between pluralism and relativism that I previously insisted upon. Relativism is the claim that the same proposition can be both true and false. The problem with such leniency is that it imports inconsistency into our belief system, and thus makes it—strictly speaking—unintelligible. In contrast, pluralism insists on consistency but acknowledges the possibility of coexisting conceptual frames which are not reducible to each other.

Pluralism therefore definitely puts constraints upon the conceptual frameworks which can coexist within the same belief system. One of the problems of the hermeneuticist conception of psychoanalysis as it has been formulated until now is that it has not seen the necessity of providing such constraints. By only concentrating on the *internal coherence* of narratives, it remained vulnerable to objections like Grünbaum's. My proposal is to remedy this state of affairs by adding constraints pertaining to what I shall call the *external coherence* of hermeneutic theories.

What I mean by external coherence can be exemplified by reference to Grünbaum's exorcist example. The force of his little story lies in the fact that the exorcist might tell a story accounting for the data quite well, and he might even have some therapeutic effect with his exorcist ritual—and yet we would not be willing even to consider whether his explanation of a woman's symptoms is correct. This unwillingness cannot be accounted for by a position claiming that the internal coherence of an explanation is the sole criterion for its acceptability.

We must therefore add another desideratum in order to delineate the conditions of acceptability for hermeneutic theories. The theory should be *consistent with accepted background knowledge embodied in other disciplines, and cohere with it*. This desideratum will probably strike the reader as quite unoriginal and even commonsensical. And so, indeed, it is. It is a standard requirement for the acceptability of any scientific theory (e.g., Quine, 1953; Lakatos, 1970; Kuhn, 1977).

I think that introducing this criterion of external coherence resolves at least part of the problem created by Grünbaum's objection to the hermeneuticist conception of psychoanalysis. The interesting question is why it has been missed by hermeneuticist authors all along. One can only speculate about the causes for this omission. The overpowering desire of hermeneuticists to detach psychoanalysis from the natural sciences as drastically as possible may have led them to focus only on criteria of evaluation which are completely internal to psychoanalysis. The attempt was to free psychoanalysis from the dependence on any information external to clinical work, thus trying to establish the uniqueness of the analytic situation as a research tool (e.g., G. S. Klein, 1973). No consideration pertaining to external knowledge was to be allowed into hermeneuticist methodology, thus leaving the internal coherence of narratives as the only criterion for their evaluation of psychoanalytic narratives.

I now want to explain briefly what I mean by external coherence and then show how it helps to make a hermeneuticist account of psychoanalysis less vulnerable to objections like Grünbaum's. The first requirement mentioned above was that a theory (using the term broadly as including narrative explanations) should be consistent with generally accepted background knowledge. This demands that if a well-established theory contains the proposition p, then the theory to be evaluated should not contain or imply that not-p.

The workings of this criterion of consistency can be exemplified in the context of psychoanalytic theory. Melanie Klein's (1946) theory of the paranoid-schizoid position implies that infants during the first three months of life have certain fantasies about persecutory objects. For an infant to have the notion of a persecutory object he must differentiate between self and nonself. It is a well-established fact of cognitive developmental psychology (e.g., Piaget, 1953) that infants in the first half year of life *do not have this distinction*.

If the Kleinian theory of the paranoid-schizoid position is to be defended, it would be necessary to show that the cognitive developmentalists are wrong. There may be alternative ways of defending the position, such as modifying the account of the paranoid-schizoid position, for instance, by placing it somewhat later in the chronology of child development. The requirement of the consistency with external knowledge demands that the inconsistency between the Kleinian account and theories of cognitive development be dealt with somehow. Considerations about external consistency have in fact been used in psychoanalytic literature. Criticisms of the sort just sketched have been formulated by Kernberg (1980) in his evaluation of Kleinian developmental theory, so that this type of reasoning is not alien to psychoanalysis. Rather these considerations for the evaluation of aspects of psychoanalytic theory have been used all along (e.g., Waelder, 1937). They have only been overlooked by the hermeneuticist metatheory of psychoanalysis (and often denigrated by analysts of all metatheoretical persuasions!).

The second requirement is that of coherence with accepted background knowledge. To prevent terminological confusion I want to mention that I am subsuming the demands of consistency and coherence under the label "external coherence" because coherence *implies* consistency: for two theories to cohere it is necessary, but not yet sufficient, that they be consistent.

Unlike consistency, coherence is a notion for which no simple, formal characterization can be given (Rescher, 1973; Putnam, 1983). In this context I can only point out some general characterization of coherence. Coherence is a *stronger* requirement than consistency. It is possible to illustrate its workings by reference to Grünbaum's little story about the exorcist's explanation of schizophrenic symptoms.

The exorcist explains the psychotic woman's confused way of speaking in terms of satanic possession. In a strict, formal sense this explanation is not inconsistent with any accepted truth of science. It does not imply the negation of any proposition to be found in the body of present-day theories. This may sound surprising at first, but I do not know of any scientific theory stating explicitly that there are no demons and no witches. Why then do we think that the exorcist's explanation is blatantly inconsistent with science?

I think that the term "inconsistent" must not be understood here in the strict, formal sense of logical incompatibility. What I mean is rather that the exorcist's explanation does not fit into the worldview implicit in present-day science. The scientific world view is not just the sum of currently accepted theories with a clearly defined empirical content. It is also a set of very general, not directly testable assumptions about the type of entities and causal relations to be found in the world, i.e., the metaphysics of science (e.g., Lakatos, 1970). The nonexistence of demons and witches is part of this metaphysical framework, within which theorizing accepted by Western science proceeds.

The demand for external coherence can also be exemplified by reference to less extreme examples than Grünbaum's exorcist story. Again, I want to use an illustration from psychoanalysis. There are two aspects of Freud's theories which were rejected by the psychoanalytic community, not because of any particular clinical evidence against, or lack of evidence in favor of them, but rather on *a priori* grounds pertaining to lack of external coherence. The two aspects were his theory of the genetic transmission of the memory of the murder of the father by the primal horde (1913) and his theory of the death instinct (1920). Both cases have been analyzed extensively by Frank Sulloway (1979). It should suffice to indicate that the theory about the genetic transmission of memories relied on Lamarckian evolutionary principles which were rejected by biology in subsequent years, and that the biological reasoning of *Beyond the Pleasure Principle* (1920) also was not acceptable to biologists. These two theories were thus rejected because they did not cohere with generally accepted background knowledge.

Let me restate briefly what the notion of external coherence is supposed to do for us. As shown, the analyst's reasoning is quite analogous to other, commonly accepted forms of reasoning. The question was asked whether the very fact of the multiplicity of coexisting therapeutic approaches does not invalidate the truth-claims of all of them. The pluralist position states that there could be many perspectives on human nature which need not be reducible one to another. However, we need constraints limiting the kind of frameworks which are acceptable as foundations for the understanding of man, lest we will not be capable of justifying why we accept a theory like psychoanalysis but reject demons and witches as concepts in our explanatory frame. The problem is that the criterion of narrative coherence of explanation is not sufficiently strong to exclude unwanted theories, as Grünbaum's exorcist example shows.

I think that the notion of external coherence does provide the kind of constraint we are looking for. It gives us the conceptual tools needed to understand why certain explanatory frames are acceptable to us and others not, although they provide explanations which are possibly quite coherent as far as their internal structure goes.

This claim can be reinforced by considering an additional component of external coherence. A theory is judged, among other things, by the extent to which it introduces explanatory principles not hitherto confirmed. The fewer such principles it uses, the better the theory is. Introducing many such principles violates the constraint of parsimony.

This property of theories can often be judged only against the background of other existing theoretical frameworks. If the theory which is to be assessed can make use primarily of explanatory concepts and laws, which can be linked to other established theories, it is better off than if it introduces concepts and laws which are totally new; in this case we judge these principles to be *ad hoc* because they have been introduced only for a narrow domain. Ultimately, such considerations can be subsumed under what I call external coherence because they concern the relationship of a theory to other accepted explanatory frameworks.

A brief illustration will show how such considerations can help to choose between competing hermeneutic theories. On what grounds can we justify a preference for some theoretical approach to dreams? The two major existing frameworks for dream interpretation are those of Freud and Jung. I assume that it would be very difficult to argue for the superiority of either of the theories by comparing their capacity to provide internally coherent interpretations of particular dreams. Given interpreters with sufficient experience and ingenuity, both schools of thought are likely to come up with rich interpretations, convincing to those accepting the theory's guiding assumptions. Internal narrative coherence is therefore unlikely to lead to arguments for either approach.

The comparison would have to proceed with an assessment of the plausibility of the guiding assumptions. In case there is independent empirical evidence for or against these, the decision may be easier, but this will often not be the case. An alternative way is thus to compare the degree of external coherence of the two theories.

An example of the kind of considerations which would be relevant in such a comparison is the fact that Freudian dream theory assumes only the existence of a personal unconscious, while Jung assumes a collective unconscious containing archetypal contents common to all of mankind. A central question in the comparison of these theories is what extent such basic assumptions cohere with our general knowledge about man. An investigation into this topic would necessitate checking current biological theories as to the possibility and plausibility of the idea that specific mental contents can be transmitted genetically.

The issue is not just one of parsimony. It is not that Freudian theory would be better off because it only stipulates one type of unconscious content. The question is whether the mechanisms by which the creation of unconscious contents is explained fits well into existing background knowledge. If Freudian theory would be more parsimonious and use only one explanatory principle, it would not be preferable to Jungian theory if the one principle were to be very implausible. This can be made intuitively clear by resorting to Grünbaum's example once again. The exorcist needs just one explanatory principle, namely, that hallucinations and dreams of schizophrenics are expressions of demonic activity. It is thus a very parsimonious theory, and yet we are not for a moment tempted to accept it because of its total lack of external coherence.

A viable hermeneuticist account of the nature of psychoanalytic theory must therefore be supplemented by an analysis of the relation of the theory to knowledge external to psychoanalysis. The historical reason for the hermeneuticist's omission of this crucial factor is probably to be found in the fact that the hermeneuticist movement was in part a reaction against the more biologically inclined parts of ego psychology (e.g., Schafer, 1976). But, as Grünbaum's objection against narrative coherence as a sole criterion for acceptability of explanation shows, the attempt to detach psychoanalysis completely from knowledge embodied in natural science leaves a crucial lacuna in the hermeneuticist metatheory of psychoanalysis. Here I could only indicate the direction in which the supplementation of the hermeneuticist conception should proceed, by introducing the criterion of external coherence. In what follows I will elaborate the topic from a slightly different perspective.

b) PSYCHOANALYSIS AS A RESEARCH PROGRAM

This essay can be viewed as an attempt to mediate between the hermeneuticist conception of psychoanalysis and the requirement for stringent experimental proof for the truth of the central tenets of psychoanalytic theory exemplified by Grünbaum's critique. I have sketched a model explaining why the hermeneuticist conception of psychoanalysis (with the emendations and clarifications proposed) indeed makes plausible that clinical work can provide some reasonably well-founded evidence for the plausibility of analytic interpretations. I have argued, though, that psychoanalysis cannot afford to sever the link with surrounding disciplines.

I am therefore inclined to agree with Grünbaum that the epistemic foundations of psychoanalysis cannot consist exclusively of clinical knowledge. The question is whether this forces us to accept Grünbaum's verdict (1984):

> In view of my account of the epistemic defects inherent in the psychoanalytic method, it would seem that the validation of Freud's cardinal hypotheses has to come, if at all, mainly from well designed *extra*clinical studies, either epidemiologic or even experimental. . . . But that appraisal is largely a task for the future [p. 278].

Grünbaum takes psychoanalysis to task for not having validated "the cornerstone" of psychoanalytic theory but I have argued that Grünbaum misconstrues the structure of psychoanalytic theory and practice as it exists today. Psychoanalytic method is far less defective than Grünbaum believes. My present concern, however, is another aspect of Grünbaum's verdict.

Grünbaum's demand for conclusive validation of the "cardinal hypothesis" seems not quite reasonable to me. Such validation cannot be achieved in a direct way. The perspective I propose to adopt on psychoanalytic theory is different. Instead of viewing its central tenets (its theory of development of the nature of unconscious processes, etc.) as hypotheses to be tested directly, they should be regarded as the *hard core of a research program* in Lakatos's (1970) sense.

Lakatos's starting point was that, as Thomas Kuhn (1962) has shown, scientists do not comply with a methodological demand formulated by Popper (1959, 1963). They do not reject theories when *prima facie* falsifying empirical data occur. Instead, the scientific community tends to take such data as "anomalies" (Lakatos, 1978, p. 49f.), which at present cannot be explained. They continue to adhere to their theoretical framework, and through additions and changes they try to assimilate the anomalies.

In Popper's view such a proceeding is irrational because it immunizes theories from falsification. In order to avoid the conclusion that actual scientific practice is largely irrational, Lakatos developed a normative model of scientific research which was meant to do justice both to the demands for testability (whether in a verificationist or falsificationist sense) as well as to the historical data about how scientists actually proceed.

The most extensive presentation of Lakatos's model is contained in his important paper "Falsification and the Methodology of Scientific Research Programmes" (1970), in which he makes a relevant statement:

> All scientific research programmes may be characterized by their "*hard core.*" The negative heuristic of the programme forbids us to direct the *modus tollens* at this "hard core." Instead, we must use our ingenuity to articular or even invent "auxiliary hypotheses," which form a protective belt around this core, and we must redirect the *modus tollens* to *these.* It is this protective belt of

> auxiliary hypotheses which has to bear the brunt of tests and get
> adjusted and re-adjusted, or even completely replaced, to defend
> the thus-hardened core [p. 48].

By "applying *modus tollens*" to an aspect of a theory, Lakatos
means that one rejects the theory if one of its consequences
(generally predictions) is falsified. The central idea of this paragraph is that the central tenets of a theory are not directly
exposed to the threat of falsification. The rationale for this
proposal is that if the hard core of theories were not protected,
no continuous research programs could evolve, since there are
always *prima facie* falsifying instances to be found. The scientific
theory has to be given a chance, to assimilate these counter-
instances within a reasonable period of time.

Popper (1963) claimed that psychoanalysis was unscientific
because analysts are unwilling to specify experimental conditions under which they would be willing to abandon their basic
assumptions, admit their theory to be falsified. Lakatos argues
against Popper that this criterion for lack of scientific methodology would lead to the disqualification of classic physics as
a science, and substantiates this point with several impressive
case studies. He shows, for instance, that Newtonians were not
willing to specify conditions for falsification of the central assumption of Newtonian physics either.

Grünbaum does *not* say that psychoanalysis is unfalsifiable.
In fact, against Popper, he takes great pains to show that it is.
His claim is that the central tenets of psychoanalysis have not
yet been confirmed. But I do not even know how such a direct
confirmation should look. Psychoanalysis at this point does not
rest on one crucial hypothesis, as it did in 1895 (for the details
of the argument see chapter 4, sections a and b). The theory
has become too complex for such direct testing.

Using Lakatos's model I propose to view psychoanalysis as
an overarching theoretical framework, which guides and suggests research in different areas like psychotherapy, psychodiagnostics, child development, perception, etc. It is quite
interesting to see that Grünbaum does not even refer to the
enormous amount of research in these areas which has been
stimulated by psychoanalytic theory. I will mention just a few

representative illustrations. Malan's work on analytic short-term therapy (1963); Exner's integration of research on the Rorschach (1974–82); Bowlby's by now classic investigations on the effects of separation in childhood (1969–80); and G. S. Klein's work on perception (1970).

It could be that Grünbaum disregards this literature because it does not validate "Freud's cardinal hypotheses" (1984, p. 278) in some immediately perceptible way. I am *not* concerned with the question whether the illustrations given actually qualify as confirmations of this or that aspect of psychoanalytic theory. This would require a great amount of detailed investigation. My point is a general, methodological one. If psychoanalytic theory stimulates research in several areas, and continues to do so, it should be regarded as the *core of a research program, which is not amenable to direct testing, but must be assessed by its overall fruitfulness.*

In earlier chapters I have been concerned exclusively with one element of psychoanalysis, albeit a crucial one, namely, interpretive work in the analytic situation. This aspect has been central to psychoanalysis in that it has generated most of its concepts and theories. But the assessment of psychoanalysis need not, and must not, rest exclusively on it.

This is no less a criticism of the hermeneuticist conception of psychoanalysis as it has emerged in the literature of the last 15 years than it is a criticism of Grünbaum's assessment of psychoanalysis. As mentioned, the hermeneuticist metatheory must be supplemented by an account of the relation of psychoanalysis to external background knowledge; moreover the tendency of the hermeneuticists to disregard all information not stemming from the analytic situation is epistemologically faulty. In addition, the assessment of psychoanalysis must also rely on extraclinical research, *which exists to a much greater extent than Grünbaum acknowledges!*

Bowlby's monumental work, for instance, combines the desiderata formulated both in the previous and the present sections. The theoretical starting point of his research is psychoanalytic, as Bowlby himself states very clearly (1969, chapter 1). Therefore his work qualifies as part of the psychoanalytic research program. It also makes extensive use of background knowledge external to psychoanalysis in order to increase the plausibility of his hypotheses—his main source being ethology (1969-80). By combining these two desiderata with an amazing richness of material and thoroughness of investigation, Bowlby has produced one of the most impressive confirmations of some of the central tenets of psychoanalytic object relations theory.

There is little doubt that Grünbaum would not consider the change of perspective on psychoanalysis which is proposed here as a satisfying strategy. His tendency is to look for some *conclusive* vindication of central hypotheses of psychoanalytic theory. And it is clear that an assessment of psychoanalysis as a research program—even if it would turn out to be convincingly positive when carried out in detail—would not provide such an unshakable foundation.

The idea of looking for quasi-conclusive evidence for a theory is seductive; it gives us the feeling that we can know the truth of well-tested theories with certainty. This ideal has been abandoned by philosophy of science in the last decades (e.g., Popper, 1959), and I am not imputing to Grünbaum that he is demanding *certain* foundations for psychoanalysis in this obsolete sense. He is, however, measuring psychoanalysis with a standard which is not quite realistic. His hope to confirm the central tenets of psychoanalysis strongly reminds one of how Popper describes a formative experience of his own (1963, chap. 1). In 1916 Einstein derived from general relativity theory a precise prediction of a previously unsuspected phenomenon (the deviation of light rays by gravitational fields), and this prediction was spectacularly confirmed in 1919 by Eddington by measurements taken during an eclipse in central Africa. Popper was deeply impressed by the fact that Einstein's theory enabled predictions which were definitely falsifiable. The clear confirmation of such a previously unsuspected phenomenon is of course a dramatic corroboration of the theory (although Popper would not use these words).

If psychoanalysis were capable of predicting phenomena no other theory predicts with precision, which would leave no doubt as to the truth of the prediction, this would satisfy Grünbaum's demands and be very laudable in itself. The lack of such precise predictions has been deplored so many times (e.g., Popper, 1963) that its mention is almost banal. But in the social sciences and the humanities such clear-cut evidential foundations for theories are actually never to be found.

In psychology it is notorious that strict experimental evidence sufficient to provide foundations for large-scale theoretical frameworks is hard to come by. Even if predictions are confirmed reasonably well, there are generally too many possible interpretations of the results to allow far-reaching theoretical conclusions. This, for example, led Newell (1973) to claim that despite the enormous amount of data produced by experimental cognitive psychology, there was no basis to be found for any theoretical framework.

While this search for precision in psychology, or in any other discipline, should in no way be denigrated, it is unreasonable to expect from psychoanalysis something which is rarely to be found in the other disciplines: clear-cut evidence for the central tenets of a large-scale theory.

In the case of psychoanalysis it might be preferable to assess the overall plausibility and fruitfulness of the theoretical framework as a whole. This is simply more realistic than Grünbaum's expectation of a clearly delineated set of data conclusively confirming the core of the theory. In contrast to the hermeneuticists, who want to limit the relevant evidence almost exclusively to material obtained in the analytic situation, the overall strength of the psychoanalytic theory is proportional to the variety of the results it produces by stimulating research. Thus my proposal to view psychoanalytic theory as the not directly verifiable core of a research program leads to a desideratum converging with Grünbaum's demand for controlled experimental research.

In summary, my position differs from Grünbaum's in the following way: I see the role of such research not as ultimately providing conclusive evidence for the foundations of psychoanalysis, but rather as a criterion for the overall fruitfulness of psychoanalysis as a research program. A concomitant of this proposed perspective is that much research which has actually been done will count as evidence for psychoanalysis, even if it does not directly confirm central tenets of the theory.

c) Psychoanalysis as a *Weltanschauung*

The time has come to step back and ask what kind of picture has emerged to mediate between the hermeneuticist intuition that psychoanalysis should not be measured by the standards of natural science and the more hard-nosed methodological approach represented so efficiently by Grünbaum's critique of psychoanalysis. The resultant position lies somewhere between the two extremes. The clinical method of investigation is less flawed than Grünbaum claims. But despite my sympathy for the hermeneuticist conception of psychoanalysis and my attempt to improve on some of its formulations, I cannot agree with its insistence that psychoanalysis can rest content with its present evidential foundation. The overall assessment of psychoanalysis as a research program is a task for the future, as I claimed in the preceding section.

Moreover, there is no doubt that this assessment, even if carried out systematically along the lines proposed, would not yield the kind of certainty about the truth-value of the central tenets of psychoanalysis which Grünbaum demands. To begin with, psychoanalysis is far from being a homogeneous and unified body of thought. Even within the boundaries of the positions represented in the International Psychoanalytic Association, there is quite a diversity of theoretical approaches—a fact which served as the starting point of chapter 6. Furthermore, there will always be room for disagreement about the extent to which findings support this or that aspect of psychoanalytic theory (Kline, 1981), since psychoanalysis notoriously cannot produce very precise predictions.

It is therefore appropriate to reflect at this point on why a research program as complex and epistemically opaque as psychoanalysis should be conducted at all. This question acquires special urgency as psychotherapeutic approaches have evolved which are theoretically far less committed than psychoanalysis, and consist of pragmatically devised methods for treatments of specific problems. Their claims for therapeutic efficiency can be tested quite easily, and they generally have no far-reaching theoretical implications beyond these claims. I am mainly thinking of approaches like behavior, person-centered, rational-emotive, reality, and multimodal therapies (Corsini, 1984) which often tend to emphasize that their theoretical assumptions are far less complex than those of psychoanalytic theory.

The most obvious answer on behalf of psychoanalysis would of course be that psychoanalysis simply is the *right* theory, the one which *really* explains the phenomena in question (Arlow, 1984). But this answer has become quite problematic for those who take a hermeneuticist view on psychoanalysis because of a tension within it, which has been clearly pointed out by Morris Eagle (1980). The hermeneuticist view does not emphasize the historical truth of the narratives evolving in the course of analytic treatments. But if the truth-value of the narratives is not crucial to the therapeutic success, why should therapists choose to interpret along the lines of psychoanalytic theory rather than according to some other framework? Why, indeed, should they interpret at all and not do something completely different, like suggestion, behavioral training, or anything else for that matter?

Eagle's point is crucial. In the "historical" view of psychoanalysis (chap. 4, sections b and c), the idea was that the patient is to be cured of his symptoms by acquiring knowledge of their biographical roots. But, as we have seen above, the modernist view of psychoanalytic interpretation strongly deemphasizes the historical truth-value of psychoanalytic narratives. Eagle's conclusion is that the logical consequence of this shift from historical truth to narrative coherence is that the only way to justify the preference for one theoretical frame over another is therapeutic efficiency. If the only really important property of psychoanalytic narratives is the extent to which they convince the patient and help him to change, psychoanalysis should concentrate on testing the mutative effects of different story lines and pick the most efficient one. If the psychoanalytic frame of reference should prove superior in this respect, this could provide the only justification for picking psychoanalysis rather than another theory.

If Eagle is right in seeing this as an unavoidable conclusion of the hermeneuticist conception of psychoanalysis, this would come close to a *reductio ad absurdum* of this view, because its emphasis is on the meaning-giving activity of the analyst, and not just on his manipulative capacity. But Eagle claims that the relativist element in the hermeneutic conception does not allow for talking about *the* meaning of the patient's symptoms and associations anyway. Therefore, only the therapeutic impact of the analyst's interventions remains as a criterion for choosing between competing approaches.

At any rate, the hermeneuticist deemphasis on historical truth seems to block the answer I proposed to why psychoanalysis should be preferred as a research program to theoretically less problematic approaches which focus almost exclusively on therapeutic efficiency. Because, if Eagle is right, psychoanalysis in its hermeneutic version could not claim more for itself as a form of psychotherapy than its efficiency. But the status of psychoanalysis was supposed to be based on its provision of the *true* genesis of psychological problems rather than only on its efficiency as a therapy, according to the claim presented above!

Eagle's argument is meant to show a weakness in the hermeneuticist conception of psychoanalysis. It must be agreed that psychoanalysis should invest more energy in controlled research on questions of therapeutic impact than has been done up until now (for a presentation of existing research, see Luborsky and Spence, 1978). This we owe our patients not only on methodological but also on ethical grounds. A patient should be allowed to expect that his therapist's choice of method be founded on reasonably well-grounded considerations.

But Eagle's query can be answered on a different level as well. If psychoanalysis is considered as an overall research program, it could well be that its assessment would lead to the conclusion that psychoanalysis still is the most powerful general framework for the understanding of the phenomena it deals with. The breadth of topics in which psychoanalysis has stimulated research is probably unparalleled by any other existing theoretical approach. If on close examination this would turn out to be the case, it might give us stronger reasons to believe that psychoanalytic narratives *do* to some extent formulate the structure of the actual biographical genesis of patients' sufferings and personality structures. We are thus led back to the necessity of going through the arduous work of appraising psychoanalysis in the manner proposed in section b.

Continuing effort and interest to be invested in psychoanalysis can also be justified in an entirely different light. In his *New Introductory Lectures on Psycho-analysis,* Freud (1933) claimed that psychoanalysis did not propose a *Weltanschauung* in any sense going beyond the demand for scientific investigation of human phenomena. It is not daring to say that Freud was not quite accurate in this statement. The extent to which Freud's work incorporates a *Weltanschauung* has been well documented by many studies (e.g., Erikson, 1963, 1964; Rieff, 1959). Actually, even a cursory review of some of Freud's later writings like *The Future of an Illusion* (1927), *Civilization and Its Discontents* (1930), his late masterpiece "Analysis Terminable and Interminable" (1937a), and even the very lecture in which Freud disclaims the existence of a psychoanalytic *Weltanschauung,* can easily convince the reader about the extent to which Freud's work embodies a general perspective on human nature (Strenger, 1989).

It is of course possible to claim that there is no intrinsic connection between psychoanalysis as a theory and whatever value systems have been attached to them by analysts (e.g., Waelder, 1962). Freud's general views on man and the world need not play any role in the assessment of his theories any more than a mathematician's political views influence the validity of the theorems he proves. In fact, authors like Rapaport (1960) have tried completely to detach the theoretical content of psychoanalysis from any consideration of *Weltanschauung.* Such attempts were strongly connected with the hope that psychoanalysis would evolve into a general psychology with a degree of formal rigor analogous to that of modern physics.

The hermeneuticist conception of psychoanalysis was in part a reaction against the attempt to assimilate psychoanalysis to the natural sciences (Schafer, 1976). In addition, it has led to a point at which it is possible to see more clearly to what extent questions of *Weltanschauung* or a general perspective on human nature are essential to the very core of psychoanalysis.

Prima facie it seems that it might be very difficult to find any common denominator of general outlook running through all the schools and periods of psychoanalysis. Correspondingly one might think that any attempt to ground one's commitment to the psychoanalytic research program on reasons of *Weltanschauung* is misguided. I do not deny that the reflections which are to follow are to some extent influenced by my own philosophical inclinations. Yet it seems to me that the hermeneuticist perspective on psychoanalysis has made salient a red thread running through the development of psychoanalysis.

In his beautiful paper, "The Psychoanalytic Vision of Reality" (1976), Schafer has attempted to characterize psychoanalytic *Weltanschauung* along the dimensions of the relative weights it gives to the comic, the romantic, the tragic, and the ironic aspects of human existence. He points out that psychoanalysis is centered around the recognition of the unavoidability of conflicts and tensions throughout the life course of every human being. The tragic perspective has a central place in the psychoanalytic view of reality. Furthermore, an ironic view characterizes psychoanalysis in its keen sense of the extent to which human beings are prone to be inconsistent and self-defeating in their attempts to deal with the essential tensions in their lives, again and again resorting to immature and unrealistic modes of conflict solution.

To my mind, Schafer captures very well one of the central tenets of the psychoanalytic outlook which has been crucial to it since its beginnings. It is probably formulated most incisively in that pessimistic masterpiece of Freud, "Analysis Terminable and Interminable" (1937a). Two years before his death Freud once again assesses the possibilities, but even more so the limits, of psychoanalysis as a therapy. He expresses doubts about the hope that a successful analysis guarantees that there will be no recurrence of the patient's neurosis. He grounds these doubts, among other things, on the insight that conflicts and tensions are bound to occur after the analysis has terminated. These will induce the analysands to return to modes of functioning given up during the course of analytic work.

The preponderance of the tragic and ironic perspective on human reality in psychoanalysis is mitigated to some extent by another factor essential to the psychoanalytic point of view: psychoanalysis is profoundly committed to think about and understand human beings as persons, as subjects responsible for their own actions and motives. This may sound unlikely at first. Wasn't Freud's great contribution to show the extent to which human beings can*not* be taken to be responsible for their own mental states since they do not even know about their existence?

There are actually two ways to view Freud's emphasis on the unconscious component of the human psyche. One is to see it as decreasing the degree to which persons can be taken to be responsible for their actions. This may to some extent be true, since indeed the psychoanalytic perspective shows that man has less control over his mental life than a Cartesian view of mind as translucent consciousness implies.

But the converse element in the psychoanalytic view of human reality is even more important, an element which has its clearest expression in the very essence of analysis as a therapy. The guiding assumption of psychoanalysis is that increased self-understanding constitutes the main factor which enables and propels therapeutic progress and change. Once the patient becomes fully aware of the aspects of his mental life previously inaccessible to him, psychoanalysis assumes that he can take more responsibility over himself and change. Psychoanalysis is *the* paradigm of a nondirective psychotherapy; the patient's insight is supposed to make it possible for him to use *his own resources* to abandon self-defeating strategies, infantile wishes, needs for omnipotent reparation, and whatever else he has come to know about himself in the course of his analysis.

Psychoanalysis is thus deeply committed to regard human beings *sub specie their potential for increasing the extent to which they take responsibility for themselves, i.e., as persons in the full sense of the word*. This commitment to the person perspective, to use Gill's (1983) term, has always been implicit in Freud's thought, even though his terminology was strongly influenced by mechanistic conceptions. Actually this perspective on man as potentially mature and autonomous was voiced explicitly in several places, most strongly so in Freud's passionate plea *The Future of an Illusion* (1927). There Freud defends the possibility of man to rid himself of illusions dictated by the regressive tendencies of wishful thinking. He is not overly optimistic about the ease with which this possibility can be realized, but he is intransigent in his insistence on man's duty to strive for maturity.

This aspect of Freud's *Weltanschauung* has remained central to psychoanalysis in its different schools. It has also become one of the centerpieces of its hermeneuticist variety. It has received different formulations by several authors. G. S. Klein (1973) describes psychoanalysis essentially as a search for hidden intentionalities and meanings. Seeking for intentionalities where none are apparent is equivalent to the attempt to widen the extent to which a human being can be regarded as an agent who determines his behavior by his own intention. It also narrows down the patient's tendency to view himself as driven by forces outside his control. In Schafer's work (1976) the same idea was put into his conception of disclaimed action. Schafer takes it to be essential to the analytic process to get the patient to see how he has disclaimed responsibility for himself by viewing himself as the victim of impulses and forces with which he does not want to identify.

The combination of the two ideas just sketched are uniquely characteristic of psychoanalysis. The commitment to take the person perspective has been discussed in chapters 3 and 4, where the methodological consequences of the fact that psychoanalysis tries to understand human beings from within were outlined. The person perspective as such is not unique to psychoanalysis. Every hermeneutic discipline attempts to understand from within. Psychoanalysis is special in that it tries to widen this understanding from within to domains otherwise excluded from it: the stories of mute suffering, which are not even recognized as stories, but only as unintelligible symptoms and character traits.

The uniqueness of psychoanalysis stems from the fact that the commitment to the person perspective is conjoined with the emphasis on the tragic and ironic aspects of human reality. Psychoanalysis does not take the attempt to understand man from within to entail that man must be seen mainly as a being concerned with self-realization, seeking for meaning and fulfillment, as some of the humanistic directions in psychology argue (e.g., Maslow, 1954; Rogers, 1962; Frankl, 1962).

The psychoanalytic emphasis on early phases of development expresses the keen sensitivity of the analytic outlook for the self-defeating, regressive tendency to perpetuate infantile patterns and events. Psychoanalysis has become *the* discipline which investigates the multiple, hidden forms of what has been called "the tyranny of the past" (Wollheim, 1984).

This outlook is what unifies the different schools of psychoanalysis. The tyranny of the past has been cast into several story lines, ranging from the oedipal drama through the terrors of the paranoid-schizoid position to the failure of forming a cohesive self. Psychoanalytic schools differ in the relative emphasis they give to those story lines, and sometimes also in more fundamental theoretical questions like the primacy of drive vs. the primacy of self psychology. But all the schools are characterized by the commitment to view human beings as persons even at points where patients do not do so themselves on the one hand, and the willingness to see the tragedies of conflict and failure in human existence and the ironies of the self-defeating ways man chooses to deal with them on the other hand.

The commitment to psychoanalysis, both as psychotherapy and as a theoretical research program, is thus more than just a pragmatic decision. I am, of course, not claiming that therapists and researchers working in psychoanalysis always go through a process of conscious, philosophical deliberation when they choose this direction. Rather, their personality inclines them to this theory and therapy. I am trying to make explicit some traits of the *Weltanschauung* underlying psychoanalysis and think that choosing psychoanalysis as a frame of reference is in part a choice to view human reality under a certain perspective.

Those, like Grünbaum, who would like to have scientific decision procedures for the choice between theories, could take these reflections as an indication for what they suspected all along—that psychoanalysis is not sufficiently scientific. In the previous section brief mention was made of the fact that one must be realistic in one's choice of standards of rigor. The pluralist position states that different perspectives on reality are possible and that there often cannot be a decision procedure for choosing between them because they are not competing theories but rather mutually irreducible conceptual frameworks. This pluralism allows for factors like personality traits, intellectual temperament, and the like to play a role in the choice of frames of reference. This does not mean that rational discussion of psychoanalysis, its advantages and shortcomings, should be avoided. This essay has been an attempt to contribute to the formulation of a framework for such a discussion. If the result does not fit the preconceived standards of philosophy of science, this should induce us to work out the confirmation of hermeneutic theories more exactly. In this way we can and should try to avoid both the *scylla* of rejecting every theory which resists precise quantifications as unscientific, and the *charybdis* of refusing to justify our adherence to psychoanalysis.

EPILOGUE

PSYCHOANALYSIS BETWEEN HERMENEUTICS AND SCIENCE

Psychoanalysis is placed between two approaches to man which Bertrand Russell (1927) once called "man from within" and "man from without." When we try to understand man from within, we consider him as a responsible subject, a person. We assume that he has a perspective of the world which determines how he acts. The perspective of each person is structured by the way he perceives and conceives of himself and others. Attempts to make this perspective explicit are called hermeneutic.

When we look at man from without, we try to determine the laws which govern man. These laws need not be part of the perspective of persons. All of us are governed by the laws of physics, chemistry, and biology, whether we know this or not. By explaining the nature of man from without we take into account that man is not only mind but also matter: he is part of the kingdom of natural laws.

Psychology in general and psychoanalysis in particular combine the two viewpoints on man. When the perspective from without is taken, our hypotheses take the form of general laws. Psychoanalysis has always relied on such laws, at least implicitly. Examples are: "every child goes through the oedipal conflict," "every person has wishes of which he is not conscious," "early interpretation of unconscious wishes evokes resistance," "every patient undergoes regression in the analytic setting," "when unconscious conflicts are made conscious, neurotic symptoms and character traits disappear."

209

The hermeneuticist conception of psychoanalysis has not sufficiently taken into account that psychoanalysts cannot exist without a set of predictive laws, even though they may only be statistical in nature. Within psychoanalysis this has been seen clearly by Wallerstein (1975, 1986a, 1986b) and Eagle (1980, 1984b). They have urged that psychoanalysis is in need of careful, controlled research for the validation of these laws.

The merit of Grünbaum's work on psychoanalysis is that it highlighted this fact once again. Even though I have disagreed with him on several crucial issues, Grünbaum's main exhortation remains valid: psychoanalysis is in desperate need of controlled research. It seems to me that this need is most urgent with respect to the question of what the curative factors in psychotherapy are.

There are analysts who say that they are willing to consider only one criterion for the progress of an analysis: the development of the analytic process as such. The patient's progress in structuring his life in more adaptive ways or his happiness do not concern them. This may often be a statement of ideology more than anything else, but such statements reflect an aspect of the psychoanalytic value system. This *Weltanschauung* is heroic and at times moving. Truth and maturity are more important than anything else.

But there is a profound danger in this position. It is possible to push it to the point where the practice of psychoanalysis becomes a value in itself. This extreme view creates an ethical problem. Most patients do not primarily want insight; they want more satisfying relationships, they want to be more successful in their work, they want to be happier. It is questionable whether the analyst's value system may be imposed on the patient, whether the psychoanalytic emphasis on inner freedom and maturity may override the patient's wishes. The second problem of this viewpoint is practical: psychoanalysis is in a constant process of retreat. Other therapeutic approaches are flooding the market, and the investment of time and money in psychoanalysis is higher than in most of them. If psychoanalysis wants to keep its patients, it must provide good reasons for choosing analysis over other approaches.

Analysts believe that their commitment to the analytic process ultimately gives the patient what he sought: less anxiety, guilt, and inhibition; more flexibility and happiness. The question remains whether this claim can be substantiated. The ethical and the practical problems can only be dealt with by investing more energy in research. We must know more about how efficient psychoanalysis is. And if psychoanalysis claims that it gives the patient something which other forms of psychotherapy do not provide, it must show that this is indeed the case. The hermeneuticist conception of psychoanalysis has not paid enough attention to this point. Psychoanalysis does rely on predictions, and no amount of convincing narrative coherence can validate them.

The second aspect of psychoanalysis has been highlighted successfully by the hermeneuticist conception. The analyst's daily work consists in understanding persons from within. The analyst is committed to viewing his patient as a person even at points where the patient himself does not do so and says, "That's just the way I am; there is nothing to be understood here." In a sense the analyst *must* impose his values on the patient at this point. He does not accept the patient's view of himself as a thing, as being subject to his character the same way a stone is subject to the law of gravitation. One of the aims of the analytic process is to help the patient assume full responsibility for who he is.

The analyst's commitment to making sense out of nonsense is constitutive of his identity as a hermeneut, as a creator of meaning. His work combines the painstaking tracing of motives and themes of the historian, the good parent's willingness to go along with the inner rhythm of the patient, and the function of the poet to present new ways of looking at life. On the one hand, we must deal with the patient's wishes to be treated as a child and to have his wishes fulfilled, and patiently point out to him time and again where he refuses to be adult. On the other hand, we must find "les mots pour le dire" ("the words to say it," in Marie Cardinal's happily chosen phrase) for him. The moving moments of analyses are those in which the patient's experience of mute pain fuses with the words he never found.

Most of us cannot rely on our poetic creativity of the moment to produce the dramatic structures and metaphors at the right time. One function of psychoanalysis is to provide us with organizing dramatic structures which help us to find meaning where the patient can only see suffering. The paradigm of these structures is Freud's tale of the oedipal drama. In the decades after Freud our store has been enriched: Melanie Klein's description of the terrors of the paranoid-schizoid and the sorrow of the depressive position; Winnicott's depiction of the infant's gradual acceptance of the separateness of the world; Mahler's story of separation-individuation; and Kohut's narrative of the success and failure of developing a cohesive self—these are the most important additions (Strenger, 1989).

Analysts and nonanalysts alike have generally not been convinced of the verisimilitude of psychoanalysis by incontrovertible evidence. The conviction the great texts of psychoanalysis engender is closer to the experience of reading great works of literature than to that of reading careful scientific publications. This is not illegitimate. As human beings and as therapists we need metaphors and narratives which help us make sense of our lives. Psychoanalysis has been singularly successful in giving twentieth century Western culture new ways of saying what human lives are all about.

This essay has tried to find a path between two conceptions of hermeneutic activity: interpretation as the *creation* of meaning and interpretation as the *uncovering* of meaning. The view of interpretation as uncovering meaning stems from the tradition of scriptural interpretation. The holy scriptures have an eternally fixed meaning and God's infinite mind has determined forever which meanings really are in the text and which are not. Hence an interpretation is right if it coincides with the meaning God has intended it to be in the text, and it is wrong if it misses this meaning. Psychoanalysis began under the spell of the archeological metaphor: there was a secret to be found in the patient's past, and it was buried in the patient's unconscious. The uncovering of the secret would bring the cure. We have seen in chapter 4 that this conception of analytic work has gradually been abandoned by many important theorists.

The alternative conception presented in chapters 5 and 6 is that of pluralism: it does not make sense to speak of *the* right way of seeing reality. Reality, human and nonhuman, can be conceptualized in an indefinite number of ways which differ in their usefulness for different purposes. This does not mean that there are no conceptual frameworks which are clearly false and useless (who would want to say that a framework containing witches is good?). But it means that there will always be incommensurable ways of conceiving aspects of reality. The choice between them is often a matter of usefulness (e.g., therapeutic efficiency). But often it is also a matter of the extent to which we experience the perspective implicit in a conceptual framework as gripping and poignant. If we feel that the perspective makes sense of our lives we are more likely to accept it.

Richard Rorty (1986) has presented an approach to Freud's achievement which takes hermeneutic usefulness as the primary criterion for acceptance. Rorty emphasizes that Freud has given us a new way of looking at ourselves and new ways of structuring our ethical discourse. Rorty is not at all concerned with the truth or falsity of Freudian theories. What interests him is its hermeneutic creativity, its capacity to generate new, interesting, and useful discourses and practices. Rorty (1980) has been the most eloquent and interesting proponent of the view of hermeneutics as creation rather than uncovering of meaning, and he has gladly embraced the relativistic conclusions he draws from such a view.

I have tried to find a way to unite two intuitions: the first is that hermeneutic activity must have constraints, and I have tried to resist complete relativism. I wanted to preserve our intuition that there is a difference between pure myth and responsible understanding, between indoctrination and rational argument. I have claimed that there are ways to do psychoanalysis which are defensible, and ways which are dogmatic and insensitive. Not all theories and not all interpretations are acceptable. Chapter 4 shows that the analyst does not simply invent a story, and that the unconscious mental states he ascribes to the patient can reasonably be assumed to have been operative in the patient's psyche. Hence chapter 4 was closer to the view of interpretation as the uncovering of meaning.

The second intuition is the pluralist insight that there are indefinitely many ways to conceptualize reality. Psychoanalysis cannot claim to be *the* truth about man, but neither can any other conceptual framework. In chapter 5 I emphasized that there are many ways to tell the patient's biography, and that the choice between versions is partially a matter of therapeutic efficiency. This and the radically pluralist approach of chapter 6 were steps toward the conception of interpretation as the creation of meaning.

The experience of psychoanalytic interpretation pulls in both directions simultaneously. On the one hand, there are experiences in which there is a distinct sense that the patient is getting in touch with something which has been there all along. This is especially poignant when a patient is flooded with an emotional response which he experiences as surging up from within as if suddenly released. On the other hand, there are the story lines which emerge from the analysis as a whole; there the element of creating a story rather than just piecing together pieces of information is more in the foreground.

The case of the "man with the absent mother" exemplified this whole problem well. Both he and I felt that there was literal truth in the biography which emerged in the course of the therapy; but I also felt that there were alternative ways of seeing things. The aim of the therapeutic process was ultimately to create the story which made most sense of the patient's present experience. My wavering between the two conceptions of interpretation is not coincidental. The discussions of interpretation in philosophy and literary theory indicate that the duality of creation and uncovering in interpretation is not specific to psychoanalysis, but that it is the predicament of hermeneutic activity in general.

The hermeneuticist authors have strongly emphasized the creative element in psychoanalytic activity. The result of this emphasis is that psychoanalysis cannot retain the simple conception of analytic work as uncovering a preexisting truth in analogy to the archeological work which uncovers hidden layers under the ground. The story lines of psychoanalysis are in part to be measured by the therapeutic effect of analytic work inspired by them. Rorty's *insouciance* with respect to factual questions like therapeutic efficiency can certainly not be shared by the practicing clinician. Rorty is concerned only with cultural enrichment; the clinician is committed to help people change. Hence, in a seemingly paradoxical manner, the hermeneuticist perspective on psychoanalysis leads us back to the question of efficiency and the need to assess it. If the psychoanalyst *creates* meaning, his criterion for the usefulness of his creation cannot be purely aesthetic; he must be able to answer the question whether his creation does what he promised to do: to relieve suffering. And this he cannot answer *qua* hermeneut alone; he needs the methods of the scientist as well.

The dialectic between the role of the analyst as hermeneut and the necessity of scientific evaluation is completed by a last point. The therapeutic efficiency of interpretations is largely a function of the experiential conviction they engender in the patient. Experiential conviction in turn is not achieved by scientific precision. It is much more a matter of poetic sensitivity and creativity. The good clinician need not be a good scientist. As emphasized before, the classic texts of psychoanalysis are mostly those which boldly presented overarching dramatic structures. Their effect on the reader is not primarily achieved by careful causal reasoning but rather by their human significance. In this respect they resemble good analytic interpretations which organize aspects of a patient's life into a dramatic structure. Hence the hermeneutic creativity of psychoanalysis is a precondition for therapeutic success.

The poetic function of psychoanalytic theory and practice is not threatened by the insistence on scientific evaluation. Experiential conviction will always be crucial in psychoanalysis. One of my goals was to show in which respects experiential conviction is both necessary therapeutically and legitimate intellectually. Another was to show where only controlled and precise scientific work can give answers which are acceptable and legitimate. Psychoanalysis is inevitably caught in the field of tension between hermeneutics and science.

Psychoanalysis is one of the important hermeneutic frames of the twentieth century, and it has had a great impact. There is a strong temptation to make convincing stories into dogmas. History is replete with great myths which once provided fresh ways to understand aspects of human existence and were turned into claims for absolute truth: the great religions, the Cartesian conception of science as certain knowledge, and Marxism are famous examples. All of these constituted advances in the history of mankind, among other things because of their critical potential. But all of them degenerated into rigid institutions which tolerated no dissent.

At times the disputes between rivaling schools in psychoanalysis have come closer to clashes between dogmas than to open discussion between searchers for truth (Grosskurth, 1986). In certain respects its training system and institutional structure resemble a religious order more than an academy which allows for critical discussion of everything which is taught (Kernberg, 1987). Some of this may be unavoidable. As Ellenberger (1970) has pointed out, Freud has revived the structure of the philosophical Graeco-Roman schools in which the disciple's achievement was not only judged by his academic proficiency. The formation of his personality and way of life were no less important goals of his education.

The analyst's personal maturity is of crucial importance for his capacity as a therapist. Hence psychoanalytic training can never be as impersonal as academic education. Neither can the analyst's achievement *qua* therapist be evaluated as publicly as scientific hypotheses have to be. Too much of his innermost personality, of his privacy, is involved. To a certain extent analytic institutes provide a space in which the analyst can open his work to scrutiny which will proceed with the necessary tact for the privacy of what he has to tell. The question is where the need for privacy is genuine and where it functions as a protective shield against critical discussion.

Psychoanalysis is at a crucial crossroad of its history. Almost a century ago it came into being by opening the unexplored territory of human irrationality to scrutiny. It developed into an institution which helped millions of people to say what had remained unspeakable throughout most of their lives. Now it has ceased to be the avant-garde movement which had to fight for recognition. Psychoanalysis was once iconoclastic. Now it has become the target of those who claim that it is a dogma.

None of the theses of psychoanalytic theory can claim conclusive evidence. None of its dramatic structures will necessarily retain their fruitfulness as tools for understanding human lives.

Freud had moments in which he was aware of the tentative nature of his hypotheses. But, as most revolutionaries, he often had to believe that his discoveries would be valid for all times and places in order to gain the energy which is needed for truly innovative work. Today we must identify more with Freud's critical cast of mind. Only if psychoanalysis is willing to rethink its foundations and to submit them to critique can it escape the fate of the systems of thought which were taken to hold for eternity and found themselves superseded.

REFERENCES

ARIETI, S. (1955). *The Interpretation of Schizophrenia*. New York: Brunner.
ARISTOTLE (1955). *Ethics*. Harmondsworth: Penguin.
ARLOW, J. A. (1984). Psychoanalysis. In Corsini (1984), pp. 14–55.
BENTHAM, J. (1789). The principles of morals and legislation. In *The Utilitarians*. New York: Anchor.
BERGIN, A. & LAMBERT, M. J. (1978). The evaluation of therapeutic outcomes. In Garfield & Bergin (1978).
BERLIN, I. (1976). *Vico and Herder*. London: Chatto & Windus.
BERNSTEIN, R. (1984). *Between Objectivism and Relativism*. Oxford: Blackwell.
BLACKBURN, S. (1984). *Spreading the Word*. Oxford Univ. Press.
BOWLBY, J. (1969–80). *Attachment and Loss*. New York: Basic Books.
BRENNER, C. (1982). *The Mind in Conflict*. New York: Int. Univ. Press.
BREUER, J. & FREUD, S. (1893–95). Studies on hysteria. *S. E.*, 2.
CARR, E. H. (1961). *What Is History?* Harmondsworth: Penguin.
COLLINGWOOD, R. G. (1946). *The Idea of History*. Oxford: Oxford Univ. Press.
COOPER, A. (1987). Changes in psychoanalytic ideas. *J. Amer. Psychoanal. Assn.*, 35:77–98.
COPLESTON, F. (1946). *A History of Philosophy*, Vol. 1. New York: Image.
CORSINI, R. (1981). *Handbook of Innovative Psychotherapies*. Itasca: F. E. Peacock Publ.
———— Ed. (1984). *Current Psychotherapies*. Itasca: F. E. Peacock Publ.
CULLER, J. (1981). *On Deconstruction*. London: Routledge & Kegan Paul.
DAHL, H. (1983). On the definition and measurement of wishes. In *Empirical Studies of Psychoanalytical Theories*, Vol. 1, ed. J. Masling. New York: Analytic Press, pp. 39–68.
DARWIN, C. (1896). *The Expression of the Emotions in Man and Animals*. New York: Appleton Press.
DAVIDSON, D. (1963). Actions, reasons, and causes. In Davidson (1980).
———— (1980), *Essays on Actions and Events*. Oxford: Oxford Univ. Press.
———— (1984). *Inquiries into Truth and Interpretation*. Oxford: Oxford Univ. Press.
DAVIS, L. (1979). *Theory of Action*. Englewood Cliffs, N.J.: Prentice Hall.
DERRIDA, J. (1976), *On Grammatology*, tr. G. C. Spivak. Baltimore: Johns Hopkins Univ. Press.

219

DREYFUSS, H. L. (1979), *What Computors Can't Do*. New York: Harper & Row.
———— & DREYFUSS, S. E. (1986). *Mind Over Machine*. New York: Free Press.
EAGLE, M. (1980). Psychoanalytic interpretations. *Nous*, 14:443–456.
———— (1984a). *Recent Developments in Psychoanalysis*. Cambridge: Harvard Univ. Press.
———— (1984b). Psychoanalysis and "narrative truth." *Psychoanal. Contemp. Thought*, 7:629–640.
———— & Wolitzky, D. L. (1986). Book review: *The Process of Psychoanalytic Therapy*. *Psychoanal. Contemp. Thought*, 9:79–102.
EAGLETON, T. (1983). *Literary Theory*. Oxford: Blackwell.
EDELSON, M. (1984). *Hypothesis and Evidence in Psychoanalysis*. Chicago: Chicago Univ. Press.
EKMAN, P. (1980). Biological and cultural contributions to body and facial movement in the expression of emotions. In *Explaining Emotions*, ed. A. Rorty. Berkeley: Univ. Calif. Press.
ELLENBERGER, H. (1970). *The Discovery of the Unconscious*. New York: Basic Books.
ELTON, G. R. (1967). *The Practice of History*. Sydney: Sydney Univ. Press.
ERIKSON, E. H. (1963), *Childhood and Society*, 2nd ed. New York: Norton.
———— (1964), *Insight and Responsibility*. New York: Norton.
EXNER, J. (1974–82). *The Rorschach*, (3 Vols.). New York: Wiley.
EYSENCK, H. (1985). *The Decline and Fall of the Freudian Empire*. Harmondsworth: Penguin.
FAIRBAIRN, W. R. D. (1952). *Psycho-Analytic Studies of the Personality*. London: Tavistock.
FARRELL, B. A. (1981). *The Standing of Psychoanalysis*. Oxford: Oxford Univ. Press.
FEYERABEND, P. K. (1974). *Against Method*. London: New Left Books.
FISH, S. (1980). *Is There a Text in This Class?* Cambridge, Mass.: Harvard Univ. Press.
FISHER, S. & GREENBERG, R. P. (1977). *The Scientific Credibility of Freud's Theory and Therapy*. New York: Basic Books.
FLEW, A. (1949). Psychoanalytic explanation. *Analysis*, 10:8–15.
FRANKL, V. E. (1962). *Man's Search for Meaning*. New York: Simon & Schuster.
FREUD, A. (1936). *The Ego and the Mechanisms of Defense*. *Writings*, 2. New York: Int. Univ. Press, 1966.
FREUD, S. (1895). Project for a scientific psychology. *S. E.*, 1.
———— (1905). Three essays on the theory of sexuality. *S. E.*, 7.
———— (1909a). Analysis of a phobia in a five-year-old boy. *S. E.*, 10.
———— (1909b). Notes upon a case of obsessional neurosis. *S. E.*, 10.
———— (1912). The dynamics of transference. *S. E.*, 12.
———— (1913). Totem and taboo. *S. E.*, 13
———— (1914). Remembering, repeating and working-through. *S. E.*, 12.
———— (1915). The unconscious. *S. E.*, 14.
———— (1916–17). Introductory lectures on psycho-analysis. *S. E.*, 15 & 16.
———— (1920). Beyond the pleasure principle. *S. E.*, 18.
———— (1923). The ego and the id. *S. E.*, 19.
———— (1926). Inhibition, symptoms and anxiety. *S. E.*, 20.
———— (1927). The future of an illusion. *S. E.*, 21.
———— (1930). Civilization and its discontents. *S. E.*, 21.

—— (1933). New introductory lectures on psycho-analysis. *S. E.*, 22.

—— (1937a). Analysis terminable and interminable. *S. E.*, 23.

—— (1937b). Constructions in analysis. *S. E.*, 23.

—— (1940). An outline of psycho-analysis. *S. E.*, 23.

—— (1950). *The Origins of Psychoanalysis. Letters to Wiehelm Fliess, Drafts and Notes: 1887–1902.* New York: Basic Books, 1954.

FRIEDMAN, M. (1962). *Capitalism and Freedom.* Chicago: Univ. Chicago Press.

GADAMER, H. G. (1960). *Truth and Method.* New York: Seabury Press.

—— & BOEHM, G, ed. (1976). *Seminar: Philosophische Hermeneutik.* Frankfurt: Suhrkamp.

GALBRAITH, K. (1974). *Economics and the Public Purpose.* Harmondsworth: Penguin.

GARDNER, M. (1984). Advance review of Grünbaum (1984), quoted on cover of Grünbaum (1984).

GARFIELD, S. L. & BERGIN, A. E., Eds. (1978). *Handbook of Psychotherapy and Behavior Change* (2nd ed.). New York: Wiley.

GAULD, A. & SHOTTER, J. (1977). *Human Action and Its Psychological Investigation.* London: Routledge & Kegan Paul.

GEERTZ, C. (1973). *The Interpretation of Cultures.* New York: Basic Books.

GELLNER, C. (1985). *The Psychoanalytic Movement.* London: Paladin.

GILL, M. M. (1982). *The Analysis of Transference,* Vol. 1. *Psychol Issues,* Monogr. 53. New York: Int. Univ. Press.

—— (1983). The point of view of psychoanalysis. *Psychoanal. Contemp. Thought,* 6:523–552.

—— & BRENNAN, M. (1959). *Hypnosis and Related States.* New York: Int. Univ. Press.

GOFFMAN, E. (1959). *The Presentation of Self in Everyday Life.* New York: Anchor.

—— (1961). *Asylums.* New York: Anchor.

—— (1974). *Frame Analysis.* New York: Harper & Row.

GOLDBERG, A. (1984). The tension between realism and relativism in psychoanalysis. *Psychoanal. Contemp. Thought,* 7:367–386.

GOODMAN, N. (1954). *Fact, Fiction and Forecast.* Cambridge, Mass.: Harvard Univ. Press.

—— (1972). *Problems and Projects.* Indianapolis: Hackett.

—— (1978). *Ways and Worldmaking.* Indianapolis: Hackett.

GREENSON, R. R. (1965). The working alliance and the transference neurosis. *Psychoanal. Q.,* 34:15–181.

—— (1966). A transsexual boy and a hypothesis. *Int. J. Psychoanal.,* 47:396–403.

—— (1967). *The Technique and Practice of Psychoanalysis.* New York: Int. Univ. Press.

—— (1974). Transference: Freud or Klein? *Int. J. Psychoanal.,* 55:37–48.

GROSSKURTH, P. (1986). *Melanie Klein.* London: Maresfield.

GRÜNBAUM, A. (1977). How scientific is psychoanalysis? In *Science and Psychotherapy,* ed. R. Stern, L. Horowitz, & J. Lynes. New York: Haven Press, pp. 219–254.

—— (1979). Is Freudian psychoanalytic theory pseudo-scientific by Karl Popper's criterion of demarcation? *Amer. Philos. Q.,* 16:131–141.

—— (1980). Epistemological liabilities of the clinical appraisal of psychoanalytic theory. *Nous,* 14:307–385.

———— (1984). *The Foundations of Psychoanalysis*. Berkeley: Univ. Calif. Press.
———— (1986). Precis of *The Foundations of Psychoanalysis*. *Behav. Brain Sci.*, 9:217–284.
GUNTRIP, H. (1968). *Schizoid Phenomena, Object Relations, and the Self*. New York: Int. Univ. Press.
HABERMAS, J. (1968). *Knowledge and Human Interest*. Boston: Beacon Press.
HARRE, R. (1983). *Personal Being*. Oxford: Blackwell.
HARTMANN, H. (1939). *Ego Psychology and the Problem of Adaptation*. New York: Int. Univ. Press, 1958.
HEMPEL, G. (1965). *Aspects of Scientific Explanation*. New York: Free Press.
HOLT, R. C. (1965). A review of some of Freud's biological assumptions and their influence on his theories. In *Psychoanalysis and Current Biological Thought*, ed. N. S. Greenfield & W. C. Lewis. Madison: Univ. Wisconsin Press, pp. 93–124.
KERNBERG, O. F. (1976). *Object Relations Theory and Clinical Psychoanalysis*. New York: Aronson.
———— (1980). *Internal World and External Reality*. New York: Aronson.
———— (1987). Institutional problems of psychoanalytic education. *J. Amer. Psychoanal. Assn.*, 34:799–833.
KLEIN, G. S. (1970). *Perception, Motives, and Personality*. New York: Knopf.
———— (1973). Is psychoanalysis relevant? *Psychoanal. Contemp. Sci.*, 2:3–25.
———— (1976). *Psychoanalytic Theory: An Exploration of Essentials*. New York: Int. Univ Press.
KLEIN, M. (1946). Notes on Some Schizoid Mechansims. In *Envy and Gratitude*. London: Hogarth Press, pp. 1–24.
KLINE, P. (1981). *Fact and Fantasy in Freudian Theory* (2nd ed.). London: Methuen.
———— (1986). Grünbaum's philosophical critique of psychoanalysis. In Grünbaum (1986), pp. 245–246.
KOHUT, H. (1979). The two analyses of Mr. Z. *Int. J. Psychoanal.*, 60:3–27.
———— (1984). *How Does Analysis Cure?* Chicago: Univ. Chicago Press.
KRIPKE, S. (1984). *Wittgenstein on Following a Rule*. Oxford: Blackwell.
KUHN, T. (1962). *The Structure of Scientific Revolutions*. Chicago: Chicago Univ. Press.
———— (1977). *The Essential Tension*. Chicago: Chicago Univ. Press.
LAKATOS, I. (1970). Falsification and the methodology of scientific research programmes. In Lakatos (1978), pp. 8–101.
———— (1978). *The Methodology of Scientific Research Programmes*. Cambridge: Cambridge Univ. Press.
LAZARUS, A. (1984). Multimodal Therapy. In: Corsini (1984), pp. 431–530.
LUBORSKY, L. & SPENCE, D. P. (1978). Quantitative research in psychoanalytic therapy. In *Handbook of Psychotherapy and Behavior Change* (2nd ed.), ed. S. L. Garfield & A. E. Berg. New York: Wiley.
MAHLER, M. S., PINE, F. & BERGMAN, A. (1975). *The Psychological Birth of the Human Infant*. New York: Basic Books.
MALAN, D. H. (1963). *A Study of Brief Psychotherapy*. London: Tavistock Publ.
———— (1976). *Towards the Validation of Dynamic Psychotherapy*. New York: Plenum.
MANN, J. (1975). *Time Limited Psychotherapy*. Cambridge, Mass.: Harvard Univ. Press.

MASLOW, A. H. (1954). *Motivation and Personality.* New York: Harper & Row.
MCCULLAGH, C. B. (1984). *Justifying Historical Description.* Cambridge: Cambridge University Press.
MCGINN, C. (1979). Action and its explanation. In *Philosophical Problems in Psychology,* ed. N. Bolton. London: Methuen.
MCINTIRE, A. C. (1958). *The Unconscious.* London: Routledge & Kegan Paul.
―――― (1971). *Against the Self-Image of the Age.* London: Duckworth.
MESSER, S. B. & WINOKUR, M. (1980). Some limits to the integration of psychoanalytic and behavior therapy. *Amer. Psychol.,* 35:818–827.
MISCHEL, W. (1968). *Personality and Assessment.* New York: Wiley.
NAGEL, E. (1961). *The Structure of Science.* London: Routledge & Kegan Paul.
NEWELL, A. (1973). You can't play twenty questions with nature and when. In *Visual Information Processing,* ed. W. G. Chase. New York: Academic Press.
NOVEY, S. (1968). *The Second Look.* Baltimore: Johns Hopkins Press.
NOZICK, R. (1974). *Anarchy, State and Utopia.* New York: Basic Books.
OGDEN, T. (1979). On projective identification. *Int. J. Psychoanal.,* 60:357–373.
―――― (1982). *Projective Identification and Psychoanalytic Technique.* New York: Aronson.
PARLOFF, M. B., WASKOW, I. E. & WOLFE, B. E. (1978). Research on therapist variables in relation to process and outcome. In Garfield & Bergin (1978), pp. 233–282.
PETERFREUND, E. (1983). *The Process of Psychoanalytic Therapy.* Hillsdale, N.J.: Analytic Press.
PETERS, R. S. (1949). Cause, cure and motive. *Analysis,* 10:103–109.
PETTIT, P. (1979). Rationalization and the art of explaining action. In *Philosophical Problems in Psychology,* ed. N. Bolton. London: Methuen, pp. 3–19.
PIAGET, J. (1953). *The Origins of Intelligence in the Children.* New York: Int. Univ. Press.
POPPER, K. R. (1959). *The Logic of Scientific Discovery.* New York: Basic Books.
―――― (1963), *Conjectures and Refutations.* London: Routledge & Kegan Paul.
Psychoanalytic Inquiry (1987). Vol. 7, No. 2. How theory shapes technique: perspectives on a clinical study.
PUTNAM, H. (1978). *Meaning and the Moral Sciences.* London: Routledge & Kegan Paul.
―――― (1981), *Realism and Reason.* Cambridge: Cambridge Univ. Press.
―――― (1983), *Realism and Reason.* Cambridge: Cambridge Univ. Press.
QUINE, W. (1953). Two dogmas of empiricism. In *From a Logical Point of View.* Cambridge, Mass.: Harvard Univ. Press.
RAPAPORT, D. (1960). *The Structure of Psychoanalytic Theory: A Systematizing Attempt. Psychol. Issues,* Monogr. 6. New York: Int. Univ. Press.
RAWLS, J. (1971). *A Theory of Justice.* Cambridge, Mass.: Harvard Univ. Press.
RESCHER, N. (1973). *The Coherence Theory of Truth.* Oxford: Oxford Univ. Press.
RICOEUR, P. (1970). *Freud and Philosophy.* New Haven: Yale Univ. Press.
―――― (1974). *The Conflict of Interpretations.* Evanston: Northwestern Univ. Press.
RIEFF, P. (1959). *Freud: The Mind of the Moralist.* Chicago: Univ. Chicago Press.
ROGERS, C. (1962). *On Becoming a Person.* Boston: Houghton Mifflin.

RORTY, R. (1980). *Philosophy and the Mirror of Nature*. Princeton: Princeton Univ. Press.

───── (1986). Freud and moral reflection. In *Pragmatism's Freud*, ed. J. H. Smith & W. Kerrigan. Baltimore: Johns Hopkins Univ. Press.

RUSSELL, B. (1927). *An Outline of Philosophy*. London: Allen & Unwin.

SANDLER, A.-M. (1985). Some varieties of transference interpretation. Read to the Second Conference of the Sigmund Freud Center, Jerusalem.

SANDLER, J. (1983). Reflections on some relations between psychoanalytic concepts and psychoanalytic practice. *Int. J. Psychoanal.*, 64:35–45.

───── DARE, C. & HOLDER, A. (1973). *The Patient and the Analyst*. New York: Int. Univ. Press.

───── & FREUD, A. (1980). Discussions in the Hampstead Clinic on *The Ego and the Mechanisms of Defense*. *Bull. Hampstead Clin.*, 3:199–212.

───── & ROSENBLATT, B. (1962). The concept of the representational world. *Psychoanal. Study Child*, 17:128–145.

───── & Sandler, A.-M. (1983). The "second censorship," the "three box model" and some technical implications. *Int. J. Psychoanal.*, 64:413–425.

SCHAFER, R. (1976). *A New Language for Psychoanalysis*. New Haven: Yale Univ. Press.

───── (1978). *Language and Insight*. New Haven: Yale Univ. Press.

───── (1980). *Narrative Action in Psychoanalysis*. Worcester, Mass.: Clark Univ. Press.

───── (1983). *The Analytic Attitude*. London: Hogarth Press.

SEARLE, J. (1979). Literal meaning. In *Expression and Meaning*. Cambridge: Cambridge Univ. Press.

SEGAL, H. (1967). Melanie Klein's Technique. In *Psychoanalytic Techniques*, ed. B. Wolman. New York: Basic Books, pp. 168–190.

SELIGMAN, M. (1975). *Helplessness*. San Francisco: Freeman.

SHERWOOD, M. (1969). *The Logic of Explanation in Psychoanalysis*. New York: Academic Press.

SKINNER, B. F. (1971). *Beyond Freedom and Dignity*. Harmondsworth: Penguin.

───── (1974). *About Behaviorism*. New York: Vintage.

SOLLOWAY, F. J. (1979). *Freud, Biologist of the Mind: Beyond the Psychoanalytic Legend*. New York: Basic Books.

SPENCE, D. P. (1982a). *Narrative Truth and Historical Truth*. New York: Norton.

───── (1982b). Narrative truth and theoretical truth. *Psychoanal. Q.*, 51:43–70.

STERN, D. (1985). *The Interpersonal World of the Infant*. New York: Basic Books.

STEVENSON, C. L. (1944). *Ethics and Language*. New Haven: Yale Univ. Press.

STONE, L. (1961). *The Psychoanalytic Situation*. New York: Int. Univ. Press.

STRACHEY, J. (1934). The nature of therapeutic action of psychoanalysis. *Int. J. Psychoanal.*, 15:127–159.

STRUPP, H. H. (1975). Psychoanalysis, "focal psychotherapy," and the nature of the therapeutic influence. *Arch. Gen. Psychiat.*, 32:127–135.

STRENGER, C. (1989). The classic and the romantic vision in psychoanalysis. *Int. J. Psychoanal.*, 70:593–610.

SULLIVAN, H. S. (1956). *Clinical Studies in Psychiatry*. New York: Norton.

TAYLOR, C. (1964). *The Explanation of Behaviour*. London: Routledge.

───── (1985). *Human Agency and Language*. *Philosophical Papers*, Vol. I. Cambridge: Cambridge University Press.

TOULMIN, S. (1949). The logical status of psychoanalysis. *Analysis*, 9:23–29.

WAELDER, R. (1937). The problem of the genesis of psychic conflict in earliest infancy. Int. J. Psychoanal., 18:406–473.

———— (1962). Review of *Psychoanalysis, Scientific Method and Philosophy*, ed. S. Hook, *J. Amer. Psychoanal. Assn.*, 10:617–637.

WALLERSTEIN, R. S. (1975). *Psychoanalysis and Psychotherapy*. New York: Int. Univ. Press.

———— (1986a). *42 Lives in Treatment*. New York: Guilford Press.

———— (1986b). Psychoanalysis as a science: response to new challenges. *Psychoanal. Q.*, 55:414–451.

WHITE, H. (1973). *Metahistory*. Baltimore: Johns Hopkins Univ. Press.

———— (1978), *Tropics of Discourse*. Baltimore: Johns Hopkins Univ. Press.

WILSON, G. T. (1984). *Behavior Therapy*. In Corsini (1984), pp. 239–278.

WINNICOTT, D. W. (1954). Metapsychological and clinical aspects of regression within the psycho-analytical set-up. In Winnicott (1958), pp. 278–294.

———— (1958). *Through Paediatrics to Psycho-Analysis*. London: Tavistock Publ.

———— (1965). *The Maturational Processes and the Facilitating Environment*. New York: Int. Univ. Press.

WITTGENSTEIN, L. (1953). *Philosophical Investigations*. Oxford: Blackwell.

WOLLHEIM, R. (1884). *The Thread of Life*. Cambridge, Mass.: Harvard Univ. Press.

NAME INDEX

227

SUBJECT INDEX

PSYCHOLOGICAL ISSUES